Strategic Alliances

Formation, Implementation, and Evolution

Peter Lorange and Johan Roos

First published 1992
Reprinted 1992, 1993
First published in paperback 1993

Blackwell Publishers
238 Main Street
Cambridge, Massachusetts 02142
USA

108 Cowley Road
Oxford OX4 1JF
UK

Library of Congress Cataloging in Publication Data
Lorange, Peter.
    Strategic alliances : formation, implementation, and evolution /
Peter Lorange and Johan Roos.
        p.   cm.
    Includes bibliographical references and index.
    ISBN 1–55786–497–7 (pbk.)
    1. International business enterprises—Case studies.   2. Joint
ventures—Case studies.   3. Strategic alliances (Business)—Case
studies.   1. Roos, Johan.   II. Title.
HD2755.5.L67   1993
658'.044—dc20   91–23298
                                                                            CIP

British Library Cataloguing in Publication Data
A CIP catalogue record for this book is available from
the British Library.

Typeset in 11 on 12pt Palatino by
Photo·graphics, Honiton, Devon
Printed and bound in Great Britain by
Biddles Ltd, Guildford and King's Lynn

This book is printed on acid-free paper

Contents

Preface

Strategic alliances are becoming increasingly important in today's intensified competitive international business setting. They can, however, present a paradox because, by definition, strategic alliances involve cooperation between two or more firms.

Strategic alliances represent a means for hungry firms to pursue their individual strategies despite limited resources in some areas. Still, these firms are not necessarily after a quick solution to their resource shortcomings, nor are they impatient in their actions. Strategic alliances require, as they typically acknowledge, a long-term viewpoint; a willingness to invest in a relationship.

Strategic alliances should be strictly seen as a means to an end – not the end itself. The basic underlying rationale, of course, is that one plus one should be more than two. These alliances should afford the partners greater likelihood of success in a competitive context than if they were to go it alone. An overall message of this book is that a cooperative approach is more realistic than a competitive approach for businesses wanting to succeed on a global level.

The major emphases of this book are on how to form, how to implement, and how to allow strategic alliances to evolve over time in order to achieve synergy.

This book is the result of four years of research on cooperative strategies and summarizes our experiences with the formation, implementation, and evolution of strategic alliances.[1]

Many people have helped us bring this book to fruition. We are indebted to the managers interviewed in Belgium, Brazil, Germany, Italy, Japan, Norway, Sweden, Switzerland, and the US, who gave so generously of their time and who provided us with a wealth of information regarding their experiences with strategic alliances.

Among all the firms that have so generously been of help in our study, we feel that one should be acknowledged explicitly, namely, the Fiat Group of Torino, Italy. The authors had the opportunity to study cooperative strategies in 29 prominent European, US, and Japanese firms together with groups of leading executives from Fiat. We have learned much from each other, and we are grateful for the Fiat Group's special input into this project.

The Swedish–Norwegian Industrial Development Fund in Oslo generously provided access to several of its strategic alliances and also provided financial support for parts of the research.

Several academic colleagues have also contributed to our efforts. We would like to thank our friends at The Wharton School of the University of Pennsylvania, the Stockholm School of Economics, and the Norwegian School of Management for their support. Professors Lars Håkanson and Jan-Erik Vahlne of the Institute of International Business of the Stockholm School of Economics, Professor Odd Nordhaug of the Norwegian School of Economics and Business Administration, Professor Harbir Singh of the Wharton School, Professor Bente Löwendahl of the Norwegian School of Management, and Professor Scott Herriot of the Maharishi International University provided feedback on the manuscript and gave valuable insights.

Ms Peggy Simcic Brønn provided editorial support and Ms Heidi Brown was much more than an able secretary, namely a superb project coordinator.

Finally, we would like to acknowledge the support from the William H. Wurster Center for International Management Studies at the Wharton School, which provided us with our research base during most of the project and also provided the backbone for our financial support during the main phases of the research project. This gave us the stability and the intellectual support so necessary to carry out large-scale exploratory research. We are indeed thankful to Mr and Mrs William H. Wurster for establishing the Center, and we dedicate this book to them with appreciation.

Oslo   *Peter Lorange*
                                          Johan Roos

To Mr and Mrs William H. Wurster

PART I
Introduction

1
Strategic Alliances in International Business

Conceptual Framework of Strategic Alliances

We can read almost daily about strategic alliances being formed between firms on a national or international basis. These alliances range from relatively noncommittal types of short-term, project-based cooperation to more inclusive long-term equity-based cooperation. But what is a strategic alliance?

In his discussion of joint venture taxonomies, Root (1987) proposes a number of other pairs of characteristics by which one can characterize strategic alliances:

* nationality and degree of interfirm cooperation
* each company's contribution from the value chain
* geographical scope and mission (in a value chain sense)
* fiduciary risk and environmental risk exposure
* relative bargaining power and ownership

One theoretical way to define strategic alliances is to look at the continuous scale between, on the one hand, transactions on a free market ("market") and, on the other, total internalization ("hierarchy").[1] This is outlined in exhibit 1.1.

The left side of the scale represents total integration of the

HIERARCHY	Mergers and acquisitions	Joint ownership	Joint venture	Formal cooperative venture	Informal cooperative venture	MARKET

Large ⟵⟶ None

Degree of vertical integration

Exhibit 1.1 Strategic alliance options in terms of degree of vertical integration with the parent firm.

activities within the wholly-owned organization. Any merger or acquisition represents a lower degree of vertical integration than the subsidiary organization. Joint ownership arrangements could represent an even lower degree of integration. Various types of formal and informal cooperative ventures are further steps along the path towards lower levels of vertical integration. At the very right end of the continuum, finally, we find the market in which we are free to exchange goods and services. There is no vertical integration. Strategic alliances can be defined as ventures along this scale.

An alternative theoretical definition of strategic alliances, according to Contractor and Lorange (1988), is based on the degree of interdependency between the parties involved. In exhibit 1.2 we list the same strategic alliance options in terms of interdependence – from high (and hard to reverse) at the bottom, to low (and easy to reverse) at the top.

It may make sense to choose a strategic alliance option based, not only on what makes immediate sense, but also on the need to develop mutual trust and confidence. A firm might wish to start out in a less committed mode and then upgrade the type of cooperative relationship over time.

The strategic alliance between the US-based firm CPC International and the Japanese-based firm Ajinomoto, initiated in 1963, illustrates this pattern. Both firms operated in the food manufacturing industry. This alliance was formed at a time when wholly-owned foreign subsidiaries were still not allowed in

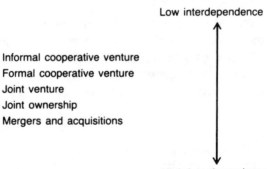

Exhibit 1.2 Strategic alliance options in terms of degree of interdependence between the parent firms.

Japan. It represented a traditional type of strategic alliance giving US-technology access to the Japanese-market. The alliance was the result of a confluence between the Japanese firm's strategy in the late 1950s to diversify and become multinational and the US firm's ongoing internationalization process. CPC International was already a successful multinational corporation with wholly-owned subsidiaries in Europe and several countries in Asia. It became increasingly evident to CPC's management that Japan was becoming an important mass market, and it was desirable to try to enter this market at an early phase. The governmental restrictions on ownership, coupled with the different food culture, convinced the US firm to aim for a traditional joint venture, based on providing its own proprietary technology in exchange for the partner's ability to provide market access. The operational responsibility was in the hands of Ajinomoto.

The alliance developed successfully and more products were added to the operations. Both partners' commitment to the venture also increased successively. Over time this led to several renegotiations which, in turn, resulted in a significant expansion of the cooperation. In fact, according to top executives from both firms, the goal became to build bridges between the Japanese firm and all parts of the US firm, particularly when it came to initiating joint research and development (R&D). It should be noted that the strategic alliance grew proportionately from both parties' points of view: the Japanese firm became more international, and the US firm could also remain competitive globally owing to the infusion of new business opportunities originating in the alliance. Today, the operations are viewed by both parties as very successful, both financially and strategically.

From the previous two perspectives discussed – degree of vertical integration and mutual interdependence – we assume that the two prospective partners see these issues the same way, that they have a commonly shared vantage point. In our opinion such an assumption cannot necessarily realistically be made. On the contrary, each prospective party has its own perspective regarding its strategic situation, which is likely to differ from the other party's perspective. This does not always lead to a common view on the vertical integration issue. Similarly, a common viewpoint on how much and what types of resource interdependencies should be striven for is not easy to obtain. This

stems from, for instance, the partners' own stakeholder considerations, historical considerations, and national and business
cultures.

To cope with this, we shall propose a two-step conceptual
scheme for the classification of strategic alliance motives and
types. The first step takes its starting point in a strategic position
perspective which leads to a set of generic strategic alliance
motives. Given these motives for the cooperative strategy, the
next step is based on a resource input/output perspective. This
will result in a set of generic strategic alliance types. The issues
at hand, as we will see, are to delineate where each party stands
on the strategic position and the resource input/output questions, and then to gauge the consistency between the two.

Generic Motives for Strategic Alliances

One way of characterizing strategic alliance motives is by looking
at the strategic positions of each prospective partner's position in
terms of two dimensions. One dimension concerns the strategic
importance of the particular business within which the strategic
alliance is being contemplated, and how it fits the overall portfolio
of a particular partner. Is this business (with its prospective strategic alliance) part of the core activities of this prospective partner,
or can it be seen as somewhat more peripheral? In IBM, for
instance, we would consider the mainframe computer business as
core, while viewing specialized computers for the telecommunications switching business as more peripheral. Similarly, in a
telecommunications giant such as the Swedish multinational Ericsson, the analog switching business is a core business, while
defense-oriented radar businesses can be seen as more peripheral.

The second dimension regards the firm's relative position in
the business it is in; whether it is a leader or more of a follower.
As a leader it would typically have the larger market share,
leading technology, or superior quality. It would approach a
strategic alliance differently than if it has a small share and is
attempting to catch up.

Exhibit 1.3 outlines the emerging strategic position framework.
Focusing on the two strategic positioning dimensions, four generic motives for strategic alliances emerge. When the strategy of
the strategic alliance is core within the parent firm's overall

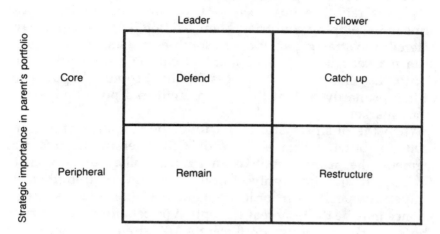

Exhibit 1.3 Generic motives for strategic alliances.

portfolio, and the firm enjoys a relative leadership in this business, the typical motive to enter into strategic alliances is *defensive*. Two major rationales for strategic alliances stem from this – access to markets and/or technology and securing resources. IBM, for instance, which for a long time resisted entering into strategic alliances, has today a number of strategic alliances, most of them with relatively small firms, for specialized software development.

Many firms in this situation enter into a small strategic alliance with an entrepreneurial, embryonic organization in order to keep track of a new technology or a particular state-of-the-art development in the field, and/or to scout out new business opportunities. An example of this is the strategic alliance between the Swedish firm SKF, the global market leader in roll bearings, and the French firm SDM to develop new electromagnetic bearings. This is an entirely new technology which is not expected to become a mass market business, but is still worth being close to for SKF. Similarly, Ciba–Geigy of Switzerland is involved in several focused strategic alliances aimed at new product development within new scientific areas, such as with Chiron in synthetic vaccines. This practice is also quite typical for many of the leading pharmaceutical firms.

Defensively oriented strategic alliances may also be necessary to secure the sourcing of raw materials and/or inexpensive products. This rationale has been a factor for many multinational firms in developing countries. Many leading Japanese firms have entered into strategic alliances in south-east Asia, and the European market leader in hard material cutting equipment, Atlas Copco, has six smaller alliances in the People's Republic of China, primarily so that they are present in a potentially enormous market.

When the business still falls within the core area of a firm's portfolio, but the firm is more of a follower in the business segment, the primary motive for strategic alliances is often to *catch up*. It may be highly critical for a firm to strengthen its competitive position in order to make it viable, and a strategic alliance may be the only realistic option (except for outright sale). The Swedish automotive producer SAAB's strategic alliance with General Motors in 1990 is an example of this. The alternative to catching up, from SAAB's perspective, would probably have been giving up! The other side of the coin is that because of the lack of full control over centrally important business strategies, volition is no longer assured.

When the business plays a relatively peripheral role in the overall portfolio, but where the firm is a leader, the main rationale is to *remain*. Here one might decide to form a strategic alliance to get the maximum efficiency out of the firm's position. Ericsson's strategic alliance with General Electric in the cellular radio field in 1989 is an example of this. This business was probably even more peripheral to GE's portfolio than to Ericsson's, but the large strategic alliance still made sense because it created more value to GE than if the business had been unloaded.[2] Ericsson's core business is in public telecommunication switches – mobile telephony is indeed related, but not part of the core as such. The large digital switches that are part of the mobile telephone systems are purchased by the strategic alliance from Ericsson. For Ericsson this was a unique opportunity to remain and to create a larger presence with the segment, particularly in the US.

To preserve a firm's continued presence in a given country the firm may have to give up full ownership and seek a local partner. Most multinationals had to do this in India, for instance. IBM, which had a wholly-owned subsidiary in India, refused to bring in local partners, and as a consequence had to withdraw from India. Access to a particular market to secure a firm's presence, and so contribute to the overall global business, may also be a motive for a project-based joint-venture-type strategic alliance. Old foreign strategic alliances in Japan are good examples of this type of strategy. During the time period between World War II and 1972, it was impossible for a foreign firm to enter into the Japanese market and retain more than fifty percent ownership. Examples of this include CPC International–Ajinomoto, Hewlett Packard–Yokogawa Electric, Hughes Aircrafts–NEC, and many more.

If the firm is more of a follower in the business area and if the particular business plays a relatively peripheral role in the parents' portfolio, the main motive for cooperative strategies is to *restructure* the business. The goal might also be to restructure the business with an eye toward creating some strength and value which might enable the parent eventually to unload this business. This might be the case for General Electric in the strategic alliance with Ericsson in mobile telephony. Another illustration of this is the strategic alliance between SKF and the Hofors–Ovako Steel Group in Scandinavia, a venture that supplies 40 percent of the steel SKF uses in its roll bearings. For SKF this is a way to unload this heavy raw material commitment, the assumption being that this raw material can be sourced from several suppliers. It is strategically no longer a viable part of SKF's portfolio.

An example from Sweden of using joint ownership to restructure a business is the case of Bulten AB, a member of the Kanthal Höganäs Group. While an important member of the Kanthal business portfolio, Bulten, a manufacturer of fasteners, only provides a fraction to Kanthal's overall profitability and in the early 1980s the situation was getting worse. In order to overcome unfavorable market conditions, to strengthen market share, and to streamline manufacturing as well as to infuse the firm with needed capital, Kanthal, through various partners and share ownerships with other Scandinavian producers, put the firm back on solid ground. Subsequently, Kanthal was able to purchase the firm in its entirety in the late 1980s and operate it as a wholly-owned subsidiary.

We have now discussed four generic motives for strategic

alliances which are based on a business position perspective –
defending, remaining, restructuring, and catching up. The
motives are functions of the relative importance of the strategic
alliance's business within the firm's portfolio and the relative
strength of the firm within its particular business segment. Let
us now move on to a discussion of what generic types of strategic
alliances could be used, given our underlying motives.

Archetypes of Strategic Alliances

Regardless of underlying motives, a fundamental concern of each
prospective strategic alliance parent is the question of how much
of its resources to put into and retrieve from a strategic alliance.
At the one extreme of the input side, it may wish to put in only
organizational resources such as people, technologies, funds,
and staff support. This assumes, however, that the basic strategic
direction for the alliance will be the one to be pursued, without
any contingencies to counteract unexpected strategic changes.
At the other extreme a parent may be willing to put in sufficient
strategic resources for the strategic alliance to adapt to an array
of potential changes in the environment. The strategic alliance
would then be able to deal with opportunities and potential
threats in a more free-standing manner. More resources, of
course, will be needed in order to allow a strategic alliance to
be self-adaptive in this way. This is in contrast to the shoe-
string type of resource commitments when only a nonadaptive,
operations-related performance is called for.

Because of the value creation within the strategic alliance, we
can also consider two extremes on a continuous dimension when
considering the retrieval of output. On the one end the parents
may take back all the output resources being generated through
the strategic alliance by, for example, retrieving all financial
profits, calling back all executives who have worked in the strategic alliance, or retaining all technological know-hows that have
been generated. At the other extreme, all of the output that is
created through a strategic alliance may be retained in the
alliance itself. This would imply that a separate organizational
entity is gradually built up with its own financial resources, its
own managerial resources, its own technology base, etc.

Given these two resource dimensions, a framework for four

archetypes of strategic alliances emerges. This is depicted in exhibit 1.4. If the parents merely put in a minimum set of resources, often on a temporary basis by complementing each other, which are plowed back to the parents in their entirety, an *ad hoc pool* type of strategic alliance makes most sense. This might be an agreement among shipowners, for instance, to trade their ships in a common pattern for a certain time charter arrangement.

Another archetype is the *consortium* type of strategic alliance. This makes sense if the parties are willing to put in more resources than in the previous case, but when the values created within the strategic alliance are still disbursed back to the partners. An example of this is a strategic alliance where two firms pursue a common R&D consortium. Each partner puts in its best technologies, scientists, etc., but the benefits go back to each of the parents after the scientific discoveries (hopefully) have been made.

A third archetype is the so-called *project-based joint venture*. In this situation the parents put in a minimum of strategic resources, entering an arrangement for jointly creating strategic value through a common organization. The resources generated do not get distributed to the parties except as financial results (dividends, royalties, etc.). An example of this is the creation of a strategic alliance in a certain country to facilitate entry into the

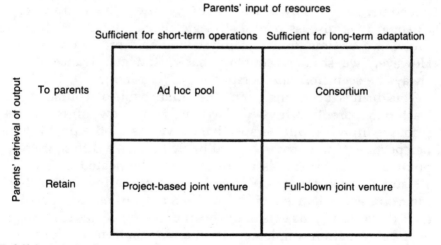

Exhibit 1.4 Archetypes of strategic alliances.

country. This becomes a strategic alliance to facilitate faster distribution of a firm's technologies.

A final archetype of strategic alliance is the *full-blown joint venture*. Here both parties put in resources in abundance, allowing the resources that are generated in the strategic alliance to be retained in the alliance itself (except for dividends, royalty fees, etc.). An example of this is long-term cooperation between partners to develop an entirely new business. This type of strategic alliance can be characterized as the creation of a more or less free-standing organizational entity with its own strategic life.

It should be pointed out that, from this perspective, a full-blown joint venture can be seen as the last resort for a firm. Some might argue that this is a too negative view of the role of strategic alliances. This is not necessarily so. If a particular party has the resources and sees the strategic importance relative to other opportunities in such a way that it makes it prudent to go it alone, then there is no reason to argue for a strategic alliance.

Proximity Among Partners

We have made the point that it is the parent's perspective regarding strategic positioning as well as the input/output of resources that dictate the form of strategic alliance. This underscores the fact that strategic alliances are a means to an end – not the end per se, and is in contrast to authors who argue for the strategic alliance as a phenomenon on its own, with its own strategic life and value. In Chapter 3 we discuss how a strategic alliance should be seen as evolving over time, thus certainly taking on a profile on its own. However, we strongly contend that a strategic alliance should always be seen from the perspective of its parents.

This brings us to the point that there will, of course, be at least two parents who will have varying viewpoints on the resource input/output perspective as well as on the positioning perspective. One party is indeed likely to have a different viewpoint on where it stands in the patterns delineated in exhibits 1.3 and 1.4 than the prospective bargaining partner. How then, can a strategic alliance be formed when the parties have perspectives that differ? This gets to the heart of the processes of strategic alliance formation, implementation and evolution. The prospective partners must negotiate a joint understanding of how their resource perspectives and strategy positioning perspectives can be reconciled. This means that there must not be too much of a mismatch between the positioning of each of the parties in terms of the discussed framework, resource-wise and/or strategic position-wise. A significant mismatch in the positions of the two parties would make it unrealistic to form, implement, and evolve any type of strategic alliance.

When there is close proximity in the way people see their positions, the basis of a strategic alliance is created. As an example, while one party may see a prospective alliance as falling into the ad hoc pool type, another party may see it as more of a joint operations type of strategic alliance. In reality there is, of course, no real clear border line between these two perspectives; it is a matter of degree of proximity between complementary perspectives.

These complementary perspectives on resource inputs/outputs positions and portfolio/business strategy positions must be maintained over time for the alliance to last. If the parents drift apart, developing larger distances between their perspectives over time, then the strategic alliance is bound to break up.

In this book the term strategic alliance refers to the four archetypes of cooperation discussed above: ad hoc pool, consortium, project-based joint ventures and full-blown joint ventures. The cooperation can involve any part of the firm's value-creating activities, that is, R&D, product development, manufacturing, distribution, or service, or a combination of these. Let us now move to a discussion of the use of strategic alliances as a tool in building international business.

The Importance of Strategic Alliances

Strategic alliances occur in many different industries and between firms of different sizes. They have numerous purposes and may involve vertical or horizontal links between the firms involved. A multitude of examples of strategic alliances can be found in the automobile, semiconductor, computer, information technology, telecommunication, robotics, air transport, and biotechnology industries, among others.

In a study of 839 collaborative agreements Hergert and Morris

(1988) have found that most such agreements were carried out in high-tech industries: automobile (23.7%), aerospace (19.0%), telecommunications (17.2%), computer (14.0%), and other electrical industries (13.0%). They also found some interesting trends regarding types of cooperations. The largest share of the agreements turned out to be joint product development (37.7%). Moreover, the vast majority (71.3%) of these ventures were formed between rivals! According to Zajac (1990), the four dominant motivations for engaging in joint ventures were:[3]

- acquiring a means of distribution and preempting competitors (35%)
- gaining access to new technology and diversifying into new businesses (25%)
- obtaining economies of scale and achieving vertical integration (20%)
- Overcoming legal/regulatory barriers (20%)

Multinational companies have also often formed what could be labelled networks of strategic alliances. This pattern of international networking seems to have taken a more structured form since the mid-1980s. To an increasing extent, partnerships are formed between companies from the three major trading blocks – US, Europe, and Japan – which have resulted in what Ohmae (1985) labelled global triads, "the future shape of global competition." Exhibit 1.5 illustrates this. Hergert and Morris (1988) have shown that the largest increases in collaborative agreements were those between companies from the US and the EEC, followed by those between the EEC and Japan, and between the US and Japan.

This triangular map does not, of course, represent the general pattern for strategic alliances. A recent example of a large alliance where only one of the corners of the triad is involved is the domestic US alliance between AT&T and Zenith, announced in March 1989, to come up with an alternative to the expected Japanese dominance in high-definition television screens. Moreover, in the European part of the triad, there is an increasing interest in cooperative strategies within Europe – especially within the EEC. An interesting early example of this is the Airbus project, which in spite of initial severe financial, political and cultural problems, has survived as an intra-European partnership. In addition, it is a well-known fact that many companies

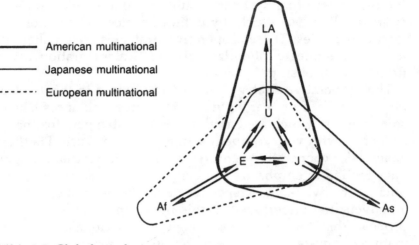

——————— American multinational

——————— Japanese multinational

- - - - - - - - European multinational

Exhibit 1.5 Global triads.
Source: Kenichi Ohmae, *Triad Power: The Coming Shape of Global Competition*, New York: The Free Press, 1985.
Key: Af – Africa, As – Asia, E – European Community, J – Japan, LA – Latin America, U – United States

from European countries outside the EEC are increasing their cooperative efforts in the EEC countries so as to not be left out of the 1992 integration. Håkanson (1989), for instance, found that Swedish companies, for reasons of political factors, tend to maintain and sometimes strengthen the R&D activities in companies they have acquired in Europe, instead of the more traditional way of closing down such activities and consolidating them in the home country.

Even though alliances between large corporations in the often large high-tech industries mentioned above typically receive the most attention in the media, strategic alliances are also a common ingredient in national and international business strategies of smaller companies. In spite of less financial involvement in absolute terms, such strategic alliances naturally can also be very important to a specific company.

This cooperative paradigm clearly seems to differ substantially from the traditional view of the multinational company operating with wholly-owned units in various countries, the focus of much previous research in strategy and management (Heenan and Perlmutter 1979) This new view suggests a distinction between internal hierarchial systems – studying one single firm – and strategic alliances, which, by definition, need interaction by at least two parties. These cooperative strategies are an alternative to classical strategies of horizontal or vertical integration, diversification, or licensing.

The cooperative strategy paradigm proposed in this book also tends to differ from earlier views on strategic alliances taken by some authors which are based on the unstable paradox that you cooperate with your competitor in a win–lose sense. Traditional analyses of cooperative ventures based on industrial economics have tended to emphasize the bargaining power of each player, often with a win–lose perspective being the outcome, along with an adversarial undertone.[4] In this book, on the other hand, we propose that there may be a legitimate rationale for a more mature, long-term, win–win emphasis regarding strategic alliances; an emphasis on more lasting relationships where benefits and costs can tip both ways in the short run but even out in the long run.

Why are strategic alliances used so extensively by large multinational firms in the implementation of their strategies? In order to try to answer this question, we would like to point out five characteristics of international businesses today:

- Increasing internationalization with tightened competitive pressure, stemming from global scale and/or scope advantages. Hence, a need to team up with partners to ameliorate resource shortages, to gain time, etc.
- Despite this internationalization, firms need to remain strong in national markets and adapt to local needs and demands. Hence, the need to have a local partner.
- Rapid technological developments leading to shorter product life cycles calling for considerable response and demand. Hence, the need to have joint R&D, to have a sufficient resource base, to put together scarce eclectic competencies, and to leverage the outputs for a broad commercial application.
- Higher demands for systemic solutions involving several types of competencies, product and/or service offerings, etc., put together into packages to make the customers succeed better. Hence, the need to bring together the best from several partners.
- The emergence of many new competitors in otherwise more traditional businesses, combined with the often strong need to reposition oneself pro-actively. Hence, the need to build strong alliance

networks – not only as a way to rapidly be in the right position to generate business but also as a defense.

All of these factors, and many others, have contributed to the increasing use of cooperative strategies. Above all, however, strategic alliances have become an important means for firms of all sizes to come up with a practical approach to increasing possibilities for being able to implement their international strategies.

For all firms, well established or emerging, making a strategic alliance succeed requires special skills. Consequently, we claim that the ability to form and implement successful strategic alliances has become an important competitive tool in its own right in many firms. This book addresses the issue of how to strengthen one's managerial skills to succeed using the strategic alliance approach.

In the study by Zajac (1990), most of the Chief Executive Officer (CEOs) responded that, in the future, their firms' interest in strategic alliances would increase (66%), and that strategic alliances were viable alternatives to mergers (67%) and internal ventures (63%).[5] These findings underscore the point that strategic alliances are here to stay.

The Challenge of Strategic Alliances

There are many examples of successful strategic alliances, in terms of both the alliances *per se* and the parent firm's perspectives. Corning Glass, for instance, has been involved in some forty strategic alliances (mainly joint ventures) worldwide during the last sixty years. In the last five years, such alliances have contributed more than $425 million in earnings. As a comparison, total 1989 sales of Corning were $2.5 billion, whereas sales for its strategic alliances were estimated at some $3 billion. The CEO of Corning, Dr James R. Houghton (1990), recently offered the following four success criteria for this strategy:

- compatible strategy and culture
- comparable contribution
- compatible strengths
- no conflict of interest

However, most of all he underlined the importance of determination and luck: "Last, it helps to be lucky. Whenever we've seen the need to form a joint venture, we've worked hard to find the right partner – then we had the patience and determination to make it work. And the harder we worked, the luckier we were" (p. 17).

There are numerous advantages to strategic alliances but, if not handled properly, such cooperative strategies can result in major problems for all parties. For instance, an article in the *Financial Times* discusses the reasons for problems in the 1989 merger-like strategic alliance between the French firm Carnaud and the British Metalbox Packaging. The strategic alliance, CMB Packaging, is the largest packaging company in Europe and the third largest in the world. Even though this article, not surprisingly, focuses on the disappointing expected short-term financial results, some attention is given to a better understanding of the underlying reasons for the unsatisfactory result. One major reason for the failure, according to the article, is that some of the two firms' subsidiaries used to be fierce competitors and consequently had difficulties working together. The CEO also pointed to large differences in decision-making styles.

An example of a problematic strategic alliance between smaller firms is the one formed in 1985 between a family-owned Norwegian firm and a Swedish firm owned by a conglomerate.[6] The main purpose of this strategic alliance was the sales and distribution of the two firms' products – garden equipment – in their respective home markets. Future joint product development was also planned. Shortly after the operations had begun, the Swedish firm was sold by its parent firm to the most forceful competitor of the Norwegian partner. Because both partners had revealed their strategic and operative plans to each other, the competitor got access to the Norwegian firm's plans. The competitor was not interested in the strategic alliance and, therefore, ensured that it was terminated. Soon after, the Norwegian partner firm went into bankruptcy.

Whatever the true reasons are for problems in making a strategic alliance work, these examples illustrate the challenge of, and the potential difficulties in, forming and implementing strategic alliances. This is further verified by several empirical studies which have found that unsatisfactory strategic alliance performance ranges from 40 to 70 percent.[7] It is, for instance, typically easier to have all R&D efforts "in house" than in cooperation with a partner or perhaps even with a competitor. It is normally much easier to run a wholly-owned company with a few independent suppliers than to manage a complex set of cross-ownership-based supplier/customer relationships. It is typically easier to manage one's own sales people than to coordinate marketing and distribution with others. It is often easier to make quicker decisions in one's own firm than to have to check first with a partner. And it is typically easier to implement decisions in a domestic firm with a homogenous organization than in a firm that has cooperative ties in several, perhaps culturally different, countries.

In addition to being based on a viable business idea, and a realistic overall strategy, a strategic alliance must be based on mutual cooperation among the parties involved. This is the *sine qua non* for strategic alliances. We need to create a climate of trust and mutual understanding of why all partners enter the alliance in the first place. This challenge ties back to such issues as what type of alliance it is appropriate to use – initially and later; what is the strategic fit with the parent firms; what are the potential synergy effects; what are the competitive advantages to each partner and for alliances as a combined entity, and so on. The partners must be mutually realistic regarding potential advantages and disadvantages so that they can create a climate of mutual trust and cooperation. It will still be natural for all parties to protect some of their core competence and possibly to have different viewpoints on a diverse set of issues such as deciding what planning and control processes to use, what people to assign, and how to approach potentially sensitive points in the contract. But the basic cooperative trust must be established and maintained from the start.

The challenge of forming and managing strategic alliances was articulated by Carlo de Benedetti, CEO of Olivetti (1990):

If you do not have the reference structure for a network organization, it is difficult to make strategic alliances work. We have to overcome the logic of the octopus and reach the logic of the network. The "network organization" requires a different organizational structure, and more important, different management processes.

Outline of the Book

This book consists of five parts. Part I consists of the introduction (Chapter 1) and a short case study of the options of Owens–Illinois and Plastic Recycling Technology. Part II focuses on the formation and evolution of strategic alliances, or what steps to take for successfully putting together strategic alliances. More precisely, the discussion centers on what the management team should consider at different stages of the process during the internal preparations within each prospective parent firm (Chapter 2). This is illustrated in a detailed case study of the formation and implementation of a strategic alliance between DEC and ITT in Europe. Then we discuss the evolution of strategic alliances once they are formed (Chapter 3). The evolutionary pattern of strategic alliances is exemplified by a case study of a strategic alliance between Mölnlycke Consumer Products and Scott Paper (UK) in the United Kingdom.

Part III of the book is on management processes. In Chapter 4 we talk about planning and control considerations, which are illustrated by a case study on the Genetics Institute Inc. Important human resource management aspects of strategic alliances are explained in Chapter 5. Some of these aspects are illustrated in the case study on Showa–Packard's operations in Japan.

Part IV covers some important contextual issues in cooperative venturing. In Chapter 6 we briefly discuss the findings from two empirical studies on cultures, management approaches and performances in strategic alliances. A case study of Fuji Xerox in Japan serves as an example of such issues. Some common obstacles to the success of strategic alliances are discussed in Chapter 7, followed by a case study of a smaller Scandinavian strategic alliance which failed. Finally, we discuss some emerging challenges, namely the notion of global-shared versus global-dominant strategic alliances. A case study of Fiat–Hitachi Construction Machinery illustrates this.

In Part V, the final part of the book, we sum up the discussions and draw some major conclusions and implications from the previous chapters and case studies. As far as possible we tie the discussion back to the four generic types of strategic alliances throughout the book.

Appendix
Owens–Illinois and Plastic Recycling Technology[1]

In 1983, Owens–Illinois (O–I), a large US bottle manufacturer based in Toledo, Ohio, had a strategic decision to make. The company, which primarily manufactured glass-related products but also plastic bottles, had recently acquired a technology which made possible the recycling of Polyethylene Terephthalate. More commonly referred to as PET, it is used to manufacture numerous products, most notably soft drink bottles. The recycling technology, however, was not yet commercialized. While recycling PET was technologically feasible, it was currently not economic. Top managers considered the option of whether to attempt to commercialize the technology and, if so, what strategic options to use.

There were several reasons why O–I might want to commercialize the technology. The pressure of political and social groups working to ban the product represented the most important. These groups, concerned with the amount of garbage going into landfills, discouraged continued use of non-biodegradable products like PET. They promoted the use of other products such as paper, glass and aluminum, which were biodegradable and recyclable, as environmentally safer and superior to plastic. The company recognized it could not ignore these efforts and, in the words of one manager, it "felt the threat of regulation." If these legal efforts succeeded, it would virtually destroy the plastic bottling industry and O–I's plastic bottling operations. O–I believed it could prevent this legislation if recycling plastics proved viable.

Second, no other company had this technology. In commercializing the technology, O–I would likely become the leader in a potentially enormous market. Many products, packaged in glass or paper in the 1960s, now came in plastic packages. The demand for plastic bottles had expanded significantly and, except for the potential legal restrictions, there were no signs that it would slow down. The demand for recycled plastic might be just as large. Third, if O–I did not try to develop the technology, they would probably not receive any benefits from its acquisition.

Commercializing the technology did not come without obstacles. First, expense represented a major problem. Developing a plant would cost in the millions of dollars. For O–I, investing the money in increased lobbying efforts, fighting the groups working to ban PET, might be more effective and economical. Second, even if O–I succeeded in commercializing the technology, the company had no guarantee of a market for the product. Unlike in glass recycling, to avoid potential contaminations, recycled plastic bottles would be recycled not into new bottles, but into non-food products. However, as a manager noted, the company "did not know if there was much of a market for recycled products." The problem of where the company would get a supply of used plastic for recycling added to this uncertainty. While systematic collection provided aluminum, glass and paper for recycling, no equivalent accumulation process of plastic bottles existed.

A third problem centered on the risk and return associated with developing the technology. While O–I would incur all the risks in developing the technology, the benefits would accrue to most companies using PET. In the middle of the value-added chain of plastic bottle manufacturing, O–I bought the raw materials from companies (e.g. DuPont), produced the plastic bottles, and sold the bottles to other companies (e.g. Coca-Cola, Pepsi-Cola, Procter & Gamble). Most of these companies are extremely reliant on PET and would be severely hampered by a ban on plastic bottles. If plastic recycling became commercially feasible, these companies would receive many of the benefits of the technology without taking any of the risks. Finally, commercializing the technology might erode O–I's position in the plastic industry. While the recycled plastic would not be used in creating new bottles, no one knew how the presence of the recycled plastic would influence the market for new plastic.

In reviewing the situation, the organizers concluded that Owns–Illinois had the following alternatives:

- Not commercialize the technology. Rely instead on alternative mechanisms, such as lobbying the government, to prevent legislation banning plastic bottles.
- Commercialize the technology. Attempt to develop the recycling technology and make it economically feasible. If it chooses to commercialize, how should it proceed? Three options are:
  - Develop the technology internally. Take the chance that the benefits of commercialization will offset the associated risks.
  - License or sell the technology to another company. Approach another company, perhaps one like Coca-Cola or Pepsi-Cola, that might have a greater interest in seeing PET recycled, about licensing the technology to them. If such a company could be found, this would spread the risk but reduce the potential gains from commercialization. The question remains whether O–I could find a company willing to agree to such an arrangement.

- Share the technology with other companies in a strategic alliance. Developing an alliance would also help spread the risk of commercializing the technology but will also reduce O–I's control. Like the licensing arrangement, what companies would join in and who would control it? For example, one of the managers questioned why the resin manufacturers, the creators of new plastic, would get involved in encouraging recycling. Also, how does this option help with the problem of developing a supply of used plastic and a market for the recycled plastic?

The decision

Owens–Illinois decided that it would pursue a strategic alliance with other companies rather than develop the technology on its own, exit the market, or lobby the government. The company realized that to develop the infrastructure necessary to make recycling feasible an alliance was needed. As a key manager in the organizing effort stated, "this was something we should all work on." As a result Bill Niehaus, a manager at O–I began the process of soliciting companies to join in the alliance. In soliciting he targeted those companies in the plastic product value-added chain and those which could commit up to $50,000 a year to research recycling technology. He convinced other companies that it was in their best interest to research recycling, and the resin manufacturers joined. They committed because it was expected that the plastic market would continue to grow, if not regulated, and the presence of recycled plastic would help reduce product costs and expand the market even further. Niehaus and the other managers involved in the discussions purposely did not contact recycling/waste management companies. They based it upon the stated belief that such an alliance "would not work if some members would make a large profit from the collaboration."

This culminated in twelve companies joining together in 1985 to create the Plastic Recycling Institute to oversee development of the alliance. In deciding how to structure the organization and where to conduct the research, the Institute focused on developing a collaborative arrangement with a university. From prior experience organizers knew that a university setting would be ideal for their interests. They also believed that in order to develop the national recycling infrastructure, it was imperative to maintain public access to the research. Conducting the research in a company might create barriers to diffusion of the technology. The organizers settled on Rutgers University of New Jersey, because it had a strong research orientation, experience with industry–university research, and the state of New Jersey agreed to provide matching funds to what was provided by the companies.

The original twelve companies (such as Coca-Cola, Continental Plastics Container, DuPont and Owens–Illinois) were joined by two more companies in signing an agreement with the university and creating the Plastic Recycling Foundation (PRF). The foundation is a legally independent, non-profit foundation. Its purpose is to sponsor research, and it does no lobbying. The companies initially agreed to contribute a total of $300,000 and the university agreed to develop a pilot plant. Owens–Illinois donated the technology to the foundation to begin developing the pilot plant.

Evolution

Since its inception, the Plastic Recycling Foundation has changed considerably, adapting to its earlier successes and new challenges. The goals have been expanded beyond the initial plan of commercializing the recycling technology to building more of the recycling infrastructure. The alliance began encouraging the collection, reclamation and reuse of plastic bottles. For example, it began programs to encourage consumers to save plastic bottles and to develop products from the recycled plastics. It has also developed additional pilot plants to research these areas.

The original pilot plant, which is about one-quarter the expected size of a commercial plant, became operational in 1987. PRF will sell the blue prints of the plant to any party interested in commercial recycling, for only a few thousand dollars. The price, about 1 percent of what it would take to develop the plant in the commercial market, is purposely kept low to encourage entrepreneurs to build recycling plants. PRF has sold many copies over the last several years.

Currently, PRF has over sixty members. The foundation is also beginning to fund research at other universities, such as Michigan State; however, Rutger remains the primary research site. The alliance has further changed in that it is now researching other forms of plastic such as Polyvinyl Chloride (PVC) and high-density polyethylene (HDPE). Finally, Owens–Illinois, now known as Owens–Brockway, has left the plastics industry. While still a member of the venture, it has sold its plastic bottling business.

PART II
Formation and Evolution of Strategic Alliances

2
The Formation Process

Strategic Intent

A strategic alliance must be structured so that it is the strategic intent of both parties that it will actually succeed. It has been argued that different strategic intents among strategic alliance partners is healthy (Ohmae 1989). One partner can, for instance, have the strategic intent of active internationalization whereas the other may want to take a seemingly more passive role as a supplier of technology. The second partner will still, perhaps, gain the benefits of more rapid dissemination of the product internationally. We feel that this is quite typical for many strategic alliances, that the goals are different, but complementary. The way to have mutual gain, even though there exists a long-term divergence in goals, is to stress the mutual recognition of these issues among the partners, so that the complementary issue becomes the common driving force in the otherwise different strategic intents.

According to Hamel and Prahalad (1989), "strategic intent" encompasses two dimensions:

- Strategic intent envisions a desired leadership position and establishes the criterion the organization will use to chart its progress.
- Strategic intent also encompasses an active management process that includes: focusing the organization's attention on the essence of winning; motivating people by communicating the value of the target; leaving room for individual and team contributions; sustaining enthusiasm by providing new operational definitions as circumstances change; and using intent consistently to guide resource allocations. (p. 64)

Hamel and Prahalad also identify three typical characteristics regarding what strategic intent means:

- It captures the essence of winning
- It is stable over time
- It sets a target that deserves personal effort and commitment.

We feel that in a successful strategic alliance both parties must have strategic intents that are reconcilable, this match being quite explicitly stated and established early on. Almost by definition the two parties will come to the table with different strategic intents – they will seek different benefits from the strategic alliance in relation to their respective strategies. The two different strategic intents must, however, be sufficiently compatible to leave room for cooperation. As we shall see, this is not necessarily easy. For instance, to establish a sense of stability over time the parties will both need to have relatively long time horizons. If one party has a predominantly short-term intention, while the other wants to be in it for the longer run, they may have difficulties in establishing a matching strategic intent. A lingering question at this point is also whether each party shows its true strategic intent. This is a question that each partner should address carefully by attempting to understand the strategic position from which each party comes. This will be discussed shortly.

In our experience, the foundation of a successful strategic alliance is laid during the initial formation process. It is at this time that the analytical and political dimensions and issues have to be dealt with in such a way that clear and realistic intents are established and that the foundation for trust and behavioral consonance is laid.

Exhibit 2.1 presents a conceptual model of critical considerations during the internal formation process. A basic premise of the model is that both the decision-making process during an initial "dating" phase and the process that takes place during the later intense phases of negotiations are of vital importance for ultimate success. Also, the model reflects both political and analytical considerations at each of these two stages. It illustrates how the formation of successful strategic alliances takes place as a gradual, complex, and mixed political and analytical process, rather than as a clear-cut, mainly analysis-based decision at one

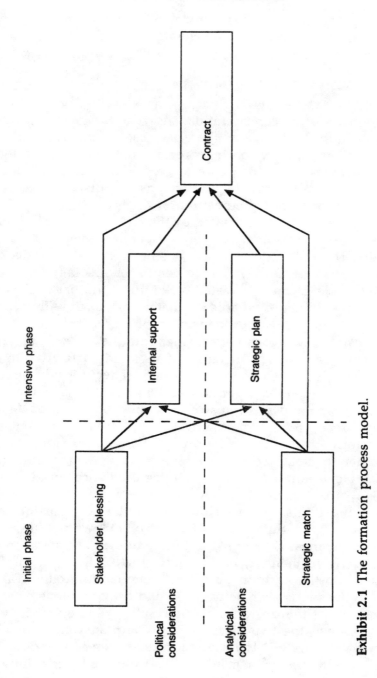

Exhibit 2.1 The formation process model.

discrete point in time. This model will be the basis for the discussion and analysis in this chapter.

Strategic Match

An initial, analytical consideration, shown at the lower left-hand side of exhibit 2.1, concerns the early assessment of the match between the prospective partners regarding two overall strategic potentials for cooperation. To a large extent this concerns the two dimensions discussed in Chapter 1, that is, resource input/output and strategic position.

The particular business created by the strategic alliance should be assessed in terms of its role in the parents' overall business portfolio. To what extent is the business truly central to the parents' portfolio? Does it play a central or a somewhat more peripheral role given the overall make-up of the parents' business activities? That is, what is the match/mismatch with respect to the two frameworks outlined in chapter 1?

The business that each party brings into the strategic alliance should also be assessed in terms of its strength relative to its competition. Is it already an established leader? Or is it more a follower, behind its competition and in need of catching up? The analysis should yield answers to questions such as: What are the broad, readily apparent benefits from this strategic alliance for each partner? How can the two parties complement each other to create common strengths from which both can benefit? How important is the strategic alliance within each partner's corporate portfolio? Are there any problems with the alliance due to its relative closeness to the core business of each partner? Are the partners leaders or followers within the particular business segment? Do they combine to create strength in an offensive manner, or is this a case of the sick joining the sick? Are the partners sufficiently similar culturally? Taken together, questions such as these should provide the answer to whether or not there is an obvious resulting strategic win–win match between the two partners. To obtain answers, it is also important to place an organisation in the partner's position and assess its own strategic considerations from the latter's point of view. The analysis at this stage should involve broad strategic matters. If an apparent win–win match emerges as truly apparent, the chances for success in implementation will increase. If this cannot be readily seen by most of the people involved, one should again reflect on whether it is worthwhile and appropriate to continue.

An example of establishing a clear win–win perspective is the strategic alliance between Yokogawa Electric and General Electric Medical Systems (Yokogawa Medical Systems), which also underscores, as we shall see, the need to reestablish a new win–win strategy as the alliance evolves over time. This alliance emerged from a successful sales agent agreement in the early 1970s. Yokogawa was very carefully selected because General Electric Medical Systems planned to make available its latest technology. By the early 1980s Yokogawa had learned so much about the technology that the firm suggested the development of a more cost-efficient and customer-adapted generation of products. Following new negotiations, the two firms agreed to form a fifty-fifty joint venture company in 1982 that would develop, manufacture, market, distribute, and service this new line of products. The new product line was immediately successful, and the operations grew rapidly. The joint venture was also able to come out with a simpler, smaller, and less expensive line of equipment, well adapted to the market. In fact, these operations subsequently became so important that General Electric Medical Systems gained clear benefits in integrating the joint venture operation further into its global strategy, where its product line would serve in a complementary manner to General Electric's other available products. In 1988, the partners agreed to increase General Electric Medical Systems's ownership share in the joint venture.

The win–win strategic match issue received a great deal of attention not only during the initial formation but also during the move from one evolutionary phase to the next when this alliance went through re-formation phases. The complementary benefits of continued cooperation for both partners were carefully reassessed at each phase. In each case a meaningful continuation of a win–win posture led to a modification in each party's role, including the ownership split. The reader might wonder if indeed this was a win–win for both parties, or if General Electric Medical Systems was the sole winner. We argue that it was also a win situation for Yokogawa Electric in that, at first, it got access to state-of-the-art technology and became part of an intense technological development effort, but later went on to benefit from being part of General Electric Medical's global strategy.

Stakeholder Blessing

A primary political consideration is ensuring that the most important external and internal stakeholders will see the general benefits from, and thus sponsor, the idea of a strategic alliance. This is illustrated in the upper left-hand side of exhibit 2.1. Needless to say, a strategic alliance can be seen as a threat among key internal stakeholders. Are key members of the top management team likely to be willing to pursue the venture by seeing how the alliance will not threaten their own power and careers? The CEOs may be hesitant if they perceive that the prospective alliance might diminish their own discretionary power (such an alliance will typically have been proposed by the firm's owners); a division manager might fear becoming lost as a small part of a large alliance; employees might fear restructuring, potential loss of jobs, or additional cultural stresses; union representatives might also see hidden agendas; and so on. To the extent that the alliance could represent a threat to any person or group, how can they be convinced to work toward the alliance's subsequent success? It is therefore critical to line up the support of the key internal stakeholders early on – the handful of persons who truly are in positions that can make or break it internally. MacMillan and Jones (1987) summarize a set of key concepts regarding how to manage internal stakeholders which seem appropriate when it comes to seeking stakeholders' support for a strategic alliance:

- One must consider the nature of the demands that will be made by the internal stakeholders.
- One must understand individual political behavior and the process by which coalitions form and evolve.
- Individuals and groups within an organization can strive to restructure conditions so that the organization pursues goals that better suit them.
- These individuals and groups tend to use manipulation, bargaining,

and coalition formation with interest groups to achieve their purposes.

- Coalitions tend to build around issues.
- Some control of coalition structure may be achieved by making different issues visible.
- To gain commitment from internal stakeholders, the political strategist must anticipate and manage coalition behavior.
- The degree of importance of the proposed strategy should determine the amount of the investment spent on the restructuring effort. Gaining commitment could take the form of finding the right way rather than winning, when the issues at hand are critical to the organization's success.

In general, these concepts concern two areas: (1) how to understand the internal stakeholders' behaviors and methods better, and, (2) how to handle internal coalitions successfully, so that the strategic alliance is given a fair chance.

External stakeholders are, of course, also important to consider early on – if not, they can stop the alliance. Critical external stakeholders are owners, board members, banks, unions, the government, and so on. When it comes to understanding external stakeholders' potential behaviors MacMillan and Jones (1987) again provide useful suggestions. They point especially at three sets of questions: First, is a particular stakeholder a dependent or a competitor? Second, should one take direct or indirect action? Finally, should one manipulate or accommodate?

In the present context, questions regarding external stakeholders that need to be addressed at this early stage in the formation process include the following. Are relevant ownership groups convinced that the venture will be desirable from their stockholder viewpoint? What will be the effect on their reputation and the response of the stock market? How will customers, suppliers, existing alliance partners, financiers, and competitors react? It is important to carry out initial preparatory efforts to increase the likelihood that major stakeholders will accept and promote the idea of a particular cooperative strategy.

These stakeholder considerations are easily facilitated, of course, if previous positive experiences, old contacts, and good reputations exist. The purpose at this stage is to ensure that key individuals and groups see the overall rationale for the alliance. If these stakeholders, at least tacitly, bless the venture at an early stage, the chances for smooth implementation increase. Conversely, if active resistance emerges among key stakeholders at an early stage, it is probably wise to call off the formation efforts then and there. A great deal of time and energy can be saved by exercising such realism in judgment.

An example of a strategic alliance where both parties established broad early stakeholder blessing is the Fiat-Geotech–Hitachi Construction Machine joint venture. The alliance idea was bought into at the top management level of both firms. A major external stakeholder, Sumitomo Corporation, acted as a catalyst in helping the parties to see the major aspects of the strategic alliance idea in a positive light.

Strategic Plan

As can be seen from exhibit 2.1, we have now completed the initial stage of the formation process. The next step is to enter the more intensive negotiation stage.

Proper analysis is, of course, essential for ensuring that the strategic alliance will be spelled out in a proper way. Paradoxically, however, analytical efforts, taken out of context, should not be overemphasized. Too often, massive analytical efforts are initiated inappropriately. Only after the initial phase is completed (see exhibit 2.1) should a more thorough, in-depth analytical phase be entered into. In order to prepare the ground for subsequent implementation, and also to avoid mistakes regarding valuation issues, it is vital and appropriate at this stage to gather relevant in-depth information, to do the proper analyses, and to develop a business plan in a systematic manner.

This first major analytical phase culminates in the development of an overall strategic plan for the strategic alliance as it is intended to emerge as a combined and continued effort by the two parties. This may also involve more detailed information gathering, and the two prospective partners should work closely together. Such joint efforts take into consideration the following: How do the prospective partners view the market potential? Whom do they view as the key competitors, and how will the alliance want to compete with them? What is the worst-case scenario, particularly for achieving planned revenue levels? What are the competitive advantages of the strategic alliance? In total, how viable is the strategic alliance idea when translated into a business plan?

It is also important to understand the joint capabilities and strengths of the two prospective partners. The prospective strategic alliance would be of interest only if it is clearly likely to succeed in producing synergies that benefit both partners. The combination of forces should enable both partners to experience a win–win result by being part of a stronger, more competitive joint entity. By plotting the value chain (Porter 1985) of two prospective partners' businesses, exhibit 2.2 shows how combinations of activities from the two value chains could create various types of synergies and thus strengths. As indicated by I, the two partners could combine their efforts along the upstream end of the value chain, e.g., through joint R&D and/or coordinated manufacturing. The major aim of this type of cooperation is to gain scale advantage, that is, to reach a more critical size jointly. Volume-based cost and capital savings could be obtained through sharing the investments. An example of this

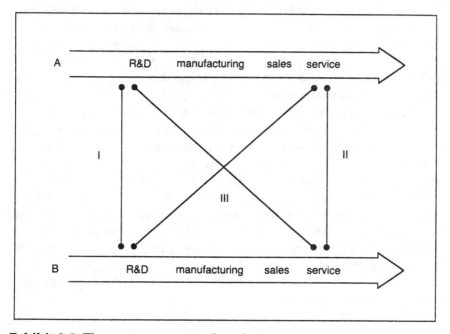

Exhibit 2.2 The two partners' value chains.

is the joint effort by Fiat and Peugeot to develop the Ducato light van. Another example is the NUMMI joint venture between Toyota and General Motors to produce cars which are sold through each party's separate distribution channels under their own labels.

In addition, critical human resources could be better utilized by working jointly. For example, teams of scarce scientists would not have to be duplicated, as in the strategic alliance between Ciba–Geigy and Chiron to develop synthetic vaccines. Cooperation also involves sharing the risks in large R&D projects and other large investments (Håkanson and Lorange, 1991).

Finally, the benefit from cooperating can also accrue to (former) competitors in businesses with overcapacity, allowing them to reduce excess capacity by combining operations while preventing the creation of excessive new greenfield capacity. This is exemplified by the alliance between ICI and DuPont in paints for the European automotive industry.

Alternatively, the prospective partners may consider how to combine efforts with regard to the downstream side of their value chains. As indicated by II in exhibit 2.2, this can be done by, for example, coordinating distribution systems, developing joint sales force activities, and/or combining both companies' product lines; in other words, developing scope advantages in the marketplace. The benefits from strengthening one's position in the market place accrue through the shared costs of building up a more dominant market presence, allowing the firm to gain momentum rapidly in key markets. Most importantly, however, combining the strength of each partner's offerings, vis-à-vis its customers, might result in an even stronger ability to serve the customers in a fully-fledged manner in the market place. The strategic alliance between Ericsson and General Electric in mobile telephony is an example of this – the products complement each other and form a more comprehensive range and capability. They are sold under a joint logo by the joint venture. Another example is the alliance between Fiat's components subsidiary Magneti Marelli and the French Matra Group in automotive components, where the products are sold through Magneti Marelli's distribution system.

It might also be advantageous for one company to combine its upstream strengths with another's downstream strengths or vice versa. This is indicated by III in exhibit 2.2. For example, one company might have a unique technology and an associated range of products that it wishes to market globally. As an alternative to investing in its own sales and distribution network in each country, which might outstrip the firm's resources, the firm could enter into a strategic alliance with prospective partners who already control market networks. The mutual gains and benefits accruing from this type of strategic alliance stem from complementarities. An example of this is the strategic alliance between Chrysler and Fiat, where a joint venture imports and distributes the Alfa Romeo 164 in the US. It is marketed through a select number of Chrysler distributorships to add upscale complementarity for Chrysler's own line.

Other reasons for these types of strategic alliances may stem, for example, from legal requirements by a host government to form strategic alliances as a condition for being allowed entry. We have already discussed this. Local ownership requirements are particularly common in certain south-east Asian countries, India, the Middle East, and Brazil. A typical well documented example of this is Corning's entry into Indonesia in a joint venture to manufacture tableware with a local partner.

Needless to say, the inverse example is the case where the firm which has a strong presence in the market place takes the initiative and contacts another firm which might have a clear upstream-type advantage in the value chain; for example, a line of better products or lower labor costs. The former might wish to form a strategic alliance with the latter to gain access to cheaper and better products than it can make itself, and that it can market through its own distribution system, keeping its market share. The benefits are gains in cost competitiveness and the securing of steady sourcing. This would also lighten the former firm's own investments in its own upstream capabilities. Through such a type of strategic alliance a firm might also get important access to the partner's technology, thereby saving time and resources by catching up with a technology leader. We find many examples of this when it comes to so-called Original Equipment Manufacturers (OEMs). John Deere used Hitachi as its OEM supplier of hydraulic excavators for a long period of time, and the relationship evolved into a joint venture. Another typical example of this type of informal strategic alliance is the long-term relationship between IKEA and its large Swedish sub-contractor Samhall. The types of supplier–customer networks that can be formed over time may be informal, in that little or no· contractual documentation exists. Still, they can be quite stable, and should indeed be seen as strategic alliances (Håkansson and Johansson 1988).

It is important that we critically assess early on the prospective benefits to each party from a contemplated strategic alliance. These benefits accrue through gaining scale, and/or scope, and/or complementarity, and they do it in different ways. For instance, benefits can accrue by gaining access to markets, gaining access to technologies, sharing risks, saving on costs, sharing investments, saving time, and/or spreading political exposure. Each party should assess how these prospective benefits satisfy its own particular strategic intent. If the prospective strategic alliance does not seem to be able to produce the benefits the partner is after, then the negotiations should probably be stopped. It should be noted that such a prospective alliance may still be a good one, but for other partners with different strategic intents.

In summary, it is necessary, as a critical aspect of the early phase of a strategic alliance formation process, to establish a clear, early understanding of the prospective strategic match. This involves seeing how the strategic intents can be satisfied, as well as reconciled, through an assessment of the sources of expected gains from a prospective strategic alliance: exactly how is value intended to be created through the cooperation? Vague and unrealistic expectations regarding the strategic match can lead to disappointments, or indeed failure, later on.

The competitive advantage of the strategic alliance must also be understood from a unified point of view. Too often the parent firms in a strategic alliance do not have a realistic holistic understanding of this. Exhibit 2.3[1] illustrates how one might assess competitive advantages for the business strategy of the strategic alliance.

Competitive strength can be created in four areas:

- Combined efforts relative to *suppliers* to create a stronger bargaining strength in this area, in terms of purchasing power and/or developing favorable long-term contracts.
- Combining efforts vis-à-vis *customers*, by offering a fuller range of

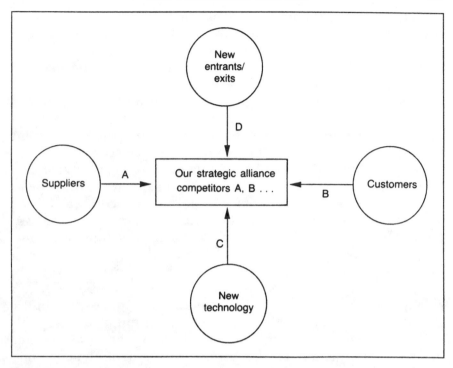

Exhibit 2.3 Assessment of competitive advantages.

products and maintaining a stronger sales force, thus being in a better position to satisfy customers' needs.
- Combining efforts to develop and exploit *new technology* by joint efforts and/or combining complementary technologies. This might lead to a possibility of leapfrogging the competitors.
- Combining efforts to achieve a size that preempts *new entrants.* That is, the creation of more effective entry barriers and/or combining efforts to diminish the number of independent players in the particular business and coming to grips with excessive overcapacity, i.e., lowering exit barriers.

It is important for both parties to identify and agree on those joint coordinated activities that are particularly critical to the cooperative strategy. Only a specifically laid out business plan can help the strategic alliance to become competitive.

If the strategic alliance is meant to support joint R&D-driven activities, for example, the two top management teams must ensure that operational integration takes place within the two

R&D functions. This must be manifested in the joint plan. Such scale synergies do not take place automatically. They require explicit endorsement of the plan by top management. In addition, a "carrot-and-stick" type of support will be needed. An analogous argument can be made for integrating two partners' efforts in the marketplace by coordinating their sales forces or product lines. An explicit plan must lay this out, and top management must approve. Again, push and encouragement from top management is vital for ensuring such scope synergies. Needless to say, it is easier for top management to go for it when they have had a chance to study an explicit business plan.

If the upstream activities of one partner are combined with the downstream activities of the other partner, it is necessary for the two parties to be glued together at the intersect point where one party's function ends and the other's begins. Here, a business plan should facilitate the basis for this. This gluing point must be watched keenly and be supported by both top management teams. Above all, however, the business plan must make sense to both parties, who otherwise might be left with only a partial view – a situation that in turn might lead to insular behavior detrimental to the competitiveness of the strategic alliance.

Turning to the major internal implementation issues that should be covered by the business plan, we must ask: What are each partner's relevant and available resources over the short and long term? What are the partners' attitudes toward long-term cooperation? How can this cooperation evolve harmoniously over time without conflicting with other strategic concerns of either partner? These considerations involve more detailed assessments regarding operational and tactical matters. If a realistic picture can be established, implementation efforts will be facilitated.

Nippon Steel exemplifies a firm that emphasized analytical considerations before it entered into a joint venture with IBM. Following the steel industry decline in the early 1980s, the firm made a strategic decision to diversify into several new business areas, one of which was "information systems." This decision resulted in the formation of several alliances, all announced in late 1988, one of which was NS & I, a relatively small venture with IBM. Nippon Steel contacted IBM directly with an invitation to form this strategic alliance. During the year prior to this invitation, however, Nippon Steel had conducted very thorough assessments regarding strategic match and operational details. The implementation of this joint venture seems to be going very well.

Internal Support

Given the analytical considerations, is it sufficiently clear who is expected to do what, and by when? A first look at this issue calls for a revisit to the political considerations. We now need to ensure that a broader range of people within the organization become committed to and are enthusiastic about the venture. This type of broadened internal "selling" is shown in the upper right-hand side of exhibit 2.1

The internal support issue concerns, above all, managers in various operational functions, who might be particularly actively involved in participating in the strategic alliance. Key questions to ask are: Has the venture idea been sufficiently explained and clearly motivated throughout the organization? Has it been presented with sufficient detail to ensure that everyone sees the tasks ahead and can focus on them as an opportunity? Has it been plausibly documented how combinations of activities are to be executed so that job security issues are addressed, and so that the strategic alliance will not be seen as a threat? Are relevant specialists motivated to carry out their specific tasks in a cooperative mode? Do the operational staffs have sufficient complementary styles to simplify their working contacts between the partner organizations?

In order for the entire organization to be prepared for quick task actions during the venture's implementation, everyone must be sold on the concept relatively early on. This diminishes the likelihood of rejection later. In a study of US–Japanese strategic alliances we found that the Japanese partners often were more forthright and effective when informing and bringing along members of their own organizations at an early stage in the strategic alliance formation process, an issue we also shall touch on (Lorange and Roos 1990).

Confidentiality considerations regarding early information

about a business deal may, of course, create problems with respect to a too-broad early organizational involvement. In certain cases, it simply may not be possible to disseminate the venture plans to a broad range of people before they are already a fait accompli. A typical example of this is the 1987 strategic alliance between the Swedish firm ASEA and the Swiss firm Brown Bovery, resulting in ABB. Only a handful of the top executives initiated and implemented the entire deal owing to a fear of insider trading in the two firms' stocks. Undoubtedly, this secrecy might have created organizational integration challenges and problems that probably, to some extent, could have been eased in the face of a more gradual and broader dissemination of information to the two organizations. It is, however, our experience that early and gradual information dissemination can be implemented more readily in those strategic alliance negotiations where stock market disclosure constraints are of little direct concern. The ASEA–BBC alliance may, from a practical point of view, be considered as very close to a merger; the two parent companies still exist but all operating activities are within ABB, the merged entity between the two prior organizations.

Outcome of Strategic Alliances

How do we really evaluate the effectiveness of strategic alliances? Shall we measure performance in terms of financial indicators?[2] In terms of survival?[3] In terms of changes in ownership?[4] Or in terms of renegotiation of the contract? Each strategic alliance obviously has unique characteristics. Therefore, it is virtually impossible to give a prescription for performance appraisal that is valid for more than a limited number of cases. Although many firms evaluate strategic alliances very much in the same way as wholly-owned divisions, such general procedures for measuring organizational performance are likely to be misleading. Traditional short-term-oriented financial measures are not valid because of, for instance, the risky setting in which many alliances are formed; uncertainties are very difficult to incorporate in the planning process. In addition, alliances have multiple parents and one of them may consider it a great success and the other may see it as a failure.

Executives seem to rank organizational performance by considering a combination of measures of performance. An example of this is the well-known survey of America's "most admired companies" by *Fortune*, where the following variables are measured: growth, profit, return on stockholders' equity, consistent avoidance of losses, consistently positive earnings, occasional improvements in operating results, good bond rating, and stable management. In our opinion, however, traditional accounting figures are statistically not sufficient to distinguish effective and ineffective firms.[5]

In an effort to grasp this problem in the strategic alliance context, Anderson (1990) developed the "input–output continuum" outlined in exhibit 2.4.[6] At the output end of the con-

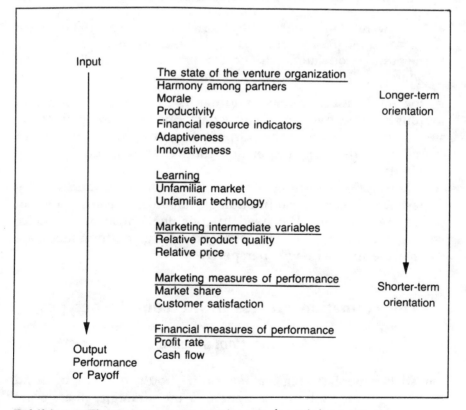

Exhibit 2.4 The input-output continuum for a joint venture.

tinuum (short-term orientation) we find the traditional result measures, for example, profitability. These are *indicators* of performance. At the input end (long-term orientation) we find variables that are determinants of performance, that is, what the organization is doing and how it achieves results. Because an organization can score well on input measures yet score poorly on the output measures, and vice versa, this input–output framework can be useful in understanding how to evaluate one's strategic alliances.

Another approach was taken by Geringer and Hebert (1991). They developed, and empirically tested, a number of hypotheses regarding the reliability and comparability of a range of objective and subjective measures of strategic alliance performance. The findings showed that:

- There was a significant positive correlation between objective and subjective measures of performance.
- There were significant positive correlations between the parent firms' and the joint venture managers' assessments of performance.
- The positive correlations also held for partners from similar national cultures.

One implication of these findings is that, in the absence of thorough, subjective performance data, one can employ objective surrogates. However, if the purpose of a strategic alliance is, for example, to develop a specific product, success might imply termination.

Although these findings can be useful for our understanding of performance appraisal in strategic alliances, we still have not solved the problem. We need to consider whose performance we are measuring, and to what extent the performances are compatible in a win–win perspective.

The Formation Process in the Four Archetypes

Ad Hoc Pool Alliance

For ad hoc pool strategic alliances, it should be kept in mind that the resources being assigned to the strategic alliance are sparse and that resources generated are expected to flow back to the parents. Similarly, we should keep in mind that it is expected that a parent sees this business, portfolio-wise, as a core business and that it expects to be a leader in this business segment relative to its competitors. An example of the ad hoc pool strategic alliance can be found in the pharmaceutical industry, where a particular leader cooperates on an ad hoc basis in tight strategic alliance designs on new business development or on R&D development. It can also be found in the electronics industry when it comes to cooperation on specific model enhancements, and it can be found in chemical firms dealing with small innovative potential competitors. As we have shown, these ad hoc pool strategic alliances tend to have a defensive nature from the point of view of the leader partner. From the point of view of the other party, the leader's nature tends to be opportunistic in exploiting the leadership it sees from being an innovator in the niche.

Given that one party typically tends to be a large established entity and the other a small entrepreneurial entity, finding a strategic match between two parties can be difficult. The important thing here is to keep in mind that one can be a leader and a strong player in the business even if the absolute size of one's firm is small.

The stakeholder blessing issue seems particularly important in that the stakeholders in the smaller firm are willing to grasp the opportunity of cooperating with a larger one, given the potential danger of being absorbed in the larger one later on. For the larger firm it may, to a large extent, be a matter of pride to be willing to cooperate with a small entrepreneurial firm in creating such an ad hoc pool arrangement.

When establishing a strategic plan for this type of strategic alliance it is important to look at the compatibility of resources, technologies, and other inputs being given by the various entities: the synergies that are contemplated should be created. In many instances the work methods of the smaller firms may differ so much from the larger ones, that technologies and market synergies are hard or impossible to achieve.

Developing a clear internal commitment to a strategic alliance and deciding when to pursue the ad hoc pool tasks among the two participating organizations are often challenging jobs. Typically, it becomes of key importance to have ad hoc meetings where the specificity of the tasks is fleshed out, and where face-to-face commitments are made among participants. This is especially important given the large differences in working styles frequently found between large, well-established organizations and small, entrepreneurial ones.

In regard to output measures, one expects specific results, such as the actual development of a particular technology, the actual creation of a particular new chip, or the actual conquering of a new market segment, to be the most important output measures. Accordingly, physical measures having to do with actually achieving the purpose of the strategic alliance are important rather than the classical financial performance output measures. Furthermore, when the physical purpose of the ad hoc pool cooperation is achieved, this strategic alliance tends to cease to exist.

Consortium Strategic Alliances

It should be kept in mind here that the resource inputs for a consortium tend to be richer, allowing more resource flexibility for adapting to new opportunities. The resources being generated in the alliance will, however, be expected to flow back to each of the parents. Typically, one finds this type of strategic alliance where the business is of core importance but where the party is a follower in a business competitive position sense.

This type of strategic alliance can be found when it comes to a more involved research consortium program among several parties, each having too small a resource base to carry out all of the research on its own. For instance, smaller rather than very large pharmaceutical firms may seek this kind of alliance, or one might find cooperation in the automotive industry among the slightly lesser players (Volvo; Renault; Mitsubishi) or within the electronics and chemical industries.

Concerning the strategic match issue in the consortium strategic alliance case, it is important that complementarities between more or less equal partners are assessed. Here, realism regarding the firm's and others' positions will be crucial. A congruence between the parties' viewpoints must be achieved. Given the fact that many of the parties may have relatively little prior knowledge of each other, and given their non-leading positions in their businesses, this strategy may involve the dismantling of many erroneous perceptions of the other party in order to delineate such congruence in the viewpoints of strategic positioning and resource input/output intentions.

The stakeholder blessing issue here is, above all, one of making sure that all key people on each side are involved, keeping in mind that more or less equal partners must create the basis for a win–win position, as opposed to creating a basis for trying to outrace each other.

In the development of a strategic plan in this case, one expects quite involved cooperation among the parties as they attempt to avoid duplication of efforts, to utilize complementary resources to the fullest, and to be realistic regarding how each other's resources can truly be best made use of. Thus, a fairly detailed delineation of the strategic actions, in a value chain coordination sense, is necessary in order to create superior quality at acceptable cost levels.

The internal selling in of the strategic alliance will require quite a substantial amount of detailed information and interaction among large numbers of members from each organizational entity, so as to create the basis for allocation of personnel to tasks within this broader-based consortium effort.

The output measures used here will partly be in the form of physical goals, such as the development of a new product, the achievement of a new R&D technology, or the penetration of a given market segment. The financial output issues will also be partly important. But above all, on the cost/resource utilization side, the key issue is to make sure that the physical outputs are being reached with reasonable financial inputs, and that these financial inputs have been incurred by the various parties in a fair way. Typical outputs in the form of revenue or profits will not normally be playing a major role within the consortium.

Project-based Joint Ventures

It should be kept in mind that project-based joint ventures typically take place where few resources are being put in by the parties, but where the resources gained are being retained in the particular joint venture. Typically the parties see themselves as leaders in the particular business segment, but also realize that this business segment tends to be somewhat peripheral in the overall portfolio strategies of the participating firms.

An example of such a strategic alliance can, for instance, be found when the parties attempt to enter a new market together, say a country which otherwise would be difficult to penetrate. One party has the market access, being initially based in the home market, the other party has the technology base. US and European firms entering into the Japanese market come easily to mind.

Regarding the strategic match issue in this strategic alliance, the question tends to be one of finding enough overlap between the perceptions of the various parties, keeping in mind that they typically come from different vantage points but still must establish a common ground. The provider of the technology must establish that it is a leader from the technology point of view but not a threat to the owner of the local market who is a leader from the market point of view. The two complementary leadership positions must be able to be matched without too extensive a threat of a win–lose degeneration scenario.

The stakeholder issue at play in this situation is that parties must overcome the fears of exposing their own strengths in order to ameliorate the other party's potential weakness (technology versus market). Hesitation from both sides is, indeed, a major reason for the lack of willingness to put in extensive resources, keeping the joint venture on a shoe-string basis until considerable trust and positive experience has been built up.

The development of a business plan typically deals with establishing the basis for the complementarities between the two parties, and documenting that the strategic alliance can be a competitive one in the local market at hand.

The organizational selling in of the strategic alliance has to do with delineating the tasks of who is doing what when it comes to, for instance, the transferring of technology from the partner owning the technology to the partner owning the market know-how. This frequently involves training, service, and other documentation issues, all being carried out on a minimum basis.

In measuring the performance of the strategic alliance, the profits and sales output measures will now become important. It is also important to keep in mind whether or not the strategic alliance is a competitive one, given that no resources have been assigned to the strategic alliance to fight unforeseen competitive eventualities. The joint operations strategic alliance will tend to be abandoned as soon as the strategic assumptions behind the alliance change. As such, one might argue for the monitoring of key strategic assumptions as one sort of output measure, complementing the typical financial measures.

Full-blown Joint Ventures

For the full-blown joint venture we recall that input resources are typically provided by each party more freely so as to allow for adaptation to new eventualities. We also recall that resources being generated tend to be kept in the strategic alliance, so as to build it up for future strategic moves. The portfolio strategy of the partners tends to be such that the business in question normally plays a relatively peripheral role in each partner's portfolio. And the partners tend to have a follower-type strategic posture within this particular business. The issue here is one of combining forces to catch up, to create much better value through a joint utilization of efforts, and, possibly, to provide a way to exit after the restructuring of one's business activities.

The strategic match between the parties in this case deals with establishing a clear understanding of the nature of the catch-up situation for both-parties. The willingness to provide ample resources will largely depend on a realization by both parties that neither of them will be able to dominate the other, and that neither of them is likely to succeed through a sparse resource infusion.

The stakeholder blessing issue, similarly, has to do with the key stakeholders on each side being willing to "bite in the sour apple," or realize that cooperation is the only realistic way. Continued independence will only be a way toward obscurity. For many stakeholders this will, of course, be hard, particularly those in prestigious businesses of long standing which have fallen on hard times.

The development of the business plan in this case, through pooling of the parties' interests in the value chains, tends to be quite elaborate. Both parties are inclined to put all their business activities in this area into the full-blown strategic alliance. This calls for a careful assessment of how the combined entity should be restructured, who should do what, what should be scaled down or up, and so on. Often such strategic plans fail because they end up being not much more than an adding together of the totality of two previously weak businesses. Needless to say, one does not gain strategic strength by combining two previously weak business strategies.

The selling in of the strategic alliance to the two parties calls for extensive and heavily involved pushing by both senior managements. Determination from the top is particularly essential here, especially since the alliance involves the merging of two separate cultures, with the subsequent laying off of people and the restructuring of the business. Getting the new organization in shape relatively quickly is absolutely crucial here.

When it comes to output measures, one anticipates the full array of financial output measures normally found in any freestanding organization: costs, revenues, sales, return on investment measures, etc. In addition, one needs to monitor carefully how the full-blown strategic alliance might be doing, relative to competitors, on measures such as market share, quality and customer satisfaction. Finally, the issue of assessing performance relative to the overall business climate is essential.

Summary

The strategic alliance formation process can be seen as evolving through two phases – an initial phase and an intensive phase. There is strong interaction between the decision-makers regarding the results of these considerations, both within and between each phase (indicated by the arrows between each consideration in exhibit 2.1). Also, there is tentative closure in the decision-making process, resulting in a "go–no-go" decision following each phase.

During the initial phase we have seen that a firm must ensure that it has the necessary acceptance and support from relevant key stakeholders. One must also be able to point out a clear, apparent significant strategic match between the partner firms. If the decision-makers are comfortable with the results of these two considerations, then the formation process should evolve into the second, more intensive phase. If not, the process should be aborted. Lack of proper attention to these considerations, and their early warning signals, can lead to unnecessary waste of time and energy on fruitless and stressful negotiations later on. Good management teams are only too aware of this. Teams that do not heed these signals easily end up wasting their top management's time.

During the main negotiation phase one must ensure that there is an understanding of, and an enthusiasm for, the cooperation throughout the organization. It is also necessary to emphasize the need for more detailed analytical efforts concerning the strategic alliance, which usually culminates in a business plan serving as a feasibility study. If the decision-makers are comfortable with the results of these considerations, a final "go" decision is likely to result. Because negotiations now have already led to socialization between the partners during the internal formation process, they will also tend to have a flying start in making the strategic alliance take off.

Ensuring stakeholder support without selling the alliance to the organization, or the other way around, will surely result in difficulties during implementation. Also, paying attention to the analytical considerations outside the context of the political considerations can lead to unrealistic conclusions. Although the analysis *per se* may yield very positive answers, it may be too narrow without the hindsight of the political dimension.

Paying attention to only political considerations, while de-emphasizing the more detailed analytical work, will probably also lead to problems, as illustrated by the 1973 strategic alliance between Joseph Seagrams & Sons and Kirin Brewery Co. in Japan. This alliance was the result of, on the one hand, Seagrams' wish to enter the promising Japanese market and, on the other hand, Kirin's wish to link up with a well-known and reputable foreign partner with complementary products. Both partners had their relevant stakeholders' blessings for the alliance and made thorough broad assessments of the strategic match. However, they appeared to have put relatively less emphasis on a detailed analysis of the market and the development of a business plan during the formation phase. Difficulties subsequently occurred, including less-than-expected sales. One reason was that the alliance's main product, spirits, turned out to be very difficult to market through Kirin's existing distribution network for beers. Over the last few years, however, sales have improved significantly, after a separate distribution plan was developed. Today the venture generates a substantial profit, with new products being added to the range.

In conclusion, to ensure smooth implementation of a cooperative strategy, decision-makers must carefully address all the four considerations discussed in this chapter, and shown in exhibit 2.1, before entering into an agreement with the partner. A thorough formation process will facilitate implementation of the strategic alliance and, therefore, increase the likelihood of its subsequent success.

An experienced strategic alliance negotiation team should now take over to formalize the contract. They must consider the major judgments of such a process, and should play out the negotiation scenario in their minds, even before actual negotiations have begun in earnest. A thorough formation process is a necessary, but not necessarily a sufficient, condition of success. The actual contract must now be fleshed out in negotiations. This matter will, however, not be discussed in this book.

Appendix
DEC–ITT[1]

On the afternoon of February 19, 1986, David Stone, Vice-President of International Engineering and Strategic Resources for Digital Equipment Corporation International, sat in his Geneva office looking out across the Rhone valley. Eight months earlier, he had briefed senior officers at corporate headquarters in the US about an effort to try out a new customer relationship. It was supposed to be based on a collaborative software development project between DEC (Digital Equipment Corporation) engineers and ITT Telecom's engineers located in four European countries. The DEC–ITT project was seen as an opportunity to try out a radically new approach to business partnerships in the information technology business. But how far could he let the experiment run?

Rumors were coming in from the financial department and from the central engineering group at headquarters, as well as from different country managers and their account executives. Everyone seemed to have a different understanding of the DEC–ITT relationship. With income from the project not even coming close to matching costs, David Stone knew that he should reassess his original strategy.

He logged on to his electronic mail system, skipped the 38 new messages and accessed his E-mail archive to re-read the eight-month-old message from DEC International's European Chairman which had been the catalyst leading to the cooperative activities with ITT:

To: D. Stone   July 15, 1985
From: P.C. Falotti
Status: Urgent

David – news from the front . . . our courtship with ITT seems to have gotten off the track. Insider tells me that Apollo has a European (Brussels ITT) confirmation for 40 workstations. Don't know if ITT is looking for a counteroffer, but we need to act fast. We might be able to make something of our "strategic relationship thinking" and link it to the recent work done by your Metaframe group. What can we do?

Background

Eight months earlier, Stone had asked a multi-functional team led by Michael Horner, part of the Metaframe "think tank," to work with ITT on a partnership arrangement. Rather than simply sell hardware and software to ITT, Mike had assembled a team to build an engineering relationship. The team would rely on DEC's new workstation and computer-assisted software engineering (CASE) technologies to transfer software development methodologies and project management know-how to ITT. Because of the potential partnership, some of the people involved believed that DEC had sold several million dollars' worth of hardware. This rumor could neither be confirmed nor simply linked to this joint software engineering project. None the less, David had committed some of his best people in the hope that a significant, long-term relationship with ITT would materialize, leading to major sales increases and useful new software tools. This activity had raised a lot of questions, both from inside the organization and from other customers with pressing needs.

Digital Equipment Corporation International (Europe)

Digital Equipment Corporation had established overseas sales and distribution in the late 1960s which eventually had led to the founding of Digital Equipment Corporation International (Europe) as a wholly-owned operating company in 1979.

DEC Europe's mission was to import, develop, manufacture, and market networked computing systems for customers in Europe. The first Chairman and founder of Digital International was Jean-Claude Peterschmitt, a polished European statesman and businessman from Switzerland. He contributed much of his time and energy to breaking down technical and economic barriers among the European states, and between the US and Europe. Peterschmitt believed that the computing industry was moving quickly from its US origins to an international computing and communications environment, and that Digital had a role to play, both as a vendor and as a developer of new technologies. See exhibit A2.1 for the development of DEC's sales and personnel.

Wherever possible, Digital International had adopted a management structure similar to that of Digital US. The parent company had been a pioneer in organizational design and development. The company structure, known as the matrix, was built around key managers, who were responsible for core product groups. In

Exhibit A2.1 DEC worldwide and European sales (million $) and personnel (thousands), 1978–85

| Year | Worldwide | | Europe (with % of worldwide) | | | |
	Sales	People	Sales	%	People	%
1985	6,686	89	1,945	29	18	20
1984	5,584	86	1,462	26	14	16
1983	4,272	73	1,074	25	11	15
1982	3,381	67	1,006	30	10	15
1981	3,198	63	935	29	10	16
1980	2,368	56	687	29	9	16
1979	1,804	44	486	27	7	16
1978	1,437	39	377	26	6	15

Europe, there was a matrix between the core product groups and geographic regions. The core product groups were built on Digital's product and technology expertise, with country managers responsible for meeting regional quotas. A major addition to the matrix were the country managers, who had overall responsibility for coordinating Digital's business activities in and among different countires (see exhibit A2.2a).

Digital's structure worked well during its period of rapid growth in Europe, protecting its product base in two major market segments (engineering and scientific computing). At the same time, the strength of its product range ensured strong growth in nearly all goegraphic segments (see exhibit A2.2b).

Product/Market Issues

Throughout the early 1980s, new competitors had reduced Digital's lead in scientific computing. In the high-end mainframe segment, IBM had recently streamlined its products into four key product groups and was offering networking capabilities. In the low-end microcomputing segment, IBM had captured Apple's early lead by introducing the personal computer (PC and PC–AT) products in its traditional strong business computing segments (see exhibit A2.3). DEC's strength had traditionally been in the mid-range minicomputer market, where it ranked second (behind IBM). Competitors such as Sun Microsystems (founded in 1982) and Apollo were moving fast in a new segment – technical workstations. Digital realized the early possibilities of technical workstations and saw them as a way to incorporate new features and technological developments into high-performance, multi-task desktop computer configurations that would sell for less than $100,000 (see exhibit A2.4). Conflicting internal product development paths hindered Digital's ability to lead in this new segment. But two bright lights were on the horizon: (1) the company's answer to the workstation market, the Microvax II, and DEC's increasing share in the emerging software development; and (2) computer-assisted software engineering (CASE) markets.

In addition, the company was ready to announce a second generation VAX system, resulting from a three-year investment of over $2 billion in research and engineering. With the announcement of several new hardware, software and service products, Digital entered what industry experts called a new product transition phase. This meant that the new hardware and software products were not quite in sync with the existing orders for

Exhibit A2.2a Digital International: Country management team, 1985 under European area management.

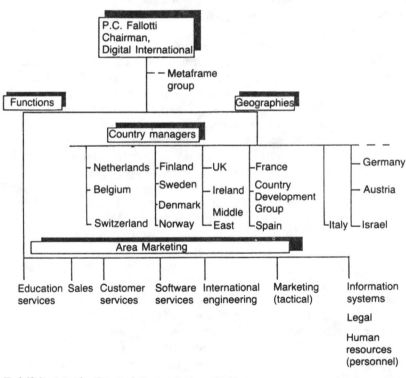

Exhibit A2.2b Digital International: European area management team, 1985.

Faced with sluggish demand for their traditional products, minicomputer makers are banking on cheaper models . . .

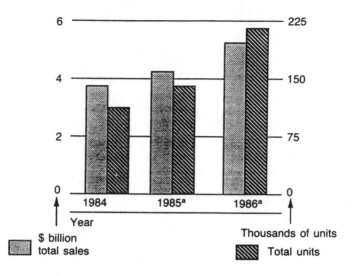

. . . but competition in this market segment is fierce.

Company	Market shares	
	1984	1985[a]
IBM	24.1%	24.5
Digital	*18.5*	*19.2*
Wang	8.4	6.7
HP	5.0	4.3
Data General	4.5	3.6
Texas Instruments	3.3	5.6
Convergent Tech.	2.1	5.7
AT&T	1.9	2.5
Burroughs	1.5	2.1
Prime	1.5	2.1
Other	28.8	26.7

Exhibit A2.3 Digital Europe: competition in minicomputer manufacturing, 1984–6
[a] estimated.
Source: Data Infocorp. DEC/ITT Indus. 1.

Exhibit A2.4 The top ten companies in minicomputers and microcomputers

Company	1985 units	1984 units	% change
Minicomputers			
IBM	3,500.0	3,500.0	NC
Digital Equipment Corp.	1,600.0	1,527.0	4.8
Hewlett Packard	1,050.0	950.0	10.5
Wang Laboratories	870.9	970.5	−10.3
Data General Corp.	799.7	840.0	−4.8
Prime Computer Inc.	563.7	479.1	17.7
Tandem Computers	533.1	477.1	11.7
Harris Corp.	470.0	410.0	14.6
Fujitsu Ltd	439.0	383.9	14.4
Nixdorf Computer	407.9	340.0	20.0

Company	1985 units	1984 units	% change
Microcomputers			
IBM	5,500.0	5,500.0	NC
Apple Computer Corp.	1,603.0	1,747.0	−8.2
Olivetti	844.5	496.9	78.0
Tandy Corp.	796.8	573.5	38.9
Sperry Corp.	742.8	503.4	47.6
Commodore International	600.0	1,000.0	−40.0
Compaq Computer	503.9	329.0	53.2
Hewlett Packard	400.0	500.0	−20.0
Convergent Techn.	395.2	361.7	9.3
Zenith Electronics	352.0	249.0	41.4

Source: Datamation 1985

equipment. This factor was felt in the marketplace, offering further possibilities for competitor encroachment on Digital's traditional customers.

The Competitive Environment for Engineering Workstations

Workstations were one segment of the general computing market. Industry analysts often identified the other segments as mainframes, minicomputers, and personal or microcomputers. Minicomputer prices ranged from $30,000 to $100,000; workstations were from $15,000 to $60,000, and personal computers from $1, 500 to $20,000.

The workstation market had emerged in the early 1980s with Apollo's introduction of its technical workstation (1981). Sun Microsystems soon followed in February 1982 with the introduction of the Sun 1, a product that included a Central Processing Unit (CPU) printed circuit board, a video board, a power supply, and a high resolution monitor. Its typical customers were universities and sophisticated end users who followed technological developments. By 1984–5 the customer base broadened to include users in Fortune 1,000 companies. Digital and Data General had both entered the market with proprietary CPUs in the workstation market, but it was still not clear whether the products would be accepted by users. Rumors of an IBM workstation were rampant, but had not yet materialized.

A key feature of the newly-defined workstation segment was rapid change. The life of a workstation design was short, 18 months at best, because the base technology of the workstation, the microprocessor, was continually improving in speed and performance.

Apollo Computer Corp. had a keen interest in redefining the market to include the new workstation segment. IBM had a virtual lock on the mainframe segment and, by then, 60 percent of the microcomputer market. The fuzzy middle ground included minicomputers, superminis and workstations, all with shifting price/ performance characteristics. Domination of this segment was still undetermined, but workstations were taking the early lead. It was still early in the game for engineering workstations, and sales would continue to hinge on both price performance specifications of the various machines and software development. One way to push software development would be to form networked engineering partnerships.

Technological Innovation in Digital: The Role of Central Engineering

At the heart of Digital's technology development process was a high level group in the United States known as Central Engineering. This team, established by Kenneth Olsen, the founder of DEC, provided the platform for developing the base technologies of the company. Central Engineering relied on current technical developments in the field and feedback from the product marketing groups to decide on its portfolio of technologies. Once Central Engineering had agreed on a five-year technological trajectory for the company's products and services, the product groups were responsible for getting the base technologies into product/market areas.

David Stone saw, early on, that the Digital–ITT relationship would not easily fit into the technical development process and plans of Central Engineering. Under normal circumstances, it should fit into one of the product/market areas – Software services and applications services (SWAS). But the Digital–ITT relationship had both a market intent and a software engineering mandate. It was working across Digital's product/market areas, trying to create its own expertise in software tool development for telecommunications companies.

Fortunately, David Stone could point to a history of joint technical development projects that his International Engineering Group had carried out in Europe. Differences in engineering approaches had given Digital Europe some leeway in its joint engineering approaches. The Engineering group of Digital Europe had written the company manual on university–industry partnerships. But university links were different from working with customer engineering groups. Sharing early knowledge with the customer in exchange for a clearer view of their current problems and future needs required a different management approach. David Stone knew that joint technical development with ITT would require having the project fit into one of the existing technical pipelines, but at the same time called for a creative market/technology approach.

Forming Policies on Strategic Alliances in Europe

The period 1984–5 had been turbulent for the world computer industry. Market growth was beginning to slow down from a 25 percent average compound growth rate to a more docile 10–15 percent per annum. Industry experts spoke of two central issues:

convergence of technologies between computing and other industrial segments such as telecommunications (see exhibit A2.5) and strategic alliances that ranged from simple technology and market exchanges to industrial mega-deals.

In Europe, Digital had received more than ten offers to form so-called strategic alliances (see exhibit A2.6). In the emerging spirit of European integration, Digital had even been approached about participating in Eureka, Esprit, and other joint technology development programs.

Digital Europe's top engineering people felt that the company was well positioned in an era of converging technologies. DEC had maintained its own proprietary hardware and software, and

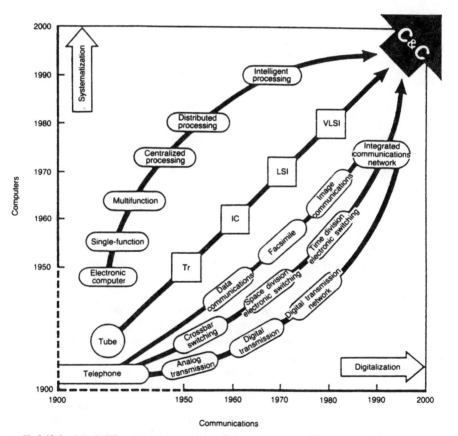

Exhibit A2.5 The convergence of computer and communications technologies: perspective on C&C Vision (courtesy of NEC Corporation, K. Kobayashi, 1985).

Exhibit A2.6 Digital Europe: Partnership approaches from European companies and national groups

---

UK
  British Telecom; Plessy

Scandinavia/Benelux
  L.M. Ericsson; Televerket; Philips

France
  CGE–TELIC; Thomson; Matra

Italy
  Olivetti; Fiat; Stet/Italtel

Germany
  Siemans; Nixdorf; Kienzle; Bosch

Pan-European
  Esprit; EC12 Interconnect Standards; National Government
  Signals in UK, Germany, France, Spain, Sweden

---

had migrated from scientific and engineering applications to a broader customer base. Digital had led the computer industry in several areas of its technical development. Ethernet networking software, an early product designed for networked computing systems, was one such technology. Digital engineers had also become experts at using their network technologies to carry out development projects simultaneously at several geographical locations.

Yet, partly because of Digital's proprietary technology path, a number of managers viewed strategic alliances as an overly complicated approach to business and technology development. Under Kenneth Olsen, Digital had become known as a "go it alone" company. In the history of the company, Digital had made several acquisitions, but all were informal agreements and true joint ventures were a new development.

P.C. Falotti argued convincingly that Digital Europe would have to develop a systematic process for evaluating the offers of potential European partners, and that such a process would require a major shift in corporate values. David Stone had asked Michael Horner and Tony Setchell to form a low-key group that would build a framework for considering partnership proposals – one that would recommend how to act. The multidisciplinary team, known as the Metaframe Group, took their mandate seriously. As Michael Horner often stated, "We were working on an industry level, seeking industry solutions." Over the next several months, they wrote a policy statement (see exhibit A2.7) and carried out analysis that considered the following issues:

- partnership approaches
- future competition
- future technology trends
- market evolution
- how Digital provides solutions for customers

The group developed a visual mapping exercise that would juxtapose the competitive and technological positions of various companies across information technology industries. The mapping tool was also used to define Digital's strategic and technical position on the map, and to suggest various possible partnering combinations (see exhibit A2.8). The Metaframe Group's work revealed that Digital's top management faced a difficult challenge: the company would have to sustain its current customer relationships, while developing new frameworks for working with customers. Joint technology development and engineering with customers was highly recommended by the team. The Metaframe process also confirmed the value of visual presentation of communication tools. By overlaying the strategies of various companies, the group could bring to the surface critical issues before making choices about new technologies and business partnering. The Metaframe Group remained an invisible task force until August 1985 when a request from ITT Europe provided David with an opportunity to take the group's abstract ideas and test them with a major customer of long standing.

ITT Corporation

ITT was a conglomerate multinational corporation that had grown enormously under the 23-year stewardship of Harold Geneen. In 1979 he stepped down as chairman of the board, having made more than 250 acquisitions and having built ITT into a vast confederation of companies comprising two thousand working units. During the same period, revenues had gone from $800 million to $22 billion, and earnings from $30 million to $560 million. The Geneen legacy was inherited by Rand Araskog on January 1, 1980. Unfortunately for Araskog, Geneen left behind a $5 billion debt accrued, in part, by his merger and acquisition activities. It was partly as a result of ITT's heavy debt burden and

Exhibit A2.7 Digital Europe: Statement of principles of the Metaframe Group

---

Vision of the Ideal – Metaframe Group, April 8, 1986

To become more productive, organizations must have a consistent philosophy of organization which empowers their employees to fulfill the company's mission. Below is Digital's vision of the ideal philosophy to achieve productivity (and high employee morale).

We believe in the dignity of the individual, the increase in his productivity which comes from associating freely with others in his organization accessing the information required by his job, and his obligation to provide information to others as he receives it. We want to help to increase the effectiveness of interpersonal communication. These beliefs lead to the peer-to-peer style of networking we produce, as well as to the management style we use: computer mediated information (notes, files, . . .) is an appropriate implementation of this style. Interestingly, this style is applicable also to computers interfacing with machines; on the shop floor we could use the slogan "liberate the Robots" to identify the power which we can add to the manufacturing process when the parts of the process are appropriately connected.

We look forward to the evolution of the business world to the "one corporation" concept, in which the information flow between departments of two different companies is as easy as that between equivalent departments in the same company. This interaction would make clear that the primary long-term added value of a company is the process which it has; if those processes are not clearly superior to those available externally, then the company should seriously consider using the external processes instead of its internal ones. This style of management would quickly lead to the distribution of processes to the place where they can be done best, just as distributed computing moves the computation to the place where it can be done best. Examples are just-in-time manufacturing which moves your inventory outside your company or external manufacturing which moves the whole process outside.

We define the mission of Digital as the production of quality information systems, products and services; where information systems are defined as "the way in which a company acquires, shares, integrates and uses data to fulfill its mission, optimize its productivity, and competitiveness and plan its evolution."

Exhibit A2.7 Continued

Vision of the Ideal – Metaframe Group, April 8, 1986

The final stage of our relationship to other companies occurs when we take the risk of agreeing to do new things together as partners. Previous to this stage, we sell products, services, architectures and then processes which we already have. The partnership commitment is to make things which both parties agree are necessary, but which were not previously part of the repertoire of either company.

We recognize that a major part of our perceived added value lies in the Digital Computing Environment (DCE), which allows high productivity in applications development, flexible restructuring of information flows to adapt to organization and mission changes, and enhanced capability for effective information management and exchange. We should therefore be developing programs to make the use of the DCE as attractive as possible to OEMs, software houses and internal company applications developers.

---

partly owing to the restructing of several ITT units that ITT was targeted and subjected to hostile takeover bids during the early 1980s. Even *Fortune Magazine* took some stabs at ITT, calling it "a museum of the investment and management ideas of the sixties."

Araskog took a number of steps to reduce the size of ITT's corporate debt. Between 1980 and 1983, ITT sold 61 companies in order to generate proceeds of $1.3 billion. He streamlined the holding into five product areas and four service areas.

Product areas

- Automotive Products
- Electronic Components
- Fluid Technology
- Defense and Space Technology
- Natural Resources

Service areas

- Insurance Operations
- Financial Services
- Communications and Information Services
- Hotels and Community Development

```
SERVICES ↑

GOVT MAIL                              TELEPHONE   VANS  BROADCAST NETWORKS   VIDEOTEX
PARCEL SVCS        MAILGRAM            TELEGRAPH         BROADCAST STATIONS   AND        PROFESSIONAL SVCS
OTHER DELIVERY     E-COM               OCCs                    CABLE NETWORKS  DATERBASE SVCS
SVCS               EMS                 IRCs                  CABLE OPERATORS  NEWS SVCS
                                       MULTIPOINT DISTRIB SVCS                           FINANCIAL SVCES
                                                                                         ADVERTISING SVCES
                   PRINTING COS        SATELLITE SVCS         BILLING AND      TELETEX
                   LIBRARIES           FM SUBCARRIERS         METERING SVCS    TIMESHARING BUREAUS
                                       MOBILE SVCS
                                       PAGING SVCS            MULTIPLEXING SVCS       ON-LINE DIRECTORIES
                                                                                      SOFTWARE SVCS
RETAILERS                                          INDUSTRY NETWORKS
NEWSTANDS                                                                       SYNDICATORS AND
                                       DEFENCE TELECOM SYSTEMS                   PROGRAM PACKAGERS
                              SECURITY SVCS


                                            COMPUTERS


                                       PABXs

                                                      SOFTWARE
                                                      PACKAGES
                                       RADIOS
                                       TV SETS
PRINTING AND GRAPHICS                  TELEPHONE MODEMS                          DIRECTORIES
EQUIPMENT                              TERMINALS                                 NEWSPAPERS
COPIERS                                PRINTERS                                  NEWSLETTERS
                                       FACSIMILE                                 MAGAZINES
CASH REGISTERS                         ATMs
                                       POS EQUIPMENT
INSTRUMENTS                            BROADCAST AND
                                       TRANSMISSION EQUIP                        SHOPPERS
TYPWRITERS                             CALCULATORS
DICTATION EQUIPMENT                    WORD PROCESSORS                           AUDIO RECORDS
FILE CABINETS                          PHONOS, VIDEO DISC PLAYERS                AND TAPES
BLANK TAPE AND FILM                    VIDEO TAPE RECORDERS
                                                                                FILMS AND VIDEO
                                                                                PROGRAMS
PAPER                          MICROFILM, FICHE    MASS STORAGE
                               BUSINESS FORMS      GREETING CARDS               BOOKS

PRODUCTS

◄─── CONDUIT                                                         CONTENT ───►
```

Exhibit A2.8 a,b Digital Europe: Metaframe – mapping the competitive positions of possible partners.
Key: ATM – Automated Teller Machine, E-Com – Electronic Computer Originated Mail, EMS – Electronic Message Service, IRC – International Record Carrier, OCC – Other Common Carrier, PABX – Private Branch Exchange, POS – Point-of-Sale, SVCS – Services, VAN – Value Added Network.
Source: B. Compaine, *Understanding New Media*, 1985.

ITT Telecommunications was part of the communications and information services area, but relied on technical know-how, especially from the electronic components group.

ITT Telecommunications and the System 12

The telecommunications industry was rapidly shifting from analog to digital switching systems, and virtually every major player wishing to compete in the global telecommunications business had reoriented their R&D strategies to move from electromechanical to digital switching technologies. Success in this technological

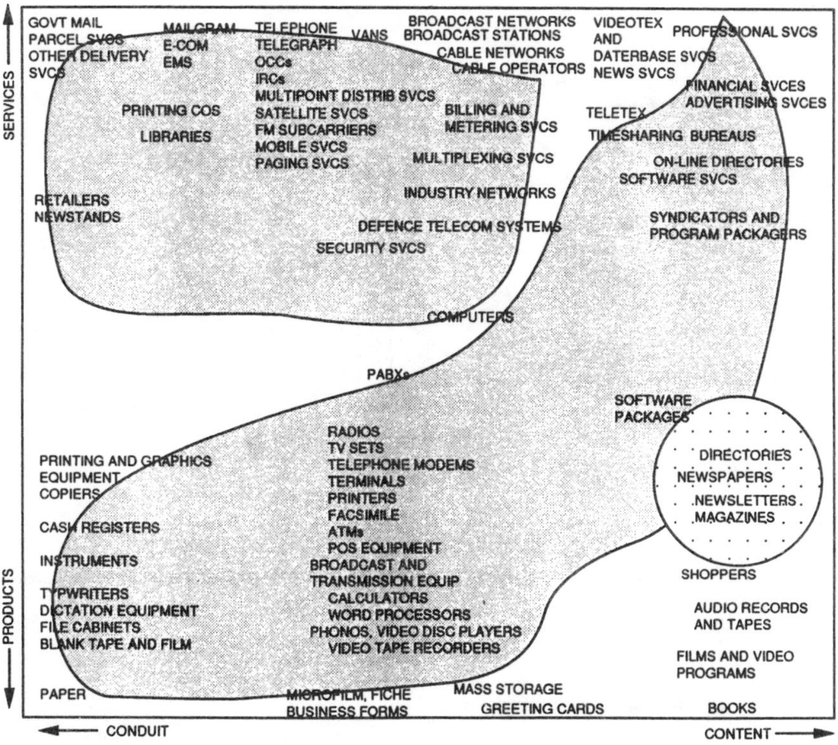
GOVT MAIL
PARCEL SVCS
OTHER DELIVERY SVCS
MAILGRAM
E-COM
EMS
TELEPHONE
TELEGRAPH
OCCs
IRCs
MULTIPOINT DISTRIB SVCS
SATELLITE SVCS
FM SUBCARRIERS
MOBILE SVCS
PAGING SVCS
VANS
BROADCAST NETWORKS
BROADCAST STATIONS
CABLE NETWORKS
CABLE OPERATORS
VIDEOTEX AND
DATERBASE SVCS
NEWS SVCS
PROFESSIONAL SVCS
FINANCIAL SVCES
ADVERTISING SVCES
PRINTING COS
LIBRARIES
BILLING AND METERING SVCS
MULTIPLEXING SVCS
INDUSTRY NETWORKS
TELETEX
TIMESHARING BUREAUS
ON-LINE DIRECTORIES
SOFTWARE SVCS
RETAILERS
NEWSTANDS
DEFENCE TELECOM SYSTEMS
SECURITY SVCS
SYNDICATORS AND PROGRAM PACKAGERS
COMPUTERS
PABXs
SOFTWARE PACKAGES
RADIOS
TV SETS
TELEPHONE MODEMS
TERMINALS
PRINTERS
FACSIMILE
ATMs
POS EQUIPMENT
BROADCAST AND TRANSMISSION EQUIP
CALCULATORS
WORD PROCESSORS
PHONOS, VIDEO DISC PLAYERS
VIDEO TAPE RECORDERS
PRINTING AND GRAPHICS EQUIPMENT
COPIERS
CASH REGISTERS
INSTRUMENTS
TYPWRITERS
DICTATION EQUIPMENT
FILE CABINETS
BLANK TAPE AND FILM
PAPER
DIRECTORIES
NEWSPAPERS
NEWSLETTERS
MAGAZINES
SHOPPERS
AUDIO RECORDS AND TAPES
FILMS AND VIDEO PROGRAMS
MICROFILM, FICHE
BUSINESS FORMS
MASS STORAGE
GREETING CARDS
BOOKS
SERVICES
PRODUCTS
CONDUIT
CONTENT

Exhibit 2.8 Continued

shift had come at a price: an Arthur D. Little study estimated that, given the shortness of the digital system technology lifecycle (5–8 years compared to 25–30 years for electromechanical systems), developers of new telecommunications switches would have to obtain 8 percent of the world market share in telecommunications switching equipment in order to break even on development costs. ITT engineers were also aware that 75 percent of digital switch development costs would be software, not hardware, related (exhibits A2.9, A2.10).

ITT had embarked on its own ambitious development project in the late 1970s: the System 12. The company had developed its own technical protocols, including the CCITT development platform, a hardware architecture and software language intended to protect the company's investment and establish a new telecommunications standard. The development project grew from the company's Connecticut laboratories to several key technology development sites in Europe, including the ITT subsidiaries.

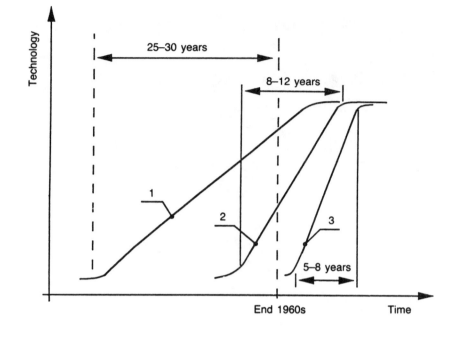

1   Electromechanical systems

2   Analog stored program control (computer)

3   Digital systems

Exhibit A2.9 Telecommunications switch development: technology lifecycles.

From Digital's perspective, ITT was confronting one of the most demanding software development projects in the history of telecommunications – its System 12 (S-12). Over 2,500 software engineers in four European locations had been working on the project for seven years, and there was no end in sight (a printout of the source code was said to fill two rail cars with paper).

The groups responsible for S-12 functional activities and engineering support were ITC Europe in Brussels and ESC in Harlow, UK, and for development and manufacture SEL in Stuttgart, Germany; BTM in Antwerp, Belgium; SESA in Spain; and FACE in Italy (see exhibit A2.11).

In the first phase of the S-12 project, it had been relatively easy to port software across programming languages and hardware

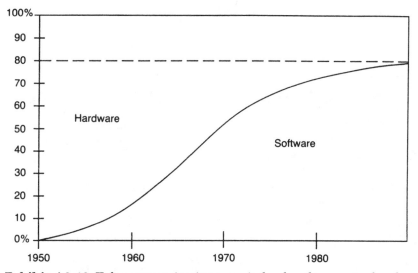

Exhibit A2.10 Telecommunications switch development: hardware versus software development costs.
Source: Ferdinand Kuznick, IMD lecturer.

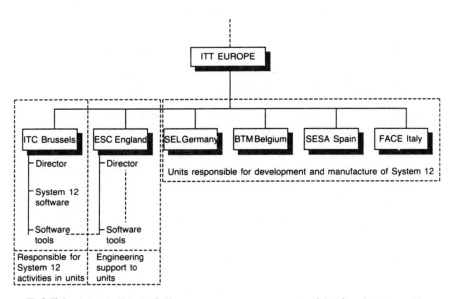

Exhibit A2.11 Digital Europe: groups responsible for System 12.

configurations. As S-12 development grew in size and complexity, subtle changes became major events in which each engineering group had to consider the changes of another group before proceeding.

When different groups attempted to work with several million lines of code, modifications became inevitable, and engineers had to overcome bugs by inserting a "patch." One engineer noted, "By the mid-1980s, we were putting new patches on top of old patches." To remedy the situation, ITT hired Tony Kenny, an ex-IBM engineer. Tony had been keen to spread the risks of any major changes in ITT's software development procedures. His solution to the slowdown in the S-12 development project was to use CASE tools.

Various factors led to questioning the potential value of ITT's long-term switch development project. These included:

- Lack of support for technological development. In the race to develop telecommunications hardware, little thought had been given to developing software processes and tools for the ongoing modification of products and services. Two presumptions proved to be false: that computer companies could provide off-the-shelf software tools to system developers, and that the cost of software development would increase at a slower rate than hardware development costs.
- Questionable market share for the System 12. The major world market for telephony, the US, was shaken in 1983 by a consent decree which resulted in breaking up AT&T's regional telephone business into eight independent companies and splitting Bell Laboratories in two: AT&T Bell Labs and BellCorp. Despite the break-up, AT&T was moving fast in developing a digital switch and would be ensured a significant market share after its introduction. The AT&T break-up created eight new competitors on the world telecommunications scene. In October 1984, Rand Araskog noted that, given the cost of the project and the increasing number of competitors, "there are doubts about the S-12's viability in the United States."
- ITT as a potential takeover target. During the early 1980s, ITT was the target of several hostile takeover attempts, each one proposing to split the company into several companies that would bring greater value for the shareholders. While Araskog succeeded in beating back each attempt, he was also required to dispose of several businesses.

The Request for BTMC and ITT (Europe)

In July 1985, the Belgian subsidiary of ITT (BTMC in Antwerp) sent a request for a tender to Digital's Belgian office. In simple terms, the offer focused on engineering workstations. Under normal circumstances, the Digital country manager would have heard about the bid request in advance. But this tender offer puzzled him. Given Digital's long-standing customer relationship with

ITT (dating back to Digital's first minicomputer purchase in 1968), the request had been hastily made, suggesting that BTMC was jumping at another new workstation offer. He was also aware of recent discussions about engineering workstations between Apollo Computer Corp. and ITT.

The country manager, being close to ITT headquarters in Brussels, had heard rumors of a "strategic agreement" being forged between Kenneth Olsen and the ITT CEO, Rand Araskog. Since the BTMC request referred to specific hardware, and because ITT was a strategic customer in several national markets, the country manager contacted David Stone in Digital's European headquarters. The ITT country manager decided to get clearer signals from senior management before proceeding.

Indeed, BTMC's request coincided with several ongoing discussions between ITT and Digital managers. Senior managers in two other ITT companies (ESC in Harlow, UK, and ITC Brussels, Belgium) had been talking with Digital about the development of software tools for the S-12. CASE tools were high on their list of needs. ITT's European headquarters (ITT Brussels) was at the center of the various proposals to work with Digital.

It was the hardware request from BTMC (ITT Belgium) that led to Pier Carlo Falotti's E-mail message to David Stone. The country manager's hunches were correct. Over the previous months, there had been several informal discussions between top level DEC and ITT personnel about hardware, software, and strategic collaboration. Digital's European Chairman, Falotti, knew that ITT was going through a strategic and technological transition. In the US, the company had successfully fought off several acquisition attempts by corporate raiders. In Europe, the System 12 telecommunications switch development project was taking significantly longer than expected. David remembered how thoroughly the Metaframe Group had reviewed ITT's situation. He wondered, "Was Digital courting a four-headed monster?"

By late summer and early fall 1985, the trade journals were full of news about an overall computer industry slump. Kenneth Olsen had announced to shareholders: "The marketplace is in turmoil. Much of the industry has been devastated in just the past two years." The main hardware vendors – IBM, Digital, Hewlett Packard, Apollo, Prime and Data General – were repositioning their products and services in the mincomputer segment. Digital's profit level was below that of one year earlier, yet it had outperformed most market analysts' expectations, thanks to cost controls and revenue growth, particularly in Europe. Apollo Computer, Inc.

had reported an after-tax operating loss of $4 million and a $14.4 million inventory write-down, resulting in a net loss of $18.4 million. Prime Computer, Inc. posted a 7 percent profit increase in a 19 percent revenue gain that went from $165 million to $196 million. Data General Corp. saw its pre-tax earnings plunge 98 percent to $800,000. More than 60 percent of the companies had lower rates of return than in the previous quarters. Most experienced wide swings in stock prices, and a number of smaller competitors either merged, formed alliances, or disappeared from the market.

Despite the overall industry downturn, there was growth in a few key segments, most notably, the emerging computer-aided design and manufacturing and workstation markets. While some industry analysts pointed to the workstation as an exciting new development in computing, others down-played its development, noting that workstations were only a reconfiguration of technologies from higher (mainframe) and lower (microcomputer) performing segments.

Apollo Computer Corporation was the founder of this segment and, along with Sun Microsystems, was one of the most aggressive marketers of engineering workstations. Their presence was only beginning to be felt in Europe. This firm had caught the eye of ITT's System 12 software development engineers.

DEC's Response to the ITT Tender Offer

David Stone had called Michael Horner, head of Engineering Strategy, to discuss ITT's tender offer to purchase workstations and related software products. David wanted to evaluate whether ITT might consider a joint technology development effort. He also saw it as a way to take the Metaframe Group's work into practice. Together, Michael Horner, the Metaframe Group and David Stone had reviewed ITT's proposed shopping list of hardware, software, and support services. As David Stone had been aware of the high-level discussions between the two companies, he advised Michael Horner to coordinate a meeting with some of ITT's European managers before they responded with a bid. In the back of his mind he was intrigued by the complex software engineering problem facing ITT. If Digital could form a joint software engineering team that would help ITT solve its problems, there would be other customers facing similar challenges.

Horner coordinated the first meeting between ITT and Digital Europe management. The primary goal of the meeting, from Digital's perspective, was to explore how the two companies might consummate a broad agreement that would lead to joint technology development. Since the top management of both companies had called for a closer strategic relationship, David Stone's proposal would be to define the boundaries of a new strategic and technical relationship. Within a few days, a hardware sale had been delicately placed on the back burner, and strategic engineering groups had been assigned from both companies.

During the initial Digital–ITT meetings, two clear camps of managers emerged on the ITT side: those who sought to purchase equipment and know-how from a computer vendor, and those who saw the opportunity to solve some larger software challenges through the newly created partnership. The ITT Engineers from ESC Harlow and SEL Stuttgart were particularly intrigued with a possible joint development effort. Michael Horner remembered the strong response from Gunter Endalee, the Chief Systems Engineer from SEL:

> Gunter was one of the brightest developers in ITT. He knew that the S-12 was a major undertaking, requiring multi-site engineering coordination. Except for announcing formal changes in software, he had given up trying to coordinate his efforts with the other ITT development groups in Europe. Digital's offer to review ITT's software development practices and propose new tools was an exciting possibility for Gunter. He never considered specific hardware and software to solve his problems. Digital had offered the conceptual breakthrough he sought.

Even after the Digital–ITT meetings in the fall of 1985, ITT's BTMC division in Antwerp had continued to push for a range of computer hardware and software products that would help the company streamline and facilitate the S-12 software development process. In their eyes, a Digital–ITT agreement would not prevent a multi-vendor solution. The computer industry press had recently focused on two new developments in computing which were particularly promising for ITT engineers: the speciality engineering workstation, and CASE tools. The heart of ITT's tender offer had concentrated on these new tools.

Michael Horner organized Digital–ITT meetings for the top twenty ITT engineers and then for each major software engineering group in Europe. Digital showed how its software tools specialists in Valbonne, France, working with ITT engineers at several locations, could redesign ITT's software development approach. But with each successive discussion, Digital also learned about ITT's lack of a common strategy for the S-12 technology development. Key S-12 engineers at the different development and engineering sites had been independently responsible for purchasing hardware and for S-12 development. Whole teams of ITT software engineers had developed separate components of the S-12 with different hardware and software standards. As one Digital engineer from Brussels, Etienne Bossard, put it: "ITT is not a company. It is a confederation of companies. As a result, technical groups do not normally communicate across the confederation, which makes for chaos when they make changes."

Applying Metaframe to Digital–ITT

The initial meetings with ITT went well. Digital and ITT engineers had agreed that a team would be assembled with the top echelons of ITT software engineers participating in introductory meetings.

Michael Horner became the European corporate sponsor of the Digital–ITT project for David Stone. Horner assembled an ITT Project Team that would implement discussions between ITT and the Metaframe Group (see exhibit A2.12). He brought in Bob Wyman from the US, one of Digital's leading software engineering experts. Bob Wyman had worked on Digital's most successful software development program to date, All-in-One. He also had an interest in extending his knowledge about CASE, and saw the Digital–ITT project as a serious applied engineering challenge. Michael Horner and Bob Wyman agreed to meet the ITT's European Managers and engineers to persuade them that DEC could assist ITT as it redefined its software development processes. From Michael's perspective, the first meetings with ITT engineers were successful. He recounted one meeting called to discuss hardware priorities: "I simply began to describe how we went about developing software. I could see they were getting excited and wanted to hear more. For the next three hours, they questioned me about Digital's approach to software development. It was clear that I was describing a brave new world."

Over a two-month period in the fall of 1985, Michael Horner and Bob Wyman travelled to all of ITT's S-12 development sites in Europe. As Michael observed:

> It was a process of getting buy-in from ITT's top management and then moving through the ranks. We targeted the first twenty people and prepared a road show. Each time, we made the following points.
> • Buying more equipment would not solve ITT's long-term S-12 problem.

Exhibit A2.12 Digital Europe: Metaframe Group and ITT Project Team

---

Metaframe Group

David Stone, Chairman
Mike Horner, Technology Specialist
Tony Setchell, Telecommunications Strategist
Haskell Cehrs, Telecommunications Specialist
Lutz Reuter, Organizational Specialist
Eric Sublet, Contracts
Renato Rattore, Italy
Jean Paul Myeller, France
Peter Kohlhammer, Germany
Bill Strecker, Corporate Strategy US
Skip Walter, Consultant (US-based)

ITT Project Team

Mike Horner, Project Manager
Bob Wyman, Consultant
Patrick Scherrer, Software Engineer
Alex Taylor, Communications
Gerard Zarka, User Representative
Theo de Jongh, Project Manager Designate
Etienne Bossard, Technology Specialist
Specialist in Antwerp
Specialist in Harlow
Specialist in Stuttgart

- DEC's knowledge of CASE tools and networked computing would be valuable if applied to telecommunications software development and, since it was a generic problem, would serve the interests of both companies.
- If ITT worked with Digital, it would be considered a privileged customer, and the S-12 engineers would be introduced to Digital's emerging technologies.
- As a result of a strategic agreement, Digital would provide equipment to key engineering sites and eventually assign a Digital engineer to work with the customer's engineers at each site.

Robert Wyman estimated that it would require around eight thousand man-years to redefine and complete the software development for the S-12. This task had to be managed among 2,500 engineers working in three to four parallel sites. As Wyman put it: "We had to network the sites and get them working together. But before ITT ever used CASE tools and workstations, we had to crash through the cultural and technical barriers."

Following the initial visits, the key sites were confirmed, and Digital began to establish network links between ITT sites: ESC Harlow, ITC Brussels, SEL Germany, and BTM Belgium. Digital, Valbonne, would serve as Digital's link to the network. Michael Horner had asked Gerard Zarka to find and configure the latest hardware and software, and to get it to several ITT European locations. Cost was not an initial consideration. Zarka was known throughout Digital Europe for his ability to get the latest equipment to the right place at the right time. He was also known less fondly by some country managers as someone who would jump the equipment delivery queue. Zarka described his efforts in Digital–ITT:

> I agreed wholeheartedly with the metaframe concept. ITT was asking for boxes. We refused. We focused on building their human-/technical links through networked computing. Why? Because we knew that more machines were not going to make them more productive. Their problem had reached a too high level of complexity.
>
> The first step had been to build and demonstrate a network. We located some of Digital's stage-of-the-art equipment: five Microvax 2-Q5 (fully loaded and networked) hardware configurations. They were the first ones shipped to Europe. The sales managers on the DEC side objected initially. We were shipping about $1.4 million of the latest technology to four countries, free of charge, and contributing who knows how many hours to the Metaframe cause. Since every country has its own budget in Digital, if a country sales person objected, we were stuck. In one case, two machines sat in customs for two months until the sales manager agreed to let us install the box at an ITT site.

The Digital Metaframe team realized that better coordination through a network was necessary for such a large and complex software development organization. Once the network was more or less in place, the teams had started to work on defining software tools that would integrate information, time, and project management protocols based on Digital's early experience with CASE tools. All of the engineer-to-engineer discussions focused on streamlining the S-12 software development process.

The team had succeeded in championing this approach at some

of ITT's sites, but some ITT engineers and managers continued to drag their feet. They wondered if Digital were trying to take over their project, and how a networked software development approach would affect different sites. How would Digital react when ITT exposed its internal processes? Bob Wyman was the recognized technical champion of the project at Digital, but attaining the role and status of project champion across companies remained inaccessible to him. Some ITT people had simply not accepted a genuine proposal coming from, in their eyes, an outsider (developers from other sites were also considered outsiders).

Michael Horner became increasingly convinced that the Digital–ITT relationship provided special opportunities for both companies. He convinced many people that his small group had developed a new approach to working with customers and business partners. Instead of focusing on getting the sale, they discussed how to solve ITT's long-term software development problems. The group had even coined the term "representative target customer" to describe and define engineering specifications for a future set of customers who would have different price/performance requirements.

He viewed their work at ITT as a prototype for future engineering-to-engineering relationships. But as an active participant in the ITT process, he was becoming aware of the differences between the two engineering cultures. He had recently asked David for more time to see whether the model would work. David remembered Michael's emphatic words: "Look, if we can get them to believe in what we do and in our approach, it is basically the same as an OEM sale. Inject the right people early on, inspire them, fund them, and wait a year for things to happen."

By the following February, eight months after members of the Metaframe Group had been assigned to ITT, the project was adrift. The tools developed by Digital were not being integrated into the ITT development process at many of the sites – different sites continued to use their own software development techniques. The network was in place, but could not seem to overcome ITT's cultural barriers.

Digital's Central Engineering in the US was asking questions about the new software development project. From its perspective the project had three problems. First, it was somewhat disconnected from Digital's Central Engineering strategy. Second, the development project itself involved a customer, requiring Digital to share proprietary software technologies and next generation hardware. And third, there were similar software tool developments going on in other parts of the company that had gotten approval from Central Engineering.

The partnership became increasingly complicated when the country management teams, who were closely linked to software services, started to hear about the project from their customers and field people. One manager contacted David Stone to find out why Digital's most advanced workstations were being shipped free of charge to ITT development labs, when his best customers were on a six-month waiting list for the same hardware.

Time for Action

David Stone had discussed the Digital–ITT relationship with his staff knowing that the product/market issues would have a bearing on what DEC could do with ITT. There was always a strong pull from headquarters in Maynard, Massachusetts, to keep technical developments and product/market segmentation close to home. Digital Europe's limited manufacturing capabilities reinforced this point. But at the same time, Digital Europe was doing comparatively well and had an expanding customer base. The country managers were generating a lot of business, and there were several advanced engineering projects and university–industry partnerships in the pipeline.

David Stone had still other reasons for being concerned about the Digital–ITT project. Very few customers had ever been in direct contact and worked together with people in Digital's engineering area. In addition, Digital's general management voiced a concern that Digital might be sharing its core technical competencies with its partners. David Stone had had to build a strong case for developing a software engineering link with ITT Europe. Perhaps he would find new ways to justify the merits of the project.

David picked up the phone to Michael Horner. Together they would decide how to proceed. As the dial tone sounded, he thought back to early 1985 when everyone was talking about alliances. He was surprised at how often he had been called to establish customer relationships. Yet, ITT Telecom had some serious engineering challenges to overcome. As soon as David Stone heard Michael Horner pick up the telephone, he said, "Michael, we'd better meet tomorrow at 8:30 to decide what to do about the Digital–ITT project."

3
Evolution of Strategic Alliances

A Generic Model for the Evolution of Strategic Alliances

When considering a strategic alliance it is useful to draw analogies with organic entities that grow and develop in nature. Just as we can observe in nature, the strategic alliance must receive energy on an ongoing basis, in this case from its parents, so that it can grow from an offspring into a working adult entity. The initial strategic alliance organizational entity needs stimuli so that it can grow and evolve. Implicit in comparing a strategic alliance with the birth and growth of a child is a need to see how the strategic alliance's relationship with its parents changes over time – from total dependence in early childhood to eventually becoming an independent, free-standing adult on its own.

There are several rationales for this evolutionary pattern, where the child grows up and the parent becomes less involved. For example, a learning process typically takes place allowing the unique traits of each parent to be picked up by the strategic alliance itself. Also, the strategic alliance is frequently under pressure to adapt to new environmental opportunities and to respond to environmental threats in its competitive arena. This often takes time, and may involve a great deal of effort, particularly if such adaptation is to take place through extensive coordination of the two parent parties.

The strategic alliance may also develop a need for its own organizational identity in order to attract, retain, and motivate human talents. The parents may develop more and more confidence in each other and in the strategic alliance as they become better acquainted and see that the strategic alliance is viable. They may then feel comfortable transferring more and more tasks to the joint venture/child.

A typical evolutionary pattern for strategic alliances is depicted in exhibit 3.1. In addition to illustrating three phases, the exhibit also pictures the gradual, decreasing closeness to strategy and decision-making from a parent company's perspective. It also illustrates the emergence of a full-blown, independent strategic alliance organization. The child becomes adult.

Let us first consider groups I–III in exhibit 3.1. During Phase I of the strategic alliance's life, one sees the alliance as a shared strategic alliance between parents with each parent having an active role. Typically these roles are complementary; one partner will be providing the technology and the other contributing the market contacts and customer access. Thus, most of the strategic alliance's physical activities get carried out by one partner or the other. The strategic alliance itself can be seen as not much more than a skeleton organization at this early stage. One might think of the strategic alliance as analogous to a strategic program being executed by different departments and divisions within a firm. In order to be successful, the program manager, or the joint venture manager, must demonstrate an ability to draw on resources from throughout the organization. Managers typically have little or no resources directly at their exclusive disposal.

After a while, however, it is often the case that one partner becomes increasingly dominant in the role of executing the strategic alliance's tasks. For instance, the partner that provides the marketing input, and in a given case also happens to be physically closest to the strategic alliance, may gradually take over a larger proportion of the hands-on activities. The other partner, who is providing the technology, may become relatively less active over time after the initial technological learning has been completed and the know-how transferred. Instead of this potentially cumbersome reliance on a distant parent, the practical solution may be that the strategic alliance itself could carry out this part of the activity. It could, of course, be the other way around, namely that the partner who provides the technology becomes relatively more active over time. Some possible reasons for this could include a new research intensity or the launching of new technological developments. After the strategic alliance

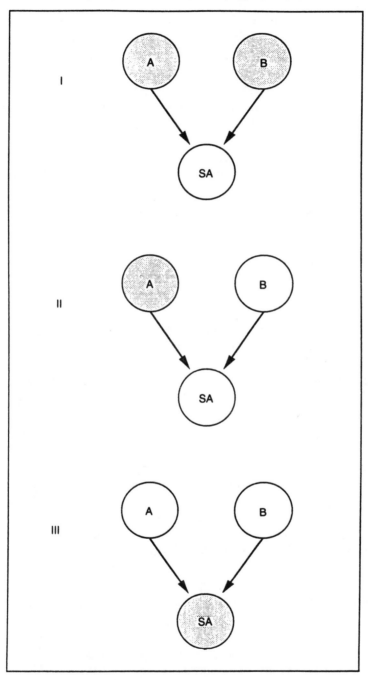

Exhibit 3.1 Stages in the evolution of a strategic alliance.

itself has been able to create a specialized marketing force on its own, based on the other partner's initial market support, training, and door-opening in the market place, this parent may now be allowed to become relatively less active.

We often see a typical evolution of the strategic alliance into a Phase II stage, where one of the partners continues performing a set of functions on behalf of the joint venture, becoming relatively dominant, while the other gradually becomes more and more passive as the joint venture organization takes over more and more of the value-creating functions on its own over time. It should be pointed out that these relative changes in parents' tasks should be anticipated in the strategic alliance agreement and should be seen as natural and pragmatic. It is not a reflection of one partner being more important and the other being relegated to secondary status. If the evolution of a strategic alliance leads to the outgrowth of such perceptions, then it goes without saying that the strategic alliance will be in trouble.

It should be pointed out that the evolution into Phase II can be slowed down, or even prevented, if both partners have a strong wish to remain active in delivering their parts of the strategic alliance's activities. This might at times, of course, be a viable option. It should be stressed, however, that over time this may require quite heavy, even excessive, coordination among the partners. Managing a business in such a hands-on fashion may indeed become too stressful in the longrun for the parties involved. The hands-on coordination between the two parties that will be called for over a long period of time may lead to a natural search by a partner to gradually "extradite" itself by transferring more and more functions to the strategic alliance itself, thereby simplifying the coordination involved for the operation of the strategic alliance. It is often the case that strategic alliances are terminated after a period of time if both partners wish to remain active; it often turns out to be too stressful to maintain this form of strategic alliance as a viable going concern concept.

It could of course also be that a strategic alliance is formed directly as a Phase II type, with one partner being relatively dominant and the strategic alliance organization performing significant tasks by itself from the start. It could, for instance, be that one partner has an active interest in a particular business and is seeking a somewhat more passive partner to provide general support as well as financing. It could also be that the more passive partner provides some sort of technology as well, particularly if the technology is of a type which is no longer core or truly crucial for the partner.

A Phase II type of strategic alliance also tends to evolve, and in this situation it may still be difficult for the strategic alliance to adapt sufficiently well to new opportunities. This is particularly true when these adaptation challenges have to be handled partly by the emerging strategic alliance's organization itself and partly by the more active parent's organization. Coordination of the split adaptation tasks between the more active partner and the growing strategic alliance organization can thereby become stressful. To cope with this, the strategic alliance *per se* can be given the lion's share of the adaptation responsibility and then the independence to carry it out.

The emergence of a Phase III-type evolution, where the strategic alliance plays the role of a more or less fully autonomous, independent entity, is often the natural next step. In this case too, it could very well be that an evolution into a Phase III stage does not materialize in practice, owing to the fact that the lead partner wishes to remain active. As one can imagine, this might lead to friction and unnecessary stress, with slow and ill-timed adaptive moves being the potential result. The termination of the strategic alliance after Phase II could also result.

There are a few caveats that may change this evolutionary path. The most important has to do with the role the joint venture is expected to play in a parent's portfolio strategy, as discussed in Chapter 2. If a core role is intended, the nature of the technology involved can be key to the evolution. If the technology is likely to become a commodity type within the near future, an evolutionary path such as the ones discussed is more likely to take place. More precisely, the partner controlling the technology will be more willing to let the alliance absorb it. On the other hand, if the technology is unique and is expected to remain so in the near future, it is unlikely that the partner controlling the technology will allow the alliance to absorb it. This leaves the parties with the options of accepting a "shared" or a possible "dominant" alliance for ever, or of dissolving the alliance at an early stage of evolution. The implication is that we need to assess carefully the importance of the technology in the alliance and whether the partner controlling it will be prepared to gradually give it up and, if so, when.

Similar reasoning can also be made when it comes to market contacts. If a partner is not willing to eventually let the joint venture establish its own market contacts, the life-cycle is likely to be aborted. It can, of course, also be that a strategic venture is formed directly as a more or less independent Phase III type entity from the start. Various partners can decide to put their activities into a free-standing strategic alliance from the start onwards, in order to facilitate the restructuring of an over-crowded, relatively mature business arena. Several partners could also decide to back a certain business idea as relatively passive investors from the start. A Phase III independent type of strategic alliance can, of course, potentially continue for a long time, provided that it remains competitive and yields a satisfactory return to the partners. Conversely, the alliance may be terminated if it does not function well enough on its own, because of not being able to document competitive success in its business area and not yielding the necessary return to its parents. If the investment that the passive partners require does not accrue, the strategic alliance would normally be terminated. Another option, of course, is that the strategic alliance is terminated as a consequence of one of the partners buying out the other – a quite normal type of event.

It is essential to understand the various types of strategic alliance initiation situations as well as the potential evolutionary patterns that might lie ahead. By understanding where one starts and what the evolutionary options and pressures are likely to be, one can be better prepared to allow the evolution to be a harmonious one. If these evolutionary issues are not addressed, one runs the risk of accidentally and prematurely terminating the strategic alliance owing to the unnecessary handicaps and stresses that will be imposed on the venture. This action could block the evolution of the alliance.

Evolution within Archetypes

When observing in more detail the generic evolutionary model just discussed, one cannot fail to be struck by the fact that there is so much determinism in the evolutionary pattern being described. This raises the question of whether such a strong, simple evolutionary pattern is generally expected to be normal and valid. We shall therefore discuss the question of evolution of strategic alliances in more detail, examining the issue in the context of each of our four generic strategic alliance models. As we shall see, very different patterns of expected evolution can be found. The generic evolution model should only serve as an input to a more tailormade, narrowly focused examination of evolutionary issues within the context of each particular strategic alliance type.

We will first discuss evolution within each of the four strategic alliance archetypes with the assumption that the archetype itself will not change in nature. For instance, how does a joint operations type of strategic alliance evolve over time, assuming that the parents' strategic positions and considerations regarding resource inputs and/or outputs do not change?

After the discussion of the evolutionary patterns for each of the four generic types of strategic alliances in a pure sense, we will look at potential evolutionary patterns when a strategic alliance might change in nature from one archetype to another. For instance, what might be the evolutionary issues if an ad hoc pool type of strategic alliance evolves into a consortium type of strategic alliance and perhaps further into a full-blown joint venture?

At this point we will make one simplifying assumption, that strategic alliances can only evolve from more simple to more complex forms, from ad hoc pools to consortia, and not the other way around. In theory, the latter can, of course, happen. In practice, however, these types of reverse evolutionary patterns will tend to lead to the break-up of the strategic alliance. Therefore, reverting to our generic model (see exhibit 3.1) we shall not discuss as a realistic issue the reverse evolution from the bottom towards the top of the figure.

Evolution of Ad Hoc Pool Strategic Alliances

In order to understand the evolution of this type of strategic alliance, through applying the framework pictured in exhibit 3.1, it should be kept in mind that no resources are being provided to the strategic alliance beyond the bare minimum, and no resources are being accumulated in the strategic alliance. It should also be kept in mind that none of the parties tends to find itself in a strategic positioning situation where the pressures towards adapting to dramatic ways of doing business through the strategic alliance are great. If the strategic alliance does not work, one can expect the parties to deal with ameliorating issues on their own, given the core nature of the business at hand and their leadership position in the business segment.

The ad hoc pool strategic alliance has a strong resemblance to the first phase of exhibit 3.1; each of the parents doing its parts of the job, and the alliance itself being nothing more than an empty mailbox. As such, one can expect little evolution beyond this stage. One might, of course, consider that the gradual building up of trust among the parties might lead to some evolutionary changes, particularly in the way the parties cooperate in executing the business activities within the pool. Still, one cannot expect the ad hoc pool to evolve beyond Phase I in exhibit 3.1.

However, if the experience with an ad hoc pool type strategic alliance is positive, and the physical objectives for the performance of this strategic alliance have been achieved, one can expect additional ad hoc pool arrangements between the partners. The most likely evolutionary patterns for this type of strategic alliance is a string of new ad hoc pool arrangements.

Evolution of Consortium Strategic Alliances

In the consortium-type strategic alliance, resources are being provided by the partners to the alliance on a more abundant basis, allowing the alliance to adapt to unforeseen opportunities. It should be kept in mind that the partners are now followers within the particular business area, and that the area is an important one within the overall portfolio of the firms. Here, clearly, the strategic alliance will tend to be, at first, and probably for quite some time, positioned in Phase I of exhibit 3.1, allowing each party to carry out its complementary role within the consortium. The actual alliance itself will be nothing more than the contract regulating who does what within each of the parent organizations. To some extent, however, one expects that coordination will gradually build up within the consortium, allowing the parties to adapt more rapidly in a synchronized manner to new environmental opportunities and to interpret performance experiences jointly, creating some sense of common learning. Still, the evolution is not expected to move far down the evolutionary chain in exhibit 3.1. Each of the parties will tend to be involved more or less as originally conceived.

For a consortium too, one would expect that the evolution is one of establishing new consortia as the old ones create the results intended.Usually this is what one sees in the oil exploration consortia where parents tend to have lasting relationships with each other, each relationship representing re-creations of complementary roles for new exploration type settings.

Evolution of Project-based Joint Ventures

We recall that for this strategic alliance, the resource inputs are held at the very sparse level, and the resource outputs are kept in the strategic alliance. We can deduce from this that the adaptive capabilities of such a strategic alliance will be limited because of the constrained resource base. The partners typically tend to be leaders in the business segment concerned but, portfolio-wise, the business within which the strategic alliance exists tends to be somewhat peripheral.

One can expect that this type of strategic alliance will follow the evolutionary pattern laid out in exhibit 3.1, and that the pressures toward evolution will be active when it comes to attempting to establish more streamlined learning to the common organization, to becoming more efficient in coordinating the uses of resources through a free-standing organization, and to adapting to new opportunities. When it comes to the latter issue, however, one must keep in mind that the scarce resource base will make adaptation difficult or impossible, at least in a larger sense. One must expect that the death rate of project-based joint ventures will be quite large, that the life expectancy of such a strategic alliance will be quite short. This is not hard to see. Given the leadership position of the various partners, they will go on pursuing their leadership positions in other ways rather than through a particular operating strategic alliance if this no longer provides a useful way to create win–win situations for the two parties. In total, the evolutionary pattern of exhibit 3.1 will tend to be manifested, but seldom throughout the entire evolutionary cycle portrayed in the exhibit.

Evolution of Full-Blown Joint Venture Strategic Alliances

The full-blown joint venture tends to be large, involving ample infusions of resources from each party and involving the accumulation of resources in the strategic alliance itself. Each party puts all of its energies into the strategic alliance in an effort to benefit positively from the restructuring that it expects will take place through the strategic alliance.

In this case one anticipates that the entire evolutionary pattern of exhibit 3.1 will take place, that over time a free-standing entity will be created, and that the parents will end up having only a financial ownership share in the alliance. This will, of course, allow each parent to exit from the alliance in quite a reasonable, financially driven way, thereby creating an exit mechanism for the strategic alliance. It is only in the full-blown joint venture that an alliance will follow the entire life-cycle portrayed in exhibit 3.1. Needless to say, however, many strategic alliances tend to be aborted in their evolution, even in this case, owing to the issues discussed in this section.

Evolution between Archetypes

We now move to a discussion of strategic alliances that might evolve from one archetype to another. We will first discuss the issue of an ad hoc pool type strategic alliance evolving towards a consortium type of strategic alliance. This, as in all types of shifts from one type of strategic alliance to another, implies changes in the way one or several parents see their resource positioning and/or their strategy positioning. It is thus important to keep in mind that it is the parents' shifting perspectives that tend to lead to changes from one type of strategic archetype to another. We are talking here about a different type of evolutionary issue than the growing up of the child/strategic alliance and the aging of the parent in the evolutionary process previously discussed.

A shift from an ad hoc pool to a consortium situation, as portrayed in exhibit 3.2, involves a shift from a strategic business leadership position to one of a follower position in the eyes of the parents. This necessitates a willingness to put in more resources so that the required resource abundance can be created, and so that the strategic alliance can adapt. Typically this type of evolution comes in the face of adverse strategic developments in the market place. Rather than giving up, by failing to respond or by failing to adapt, the partners may have developed enough positive feeling for the potential to win through further cooperation that they want to upgrade the ad hoc pool to a consortium.

A quite analogous situation can be found when a strategic alliance evolves from a project-based joint venture situation to a full-blown joint venture (exhibit 3.3). Here, too, the difficulty of maintaining a leadership position by means of the partners' business strategy, while facing the fact that they may be slipping into a follower's position, tends to be the driving force. See, again, exhibit 3.1. The same negative evolutionary force is thus at play, forcing the partners to face up to the fact that they have

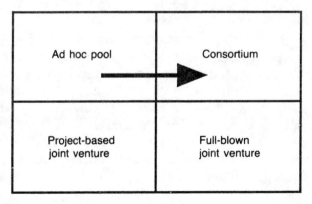

Exhibit 3.2

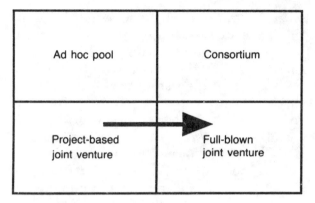

Exhibit 3.3

lost leadership and are now followers, and that only a more involved full-blown joint venture participation through significant infusion of resources will be the way out.

A fundamentally different type of evolutionary pressure takes place when an ad hoc pool cooperative arrangement develops into a project-based joint venture cooperative arrangement (exhibit 3.4). Here the change in the parents' strategy perception has to do with re-prioritizing the business in question at the portfolio level so that it gets assigned a less critical role, from core to peripheral. The issue is one of recognizing that the purpose is no longer one of necessarily taking all of the resources out of the strategic alliance but of allowing it to retain some of its resources. A similar situation can be seen when a consortium type of strategic alliance is evolving into a full-blown joint venture (exhibit 3.5).

The typical reason for a strategic alliance business moving from core to peripheral has to do with the fact that the overall core competencies of the firm do not tend to be maintained through a strategic alliance. It is a life-cycle consideration which leads the firm as a whole to redeploy core competencies into new core businesses, allowing the strategic alliance to become less critical over time. Few firms will, of course, strive for generating core competencies and core dependencies which are imbedded in a strategic alliance.

Finally, let us discuss the possibility of moving from a very loose ad hoc pool strategic alliance arrangement to a full-blown

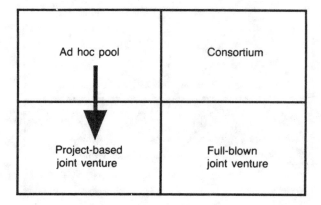

Exhibit 3.4

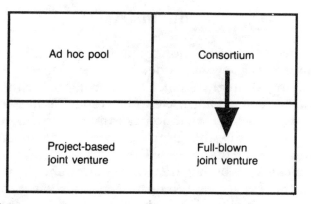

Exhibit 3.5

joint venture. Needless to say, such an evolution tends to take place either via a consortium route or a joint operations route. Such an evolutionary pattern involves simultaneously reclassifying the importance of the business within its portfolio and facing up to the deterioration of the business's competitive position. The response to these two moves, one typically leading the other, is the possible development of a full-blown strategic alliance (exhibit 3.6). The typical evolutionary trajectory of exhibit 3.1 starts to take place, after the full-blown joint venture is in place. As such, one can see ad hoc pool arrangements ending up in a Phase III evolutionary position as shown in exhibit 3.1.

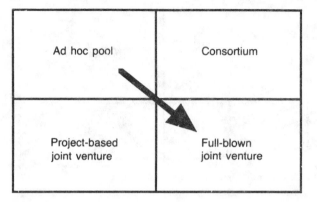

Exhibit 3.6

Summary

The tendency for an evolutionary pattern to exist has important implications for how we understand key aspects of forming and managing strategic alliances. For instance, at the outset of forming a strategic alliance, we must recognize not only who is doing what, but also at what point in time these task roles might shift. In other words, the formation process should include an open discussion of the expected dynamics of the venture. The decision-makers in both parent companies should not be surprised at the subsequent requirements for task adjustments which may result in an increasingly independent entity.

The evolutionary path also has to do with a specific product's stage in the product life-cycle. If the nature of the product is such that it is not likely to become commodity-like in the near future, it is more difficult to see how a strategic alliance will evolve into an independent organization. Such an evolution would require that both partners give up all relevant know-how to the strategic alliance and have no hands-on control over proprietary know-hows. This might jeopardize a unique and important revenue-yielding technology or know-how.

If the product is likely to become a commodity, on the other hand, there is much less of a problem with the creation of an independent entity. In this case, we might expect that the specific know-how is already more broadly diffused in the industry and, therefore, may be of less strategic value. The evolutionary perspective is also consistent with other authors' findings. In her concluding remarks, for instance, Harrigan (1986), stated that "joint ventures are a transitional form of management – an intermediate step on the way to something else."

Appendix
Sancella, Ltd[1]

Introduction

This case examines Sancella, Ltd, the strategic alliance between the Swedish firm Mölnlycke Consumer Products and the British-based subsidiary of the US firm Scott Paper Company. Initiated in 1977, this venture involves both the production and the marketing of sanitary products (sanpros) in the UK.

This case illustrates a vertical upstream–downstream joint venture where one partner supplies technology (Mölnlycke) and the other markets the products (Scott). The basic venture model has been used in a number of Mölnlycke Consumer Products ventures worldwide. An important feature here is the illustration of a joint venture's dynamic evolution – brought about by changes in the parents' overall strategy. In addition, the case demonstrates (1) the difficult managerial tasks of coordinating a combination of wholly-owned subsidiaries and joint ventures, and (2) how difficult it is for a joint venture to evolve toward independence.

This case comprises three parts. The first part briefly describes the two parent firms and the UK sanitary protection industry. The second part discusses both parties' strategic rationales for entering into this joint venture and its design. The last part analyzes both the dynamic evolution of this venture since it was formed in 1977 and its future outlook.

The Swedish Parent Firm: Mölnlycke Consumer Products AB

Based in the town of Mölnlycke, east of Göteborg, Mölnlycke Consumer Products is one of six independent divisions of Mölnlycke AB. This division develops, produces, and markets baby diapers and external (pads and panty liners) and internal (tampons) sanitary products. Internationalizing its operations at an early stage resulted in wholly-owned subsidiaries in five Western European countries: Denmark, Norway, Finland, the Netherlands and Belgium. The firm, with high market shares in all products, is either the market leader or second-best in all these markets. In fact, the company considers Western Europe as its home market. It also participates in seven international joint ventures. Of its total 1988 turnover of $450 million, one quarter was related to all its joint venture operations. Of the firm's 1,900 employees in 1988,[2] 700 were employed in the joint ventures.

In 1975 Mölnlycke AB was acquired by Svenska Cellulosa Aktiebolaget (SCA), one of the largest paper mill companies in Sweden. Two years earlier, Mölnlycke AB had acquired SCA's hygiene division. It should be noted that SCA's strategy is, and has been, to expand downstream with more value-added consumer products. To a large extent, this strategy is implemented through the Mölnlycke Group.

The British Parent Firm: Scott Ltd (UK)

The history of Scott Ltd (UK) began with a joint venture – called Bowater–Scott – between the US-based Scott Paper International, Inc. and the British company Bowater Industries PLC. Bowater–Scott's major business was to produce, distribute, and market various types of tissue, but primarily bathroom tissue. Scott Paper Company is one of the world's leading manufacturers and marketers of sanitary tissue paper products, with operations in some twenty countries. Hence, the joint venture was a direct extension of Scott's operations, that is, distributing one of the US company's most important products.

Originally Bowater–Scott shares were held equally by both parents. In mid-1985, however, Bowater Industries' shares were acquired by Scott Paper International, Inc. Consequently, Bowater–Scott is now a 100 percent subsidiary of Scott Paper, named Scott Ltd (UK). Its total sales in 1988 were £260 million; and it employed, on average, 2,800 people.

Industry Structure

The UK sanitary protection industry is characterized by a few large competitors, a relatively high level of competition, slow growth, and somewhat conservative buyers. New entries are restricted by the high costs involved in developing the appropriate technology. The 1989 ranking of the joint venture and its most important competitors in the UK market are listed in exhibit A3.1. These companies totally dominate sales, with a combined market share of approximately 75 percent.

The Joint Venture: Sancella, Ltd

Sancella, Ltd was formed by the hygiene division of SCA in 1970–1. Its operations included manufacturing in its own production plant and distributing and marketing sanitary protectives in the UK. In 1973, SCA decided to sell its hygiene division, including Sancella, to the largest hygiene company in Europe at that time – Mölnlycke AB. As part of the agreement, however, SCA became one of Mölnlycke's largest owners. Two years later, the two parties reached an agreement whereby SCA acquired the remaining shares of Mölnlycke. For Mölnlycke, this meant both a secure supply of raw materials and access to SCA's financial resources and technical know-how in the raw materials area. For SCA, the acquisition was a vertical downstream integration towards high value-added consumer products, based on SCA's raw materials.

Sanitary protectives, which traditionally had been sold only through pharmacies, gradually became available in food stores during the mid-1970s. This change in consumer patterns caused problems for Mölnlycke Consumer Products' sales organization, that is, Sancella, and plans for a cooperative strategy evolved. Concurrently, as Mölnlycke Consumer Products undertook a search for a potential partner in the UK market, the head of international operations by chance met a Bowater–Scott representative in Australia, resulting in the initiation of the Mölnlycke Consumer Products–Scott operation in several countries. Sancella was transformed into a joint venture between the two firms in 1977.

Exhibit A3.1 1989 ranking in the UK sanpro industry

	Towels	Panty-liners
1	Kimberly–Clark	Johnson & Johnson
2	Sancella	Sancella
3	Lilia–White	Kimberly–Clark

Strategic Rationales

It is essential to understand the two parent firms' strategic rationales for forming this joint venture, as their rationales direct the joint venture's design. In this context, Sancella was already an established hygiene company with its own production plant and distribution and sales organization.

There were at least two basic business strategy rationales for Mölnlycke Consumer Products to change this situation and transform Sancella into a joint venture with Bowater–Scott. First, it would have been very costly to adapt the existing Sancella marketing and sales organization to the changes in sanitary protection consumer patterns which occurred in the UK during the mid-1970s. A cooperative venture with a larger existing local sales network would, consequently, both reduce the risks and costs of marketing and sales and, at the same time, it was hoped, offer access to new parts of the market. This would also save time in penetrating the market with Mölnlycke Consumer Products' own product lines by combining existing technology and local market know-how.

Sancella's products are sold with Mölnlycke's brand names. Hence, Mölnlycke Consumer Products clearly continues to have a strong interest in the very business that the joint venture is engaged in.

On the other hand, one of Scott's (UK) major business rationales for this product diversification appeared to have been the potential economies of scope in the sales force, by combining the company's existing tissue products with more "interesting" hygiene products. Even though Sancella's hygiene products constituted only a small portion (5 percent) of total sales, the sales representatives found it stimulating to be able to discuss more than "tissue" with their potential customers. Another business rationale might have been that through the cooperative venture, Scott (UK) would have indirect access to advanced sanitary protection technology.

When the venture was formed in 1977, there were probably many more strategic business rationales for cooperation than the few mentioned above. For obvious reasons it is difficult to make a correct in-depth analysis of these rationales today. As we will discuss later, however, these rationales are currently not the same.

Joint Venture Design

Mölnlycke Consumer Products had no prior experience with joint ventures but did have extensive experience with licensing agreements. The model used in the Sancella deal was later used for setting up other Mölnlycke Consumer Products international joint ventures in Australia, Hungary, the US, Mexico, Colombia, and Thailand: a traditional upstream–downstream cooperation where one party provides the technology and the local partner is responsible for marketing and sales. The conceptual structure is shown in exhibit A3.2.

Three legal contacts stipulate the terms of the cooperation: the joint venture agreement, the licensing agreement, and the service agreement. First, the basic *joint venture agreement* defines Sancella's operation for the production and sales of external sanitary protection. (There are clauses covering the possibility of broadening the product base with other sanitary protection products.) This agreement also regulates how to split returns between the two partners. Second, the *licensing agreement* gives Sancella free access to Mölnlycke Consumer Products' technology, present and future, within this area. In addition to compensation, it regulates issues such as research and development and relevant products and their quality. The agreement also includes stringent secrecy

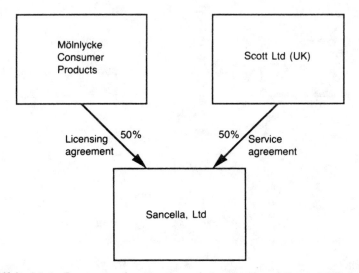

Exhibit A3.2 Conceptual structure of the Bowater–Scott–Mölnlycke joint venture agreement.

clauses to protect Mölnlycke Consumer Products' black box – their sanitary protection knowledge know-how.[3] Finally, the *service agreement* specifies the services provided by Scott (UK), e.g., administration and distribution.

See exhibit A3.3 for the resulting organizational structure. The board comprises six people, three from each parent company. In addition to its managing director, Mölnlycke Consumer Products is represented by the head of international operations and the production manager. Scott (UK) is represented by its managing director and Sancella's managing director and manufacturing manager. Both partners formally control 50 percent of both shares and board seats and, consequently, both have equal power because all decisions require a majority.

Because Sancella is integrated into Scott's (UK) organization, staffing poses an interesting management and control issue. The first general manager of Sancella was, at the same time, head of finance at Bowater–Scott, i.e., the part-time manager of Sancella. The present manager allocates 80 percent of his time to Sancella and the remaining 20 percent as manager of another of Scott's (UK) subsidiaries, as agreed upon by the two parties. Four of six heads of Sancella's departments are Scott (UK) employees, spending 10 to 20 percent of their time at Sancella. The remaining two managers of marketing and manufacturing are full-time Sancella employees. Sancella's management committee comprises the

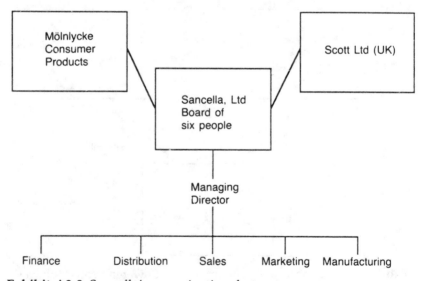

Exhibit A3.3 Sancella's organizational structure.

heads of finance, marketing, manufacturing, sales, distribution, and the general manager.

This brief analysis of Sancella's design leads to two major conclusions. First, owing to both physical proximity and the high level of Sancella's integration into Scott (UK), the latter parent firm appears to have a relatively high degree of operational control over the joint venture. On the other hand, Mölnlycke Consumer Products seems to have a great deal of strategic control over Sancella: it is responsible for research, product development, and present technology as well as upgrading this technology. Also, the brand names of the UK manufactured products are controlled by the Swedish parent firm.

The First Ten Years: 1977–87

When Sancella was formed in 1977, each partner had an active role to play. Mölnlycke Consumer Products provided the Swedish technology and the existing production plant in England. Bowater–Scott provided its unique distribution and sales network for tissue products. Both inputs were complementary; and synergy effects were expected to occur. At this early stage, Sancella comprised the production plant in north-east England and a few individuals at Bowater–Scott's head office south of London. Hence, Sancella was originally of greater importance to Mölnlycke Consumer Products than to Scott (UK), because it was a means by which to penetrate the UK consumer market. Although a sister organization to Mölnlycke Consumer Products, Mölnlycke Hospital Products, was already operating in the UK market, the latter firm's sales force was oriented towards healthcare institutions. Therefore, no other reasonable alternatives were available.

Sancella's sanpro sales made up only a small percentage of the total sales of Bowater–Scott, whose operations concerned tissue. Consequently, Sancella was dominated by Mölnlycke Consumer Products' interests. This situation is similar to the Phase II stage discussed in exhibit 3.1, where one of the partners typically is more dominant while the other may be more passive. In this case, however, the dominant situation did not result from an evolution but from the basic premises of the cooperation.

There had been, of course, periods of stress between the partners during the first ten years of cooperation. However, the situation began to change within the last two of the ten years. Mölnlycke Consumer Products has become an increasingly successful multinational company, with the full support of its upsteam parent firm, SCA. Even though its base is the Nordic countries, the firm is rapidly expanding its international operations. In fact, the company considers the whole of Western Europe to be its home market. Sancella was the first joint venture agreement; but, in addition to its wholly-owned subsidiaries in Western Europe, the company is now involved in seven joint ventures worldwide. It should be noted that Sancella is the only partly-owned subsidiary in Western Europe.

Among the Mölnlycke Group's acquisitions over the last few years has been the tissue company Lilla Edet, a 1985 acquisition that turned Mölnlycke into more of a direct competitor with Scott Paper International, Inc. – whose core business is tissue – at least in this particular product area. This situation was articulated further by Mölnlycke's 1989 acquisition of Laakirchen, an important producer of lightweight coated paper and tissue in Austria.

The joint venture with Bowater–Scott, on the other hand, became the wholly-owned Scott Paper International, Inc. subsidiary Scott (UK). The previously mentioned change in corporate strategy has resulted in more centralized operations in fewer countries, with Europe as a priority area. This change has also included expansion of the product range from sanitary tissue products into the broader area of personal care and health – a product area close to Mölnlycke's core business.

A Major Event: Mölnlycke's 1988 Acquisition of Peaudouce

In January 1988, Mölnlycke announced that it had acquired the French multinational corporation Peaudouce for US $3 billion. A major participant in the European baby diapers industry, the French company is also active in the sanpro industry. This was a significant step in Mölnlycke's strategy to strengthen its position both in the personal care and health business area and in the European consumer market. In fact, Peaudouce was as big as Mölnlycke Consumer Products (including its joint ventures) in both turnover and number of employees.

This acquisition also increased the number of subsidiaries within the Mölnlycke Group. In addition to the French operations, Peaudouce included manufacturing plants and distribution networks in the UK, manufacturing and distribution via a joint venture in Greece, and sales operations in Belgium, the Netherlands, West Germany, and Ireland. Of its eleven manufacturing plants, nine were located in France.

Before the acquisition, Mölnlycke was present in the UK healthcare market only via its Hospital Products subsidiary. As we mentioned above, this is a very different market – aimed at institutions, not directly towards consumers. Thus, its sales force has been unable to combine with that of Sancella, which is oriented towards customers only. The situation is somewhat different today in that Mölnlycke has access to a consumer-oriented sales and distribution network through Peaudouce. Although this network is only half the size of Scott's (UK), the point is that Mölnlycke has the ability to utilize this sales force. In other words, Mölnlycke is now in the position of having a double presence on the UK consumer market – via the Sancella joint venture and via the wholly-owned Peaudouce.

The Present Situation: Cooperation and Competition

Both companies' evolutions and changes in corporate strategies in the late 1980s clearly imply a shift in the strategic rationales regarding the joint venture. The general impression is that because Sancella's operations clearly coincide with Scott Paper International's interest in personal health and care, the joint venture has become of greater importance to this firm, i.e, of greater strategic importance. At the same time, Sancella remains of great important to Mölnlycke Consumer Products for the reason mentioned above. This evolution represents a shift towards a more shared type of cooperation, similar to the Phase I stage discussed in exhibit 3.1, where each partner normally has an active and complementary role to play.

The competition within Peaudouce's product segment had a tightening effect on the UK market during the first part of 1989. In fact, competition throughout the European baby diaper industry has become much stronger. This can be explained, in part, by the fact that in the late 1980s one of the major participants in the industry, Procter & Gamble, lost but is now trying to regain much of its market share in Europe. Logical consequences of these efforts have been increased competition and significantly lower price levels, which, of course, have posed problems for Peaudouce and other competitors in the industry. On the other hand, in early 1989 Peaudouce introduced to the UK market, a new, environmentally safe, disposable baby diaper, based on one of Mölnlycke's unique raw materials (CMTP) which became such an enormous success that it has been necessary to set distribution quotas for the retailers!

From Scott's (UK) perspective, the basic rationales for the joint venture remain, i.e., the possibility of complementing existing products and being part of the interesting sanpro industry. Given the Peaudouce acquisition and the resulting sales organization, questions have been raised regarding Mölnlycke's long-term intentions in the UK. Will this sales force be utilized? If so, in what way? What will happen to Sancella's manufacturing plant?

Another issue concerns the success of Peaudouce's new type of disposable baby diaper in the UK, which could result in increasing demand and, indeed, pressure from British consumers on the tissue manufacturers, e.g., Scott (UK), to introduce similar environmentally safe, disposable tissue products. The crux is that the CMTP-based tissue is of inferior quality.

PART III
Management Processes

4
Planning and Control Considerations

Introduction

In this chapter we shall address the challenge of developing planning and control approaches and processes in strategic alliances. Strategic planning continues to be a controversial activity in many corporations. On the one hand, most executives acknowledge the need to strengthen their organizational ability to adopt to new environmental conditions, and many commonly view strategic planning as a key vehicle in this respect. On the other hand, strategic planning is often seen as a too mechanistic process which can foster shallow thinking and lack of true understanding. The formidable challenge of strategic planning is exemplified by the following quotation: "Trying to predict the future is necessary but impossible" (Chang 1990).

Given the fact that several organizations are participating in a strategic alliance, strategic planning and control are certainly not easy to carry out. Still, with the need to achieve goal congruence, to avoid information asymmetry, and to reach consensus regarding how to take corrective measures and adapt over time between several partners, there is no doubt that strategic planning processes can help us in the implementation of strategic alliances. We will discuss four important aspects of strategic planning and control processes in this respect:

- the setting of objectives for the strategic alliance network as a whole
- developing strategic programs for implementing particular objectives
- delineating the near-term tactics in relevant budgets

- monitoring of bottom-line progress, longer-term strategic progress, and protection of the firm's core competencies.

Objective-Setting

Because a number of firms can participate in an alliance, it is crucial that the objective-setting process allows for a sharing of outlooks regarding goals; that a common information base is established; and that the process is highly interactive, based on broad representation among all the relevant focal parts of the organizations. This ensures buy-in regarding the pursued strategy, establishes goal congruence and avoids information asymmetry (Lorange 1980).

Forming a representative top management committee is a key to the objective-setting process in order to work out the basic goals for the strategic alliance network. Such a group should, of course, follow up the objectives that have already been agreed upon as part of the formation process, as discussed in Chapter 2. Often the formal agreement can be based on quite a detailed set of stated objectives as well as a business plan. However, the degree of articulation necessary when operationalizing the objectives may be less. The senior management group must take off from this starting point, transforming the strategic intent into reality. This involves elaborating on the particular business objective by further analyzing the attractiveness of alternatives within the basic business niche, identifying specific ways of penetrating these niches in terms of the more detailed products/services to be offered, and articulating the means of reaching the various customers with the products and/or services. The senior planning committee, which is formed to lay out the objectives, must also have the necessary political clout to ensure sufficient stakeholder blessing.

A strategic alliance can realize significant additional advantages from the outputs of such an eclectic planning committee formed from members of several focal organizations, in that such a committee can become a vehicle for releasing new levels of creativity. Too often, objective-setting in many organisational contexts tends to be unimaginative, even degenerating over time, because conventional, extrapolative thinking is allowed to dominate. This is not the way to carry out the partner's strategic intent. The potential benefits of bringing together key executives from each of the focal organizations into a creative "group think-tank atmosphere" can be substantial (Lorange 1984; Mason and Mitroff 1981).

Strategic Programming

Strategic programming (outlining how to carry out the various objectives, and who should carry them out) must now be tackled, and it must be done with great care. The implementation of a particular strategic program involves co-operation among executives from several functional lines. For example, the R&D function must co-ordinate its efforts with the manufacturing function, specifying products that can be produced, first in a pilot plant stage and then in a full-scale mode. Developmental efforts must be co-ordinated between R&D and the distribution and marketing functions, so that the product developed corresponds with the needs of the customers in the market place. There are numerous examples of strategic program implementation efforts which underscore the strong need for cooperation and co-ordination among various organisational functions in these activities. Typically, cooperation is difficult enough in normal organizational set-ups, where kingdom mentality and functional blindness can often hamper strategic programming. When these responsibilities are being shared among several focal organizations, the question of realistic cooperation becomes even more crucial (Lorange 1980).

The strategic alliance between San Miguel and the New Zealand Dairy Board regarding local manufacturing of cheese products in the Philippines provides an example of the difficulties in coordinating strategic programming. The two partners were unable to establish punctual and stable production, owing to delays in the supply of raw materials from New Zealand. The resulting set of delays significantly helped competitors to gain market share. The coordination challenge was perhaps particularly formidable for the New Zealand Dairy Board because of its many joint ventures in a number of the south-east Asian markets, all with their particular implementation challenges and raw material needs.

To handle this issue, one must, above all, take great pains to identify who is responsible for doing precisely what. Choosing appropriate team members in the ad hoc project organizations mandated to carry out particular strategic programs is crucial. The focal organization which should have the lead role in what aspect of the implementation of a particular strategic program is also important. Here, the basic agreement stemming from the formation process will hopefully be specific enough to cut down on ambiguity. The senior management planning team responsible for the overall objective setting should be a driving force for diminishing ambiguity, by further prescribing the strategic programming tasks. For each basic strategic program a separate project team should be formed. Each of these teams, representing the fitting together of complementary functions from each of the focal organizations, should report to the overall senior management planning committee.

In addition to establishing a clear picture of the roles of each focal member organization in each of the strategic programs, it is also essential to consolidate the various planning roles of each focal organization. This is important so that each is clear about the totality of planning roles it is expected to play in carrying out the various parts of the several strategic programs in which it is involved. Consolidating planning roles might uncover capacity problems or the deficiency of managerial strengths needed to meet commitments.

We shall now discuss how to cope with the resource availability issue through so-called strategic budgeting (Chakravarthy and Lorange 1991).

Strategic Budgeting

Carrying out a strategic program requires available resources, in the form of managers, technologies, and funds. Such resources must be explicitly set aside by each of the focal organizations. The reality of effecting a particular strategic plan will largely depend on the ability of each focal organization to mobilize the necessary resources to do its part. As we have noted, we need to consider several types of resources. Most importantly, each organization must be willing and able to nominate and release the necessary human resources. Competent executives always tend to be scarce and in high demand. If a participating organization is unwilling to nominate its best people, and instead resorts to releasing its second- or third-string executives to the cooperative venture, then there is a serious risk of being unable to implement a particular cooperative strategy.

Another type of strategic resource that must also be made available is relevant technologies, together with the technical support people in question. Examples of this resource include the availability of laboratory time, experimental access to pilot plants, access to market testing through sales and distribution networks, and so forth. If the various participating organizations cannot make these available immediately (say, because of their need for such resources in other connections), then the implementation effort can run into trouble.

Finally, there is clearly a need to set aside sufficient financial resources for carrying out the various strategic programs. Each focal organization must be able to earmark enough financial resources for its part of the job. And these financial resources must be protected from "fire-fighting" demands that may arise within the parent organizations themselves.

The strategic budgeting phase requires that the various participating organizations actually set aside the necessary set of resources for making the cooperative strategy work. This phase can be the acid test of whether the cooperative organization will have a realistic chance of succeeding. Too often, there is a tendency to under-allocate critical resources to the cooperative venture, and/or to commit resources only on general terms, without actually nominating the executives in question, earmarking the resources clearly, etc. The existence of a realistic strategic budget needs to be affirmed by the overall senior management planning committee. It should also be a focal point of discussion for the board of directors of the strategic venture, if such a board is established. A lack of realistic, top-level attention to tangible, explicit resource allocation can lead to serious problems for the cooperative strategy. Such a lack can be a symptom that the strategic intents of various partners were not in fact as strong as anticipated. (Håkansson et al. 1980).

Control and Protection of Core Competence

In a strategic alliance, both parties, through their unique contributions of inputs, cooperate to create a business entity which is presumably better than if each party operated on its own. The notion of creating added strength by combining complementary resources is critical. Such a combination of efforts does, however, imply that the parties must play with reasonably open cards. This can create a dilemma in many senior executives' minds regarding what might happen after the termination of a strategic alliance, or after it has failed.

A partner must remember that a strategic alliance can break up for a variety of unforeseen reasons. It is reasonable, therefore, that a partner maintain for itself some unique proprietary skills and know-hows to be used as latent protection against the other partner in potentially adverse circumstances. This action is called creating a black box, and may be particularly crucial if excess importance is attached to it in a given partner's portfolio strategy.

The easiest way to maintain such a black box is simply to not give away much of the firm's unique competence at the outset. In other words, the firm does not share all the basic technology or market contacts, but simply performs these functions on its own on behalf of the alliance. For example, as described in Chapter 3, Appendix, Mölnlycke Consumer Products of Sweden is involved in seven strategic alliances worldwide for the local production and marketing of sanitary protectives. In all of these alliances, Mölnlycke shields its core competence, its technology, by keeping total and strict responsibility for providing and maintaining the manufacturing equipment. This is also the approach of Tetra Pak, a major player in global food packaging materials, which actually owns and services packaging machines and receives its revenues through the sale of specially coated and printed paper for the machines to its partners. In another example, Coca-Cola manufactures its syrup, based on a secret formula, in its wholly-owned plants and distributes this to its franchising partners.

Another important way of creating an effective black box is to integrate many discrete activities into a systematic totality where each is relatively modest when seen in isolation. This might include, for instance, some product know-how as well as some manufacturing process know-how, both possibly tied to ongoing research and development efforts and competencies that are being maintained by a parent. In the same vein, there may be various types of software, management processes, financial know-hows, training, maintenance support, human resource support, and other services that a partner can give to the strategic alliance. Separate agreements can be entered into which regulate the use of each of these services. When all of this is managerially put together into a single, coordinated concept, it easily becomes a formidable source of protection for a partner, making it much harder for the other partner to break away from the strategic alliance. If a partner wishes to break up specific parts of the agreements it risks the deterioration of the entire relationship.

A black box position must, of course, be maintained and upgraded over time in order for it to remain unique. It may, for instance, be necessary to provide additional research on an ongoing basis to continue to improve one's technology lead and unique know-how regarding the market place. If not, one might end up having to give up more and more of one's core competencies simply to remain of interest to the partner. An example of this is the 1963 strategic alliance previously discussed between CPC International and Ajinomoto in Japan. Over time, Ajinomoto learned more and more of CPC's technology, and the latter gave up more and more access to its international network to the former in order to remain an equal partner. Conceivably, with more relative power swinging in the direction of Ajinomoto, it could become relatively easier for this firm to renegotiate a more favorable contract or even break off entirely to pursue a wholly-owned strategy.

During all of this we must keep in mind the assumption that we want the strategic alliance to succeed. It should be assumed that all parties genuinely want to cooperate fully to make the joint venture work, but the development and maintenance of a black box can represent a stress factor to the cooperative spirit. Each partner should also recognize that a reasonable black box protection is quite legitimate, and it should not be interpreted as a provocative move. It is a delicate and potentially stressful effort to determine the degree of protection needed to maintain some discretionary strength so that a firm may not be taken hostage by its partner. Even though the term "terror balance" is (happily) not used much today, it is exactly analogous to what is meant by effective black box protection – the term is indeed very appropriate in the context of strategic alliances.

Non-Financial Strategic Control

We see that having a strong black box position gives a partner a sense of strategic control over the direction of the strategic alliance. There are, however, other useful sources of non-financial strategic control. It is important to recognize that control of a strategic alliance does not typically happen primarily by means of enforcing legal control (Killing 1983; Schaan 1983). As experienced by many firms, legal contracts alone do not make alliances work, and majority legal ownership does not equal effective control. It is also imperative to understand that a power-based attitude toward control does not induce a cooperative spirit in the strategic alliance. In fact, if both parents attempt to maximize control this way the alliance will surely be doomed to fail. Control must be based on dimensions other than traditional legal rights and outright exercise of ownership voting power. For example, a major European corporation in automotive components exercises strategic control of its strategic alliances by being heavily involved in the planning process and in the follow-up reporting on strategic progress. It is thereby in a good position to influence its partners up-front.

Another way to maintain a sense of control is to be careful in assigning key people to the strategic alliance. In fact, the stronger the people we can assign, the better from a control viewpoint. Strong managers are typically mature enough both to contribute to the strategic alliance and to look after the parent's interests. A key to success for such executives is to be able to maintain their integrity and not be seen as disloyal by either of the parents in the alliance – to contribute genuinely so as to make the strategic alliance work.

The board of directors also represents an important source of control. It is usually an advantage to assign to the board executives who are also active in a parent's own business, particularly if the parent remains active in the same business. If a strong portfolio strategy interest exists, it is important that senior corporate-level executives are involved, so that the partner's strategic intents continue to be actively pursued. Active board participation by relevant members of the parent's organization can be a particularly strong source of control.

As we have noted, it is also crucial that each partner's responsibilities are clearly spelled out, and that, for control purposes, their delivery on these commitments is monitored. If routine monitoring is established, one can better cope with potential problems in their infancy and resolve them before they become too sensitive.

A pragmatic problem-solving atmosphere is also an important part of good strategic alliance management. Avoiding sensitive issues for fear of upsetting a partner is not a workable solution: it only aggravates problems later on, and can lead to loss of control.

There must also be strong partnership agreements among the parties regarding how to share sensitive output from the strategic alliance, such as technological ownership and/or the handling of geographical territory issues. There should be a monitoring mechanism in place to establish that no one breaks such strategically sensitive aspects of the agreement.

Although agreements should be backed up by black box arrangements, this is not sufficient alone: strategic surveillance is necessary. Again, one can see the analogy with power balance settings in international political treaties.

As an additional measure to enforce territorial control, it is important to pay attention to the manufacturing capacity of a strategic alliance. If the manufacturing capacity is larger than the assigned territory needs, there will always be the temptation for the strategic alliance to export into other territories, potentially creating conflict. Capacity expansion decisions should be carefully planned and controlled. Arco Chemicals, for instance, has a number of joint ventures for making gasoline additives in the Far East and in south-east Asia. Each joint venture is set up to cover its local national market. The maintenance of price stability is dependent on the capacity balancing of each joint venture, so that no one will be under pressure to export into other territories. Typically, the capacity expansion decision is a particularly important prerogative for the board to keep control over.

In most of our discussions regarding non-financial approaches to maintaining control in a strategic alliance, we have assumed that there has been a joint ownership of assets in the joint venture. Many strategic alliances do, however, function without actual joint investments by the parents. They can be cooperative networks of various sorts. Such cooperative networks tend to function and hold because of social contacts and interpersonal relationships. But these types of networks typically take a long time to establish. They are frequently found in supplier–customer relationships in industrial marketing. It will be social norms, commonly established expectations, and an appreciation of seeing takes-and-gives over a longer time period, that establish the control mechanisms in such networks (Håkansson 1980).

One approach to further institute stability in such potentially, relatively loose networks, and thereby exercise more tangible strategic control while protecting core competencies, is to take a minority, cross-ownership financial stake in the partner(s). While this will not be sufficient for a firm to dictate its views to the partner, it should be seen as a complement to the social control as it signifies a long-term commitment. By being tied up with the partner in a more binding way, the parties might be even more compelled to find cooperative solutions to specific issues and problems in a win–win spirit. For example, as of early 1991, SAS had an equity stake in several of its strategic partners. This in no way gives SAS much of a legal say; however, it does signal a strong commitment to the joint long-term success. (SAS is a strategic alliance between the national airlines of Denmark, Norway, and Sweden, with two-sevenths, two-sevenths, and three-sevenths ownership, respectively.)

Financial Control

Having established the basic direction for the strategic alliance (manifested in a set of objectives), an accompanying set of strategic programs, and the necessary strategic budgetary resources for implementation, we are ready to discuss the various financial control vehicles necessary to assess the progress of the various strategies and which complement the non-financial controls discussed in the previous section.

Financial control must, of course, be made as compatible as possible with both parents' control systems and needs. Hopefully this can be done without actually installing two separate control systems, as this might create excessive paperwork for the joint venture – an activity that might not necessarily enhance the likelihood of success.

What dimensions should the financial control system focus on? There are some variables, which are primarily associated with tracking short-term performance, and it is important to monitor the revenue figures tightly in order to get a measure of the strategic alliance's ability to create transactions successfully in the market. But other factors, while less obvious, are equally important and we shall primarily focus on these:

- critical underlying assumptions
- scanning the environment
- strategic program progress
- assessing competitor and customer responses
- strategic budget expenditures

It is very important to monitor the critical underlying assumptions behind the particular objectives at hand. This means constantly reassessing whether the basic direction is still valid and obtaining early warning signals for when it is necessary to modify a particular strategic direction. One set of critical assumptions centers on basic growth suppositions, such as where a product is situated on its life-cycle curve, and calls for re-examining the outlook for future sales. Competing products, innovations, changes in consumer trends, and/or demographic changes are essential to monitor in this regard. Other vital issues might concern changes in distribution patterns, changes in business–government relations, and so on. Finally, changes in the competitive structure of the industry such as a new entrant or the emergence of competing strategic alliances, will be important to keep track of.

The task of scanning the environment should be articulated to the extent possible and assigned to various executives within the strategic alliance. Moreover, the planning committee must meet on a regular basis to discuss the potential implications of changes in critical environmental assumptions. It should be made clear that the responsibility for tracking these assumptions rests with all of the organizations involved in a strategic alliance. Too often there can be confusion on this point, with one partner assuming that the monitoring of a particular set of critical underlying assumptions behind a given objective is being done by the other partner, say, the organization most heavily involved in the distribution and sales of the product. All cooperative arrangements can become a sleeping pill for many alliance members, leaving them unaware of, or insensitive to, signals from the market place.

In controlling the strategic program progress, there are two sets of issues that require attention. First, each parent organization must monitor the focal organization to see that it is carrying out the various roles that have been assigned to it, relative to each given strategic program. As discussed in the section on strategic programming, the issue of who is doing what can become quite complicated. It is imperative to follow up carefully, seeing that every participant is doing his or her share as intended (Lorange 1984). Project management milestone control would be useful here. Furthermore, wherever it becomes clear that a particular focal organization is not able to carry out its role, the repercussions on the entire strategic program should be examined, so that ameliorating modifications can be instituted. This can eliminate the delays which might otherwise plague the strategic programming efforts.

The second issue in controlling the strategic programming effort centers on monitoring the critical underlying assumptions behind a particular strategic program. This primarily involves reassessing reactions from the environment, those of competitors as well as customers. Are the competitors responding with countermoves to our particular strategic program? If so, do we need to modify our approach? Similarly, are the customers accepting our particular strategic program as we expected? If not, how can we modify our approach?

Strategic alliance organizations often tend to be sluggish when it comes to assessing competitor and customer responses. This is generally because so many executives need to be involved, very often without sufficient benefit of clear task delineation and definite responsibility assignments. The ability to react to such responses is too often tentative. Careful monitoring of competitor moves and customer responses is as crucial for strategic alliances as for any other organization.

Strategic budget expenditures also require careful monitoring. The key executives committed to the cooperative strategic program must actually be assigned to the tasks at hand. Very often, these key executives are loaned back to a given parent organization to "firefight" within their particular organizational domain. Similarly, the financial resources necessary can be held back in response to emerging strategic opportunities that a particular parent organization subsequently sees for itself. It is important that the other partners in the cooperative network be able to apply sanctions, if a particular partner organization should deliberately undermine the agreed-upon cooperative trust by not applying the promised strategic resources. These sanctions can be in the form of penalty payments for not living up to the contractual commitment.

Tailoring Planning for the Four Archetypes

It should be kept in mind that planning in ad hoc pool strategic alliances consists merely of sorting out the joint rationale of working together, assuming no resource slack and no development of an independent organizational entity cum strategic alliance. The issue here is further flavored by the fact that one of the parties tends to be large and well-established and the other small and entrepreneurial. The development of a joint plan needs to focus on creating clarity regarding the compatibility of efforts, technology, and tasks, among other things. Difficulties regarding definition of standards, cultural differences, and differences in formalization of the organization versus entrepreneurship, also need to be captured in planning this ad hoc pool stage.

When it comes to the consortium situation, many of the same issues that have been discussed in the previous paragraph also are at work. Here, however, one should keep in mind that the parties tend to be more even in size, and the consortium tends to be larger and more all-encompassing in scope. The sheer articulation of how scale and scope advantages are created, and how to develop strategic programming which allows each party to understand who is doing what, becomes particularly important.

For a project-based joint venture, the issue is one of developing a sense of planning to allow the transfer of know-hows through the common skeleton entity with minimum efforts and with no more additional resources than intended. Here the planning must emphasize training, institutionalization of know-how transfers, and servicing routines.

Finally, when it comes to a full-blown joint venture, the strategic planning is more or less similar to what one would find in a full-blown organization, one which has been created through an ordinary merger.

Tailoring Control for the Four Archetypes

For the ad hoc pool strategic alliance the only control measure to follow is observing whether the intended output from the pool efforts has been achieved or not. This measure can be enriched by setting control points initially agreed upon by the partners, e.g. technological development, level of customer satisfaction or market share.

The consortium type of strategic alliance uses the same types of control measures as the ad hoc pool. Here, however, the question of resource utilization becomes crucial, particularly on the cost side. The question of equity relative to each partner, so that potential freeloading temptations can be arrested, becomes critical.

For the project-based joint venture, performance outputs of a financial nature become the key control dimension; costs, sales, profits, but not return on investments (given the fact that the resource base left in the strategic alliance tends to be kept intentionally small). In addition, some measure of strategic fit should be controlled to determine whether the strategic assumptions behind this type of alliance are still valid. This allows the parents to assess whether the output measures of performance are satisfactory or not, given the business climate and its changing environment.

Full-blown joint ventures use output measures such as the

ones discussed for project-based joint ventures, complemented by output measures calculating return on investment, and coupled with strategic control measures dealing with adaptive responses to moves from competitors and reactions by customers. Finally, here too, some measurements of changes in the general business climate should be employed.

Planning Implications of Relative Business Position

Throughout the discussion in this chapter we have pointed towards the importance of appropriate planning and control, irrespective of what type of strategic intent the partners might have in connection with the strategic alliance. We now point to the need to tailor the planning and control approaches, so as to support better the particular strategic requirement a partner might have. It is not enough to follow a comprehensive planning and control approach. The emphasis and approach also need to be tailormade further in order to provide appropriate support for a given strategic intent.

We recall from our conceptual scheme in Chapter 1 that the type of position that a partner may have depends on how it sees the particular business, vis-à-vis the strategic alliance, in a competitive business strategy context and in a corporate portfolio strategy context.

In a situation where there is a strong business position, as well as a core role for the business within the firm's portfolio (a defensive strategic intent), we expect a relatively strong emphasis on the development and maintenance of a black box position. Similarly, even though strategic alliances in such situations tend to be relatively small, we expect heavy non-financial control because of the importance of the strategic alliance. In light of the small size, however, we do not expect a too heavy emphasis on financial control nor on formal strategic planning.

In contrast, in a situation where there is a relatively weak business strategy position combined with a core portfolio strategy position (a catching-up strategic intent), we do not expect as heavy an emphasis on the black box dimension. Often such strategic alliances can be quite large and complex, needing formal planning and quantitative control.

When it comes to a situation where there is a strong business strategy position coupled with a peripheral portfolio role (a restructuring strategic intent), we do not expect as much emphasis on non-financial controls so that senior management involvement is limited. Planning and financial control should emphasize the support of restructuring efforts, with particular emphasis on strategic programming efforts needed to reach the strategic intent.

Finally, in situations where there is a relatively weak business strategy position coupled with a relatively peripheral portfolio strategy role (a strategic intent to restructure with an eye to exiting), we expect neither much non-financial control nor many attempts to establish a strong black box position. Rather, the emphasis is on planning and financial controls consistent with the size and complexity of the particular strategic task. Relatively limited planning efforts can often be used, letting the stronger partner take the lead, with basic financial control being the sole remaining emphasis.

Planning Implications of the General Evolution Pattern

Tailoring the Management and Control Mode

Let us start out by considering what might be an appropriate mode of management control during Phase I (exhibit 3.1) of a strategic alliance's evolution. In this phase both partners play active, complementary roles. As already noted, this form of strategic alliance can be realistically compared to a strategic program being executed through the cooperation of several departments and divisions internally in a corporation. The critical mode of management and control here is securing hands-on coordination, making sure that it is clearly delineated who is doing what, and at what point in time. The control should center on achieving milestones, and pursuing a traditional project control mode when running the strategic alliance.

When it comes to Phase II of the generic strategic alliance

evolution model, the so-called dominant type of strategic alliance, the management and control approach changes to reflect that one of the partners now remains relatively active within the growing strategic alliance. There is a need for hands-on control in the relationship between the more active partner and the emerging free-standing strategic alliance organization that is gradually being established. This is analogous to the project-based management and control already described for the Phase I situation. However, coordination will now be primarily between one partner and the emerging strategic alliance organization. In addition, control routines must now also be put into place to satisfy the needs of the relatively passive partner. This is comparable to a responsibility center-based control approach. In this situation, it is important to have in place some sort of decentralized financial control, similar to what a firm might have implemented for wholly-owned subsidiaries. For the more passive partner, emphasizing return on investment, profits, costs, etc., will have to be gradually phased in through control routines.

In the Phase III evolutionary stage, with its so-called independent strategic alliance, both partners now play relatively passive roles vis-à-vis the strategic alliance organization. Thus, both partners now need to rely on decentralized responsibility center control while benefiting from the control system already put in place during Phase II.

In total, we see a need to change the control emphasis of a strategic alliance as it evolves from the hands-on physical control mode to a more decentralized financial control form. It goes without saying that the executives involved in the management of the strategic alliance from the two parents' sides must be sensitive to how they should shift their emphasis on control over time. If they continue to maintain a heavy hands-on type of control, the long-term success of the strategic alliance might eventually become frustrated.

Strategic Planning Changes

One of the critical challenges of any new organization is adapting to new opportunities that emerge in the environment. Adaptation is necessary in order to steer clear of prospective dangers and adverse developments that might emerge in the environment, possibly from competitors or from unforeseen shifts among one's customers. Strategic planning plays a crucial role in preparing an organization to be ready to adapt to new opportunities. As discussed earlier, a well-perceived planning process not only helps to spot such opportunities and threats, it also facilitates the delineation of how the organization's current know-hows and resources are re-deployed to take advantage of emerging new business opportunities.

A strategic planning process helps the organization both to build up new businesses for the future and to maintain the present business base. Both activities must continue on a parallel day-to-day basis, carried out largely by the same management team.

When it comes to a strategic alliance's attempts to meet its adaptive challenges, the issues just outlined can become more complicated owing to the fact that several partners are involved, creating, at least potentially, a more cumbersome decision-making process. The partners may have different viewpoints as to what the adaptive challenges are. They may, for instance, not see the environmental signals in a similar way. The fact that several partners are involved also slows down the process of reacting to opportunities and threats. Pro-active thinking regarding how to adapt becomes much harder to develop. Different partners may, in fact, feel more inclined to stick to the assumptions that were set out at the time the strategic alliance was entered.

Considering, for now, a Phase I-type shared strategic alliance, we know that the adaptive challenges typically rest heavily with both partners. Each partner has to be responsible for looking after those parts of the value-creating chain that falls under its jurisdiction. A prospective problem here will often be an only partial view by each partner of what is really happening to the overall business, because each partner typically will only focus on parts of the value chain. A common planning process which coordinates the partners' view points on the evolution of the overall business vis-à-vis its competitive environment is necessary.

For a Phase II situation, with one partner relatively more dominant, the adaptive challenge rests on the shoulders of this partner, together with the emerging management team of the strategic alliance itself. Here, an important issue is the development of a planning process which allows a common viewpoint to develop around key competitive issues, customer moves, technology shifts, etc. The process has to satisfy a dual set of purposes – an identification of what appropriate adaptive moves to take, and the facilitation of internal agreements among the members of the strategic alliance organization and the dominant parent organization regarding how to identify, split, and realign tasks and roles.

In a Phase III strategic alliance, the strategic planning process is embodied in the strategic alliance so that it can carry out its own planning autonomously. The design of the planning process for this situation is quite similar to what we find in an independent company or wholly-owned subsidiary. Emphasis must, of course, be put on developing a dynamic strategic thrust that is satisfactory in the eyes of the parents when, for example, it comes to the alliance's ability to finance its own growth.

The design of the strategic planning process should be conceived in such a way that it pro-actively anticipates the changing needs for the planning support as a firm moves from Phase I to Phase III. The shift should be from a heavy emphasis on project planning, as if the strategic alliance is being considered as a strategic program, to a gradual building-up of a complementary business planning activity. By the time Phase III is reached, this planning form is the dominant one. Failure to manage the evolution of the planning process leads to dysfunctional performance by the strategic alliance.

Summary

In this chapter we have considered the management processes and the systems dimensions unique to strategic planning and control in a strategic alliance. Establishing a realistic planning and control system along with complementary managerial processes can strengthen the odds to make the strategic alliance work. Without such a consistent approach to systems and processes, it is difficult for the strategic alliance to succeed. For instance, as we have seen, classical budgetary control is necessary, but it is not sufficient alone to address the critical control issues adequately. Neither is the establishment of a strong black box position nor a terror balance approach alone sufficient. It is an integrated approach to planning and control, based on a complementary set of approaches with a relatively large set of executives from all parent organizations involved, that ensures that the strategic alliance stays on its track. In addition, when it comes to these issues, we see that differences in strategic intents can lead to shifts in what to emphasize. It does not make sense to strive for the development of a black box position under all strategic intent settings, for instance. Similarly, senior management's involvement through non-financial controls and through the strategic planning committee only makes full sense when the strategic intents are such that they merit it. The size and complexity of the strategic alliance also plays a role regarding the relative emphasis on formal planning and control.

Appendix
Genetics Institute Inc.[1]

Gabriel Schmergel, President and CEO of Genetics Institute Inc. (GI), listened intently as Gustav Christensen, Vice-President for marketing and business development, outlined the various forward integration options available to the three-year-old Cambridge-based biotechnology firm. The company was at a crossroads in early 1985. With deadlines approaching on the exercise of contractual options to manufacture a portion of the commercial needs of certain products licensed to client companies, GI had to develop a manufacturing capability in order to exercise these options. Given the timeline for approval by the Food and Drug Administration (FDA), addressing the manufacturing issue would be a top priority for GI's management in the coming year. For one of the biotechnology industry's five largest firms, the time had come to begin looking at the various alternatives.

The previous year had seen the beginning of a shift in GI's basic philosophy. Founded in 1980 as an R&D company with products licensed out to clients for clinical development, manufacturing, and marketing/distribution in exchange for royalties on sales, GI was now poised to take the crucial step into manufacturing and move toward becoming a fully integrated company. That bridge had already been crossed, Gabriel Schmergel knew, but it had not been easy. Initially some of the senior scientists who had a significant influence on the company's affairs, questioned the rationale. Only after "an enormous amount of soul searching" did GI management decide to move away from the company's original strategy.

Gustav Christensen favored a joint venture to build a plant for commercial manufacture of protein therapeutics with one of the world's largest pharmaceutical companies. The idea had a lot of merit, but it would require thorough scrutiny and analysis, as would all the available options. Of one thing Gabriel Schmergel felt sure. At this point, no longer was it a question of whether GI should get into manufacturing. The issue was how to implement forward integration, and what was the best route to take. This issue had been evaluated and reevaluated several times throughout late 1984 and early 1985.

The company

Genetics Institute was founded in December 1980 by two Harvard professors and biochemists, Dr Mark Ptashne and Dr Thomas Maniatis. Harvard had previously approached Dr Ptashne with a view to starting a university-sponsored genetic engineering company, but abandoned the idea when controversy arose on campus concerning the propriety of even limited equity funding of such a venture. The two scientists decided to go ahead with the idea independently and recruited Gabriel Schmergel, a 1967 Baker Scholar from Harvard Business School and former President of the International Division at Baxter Travenol Laboratories Inc. to run the company. The new CEO asssembled a management team with extensive experience in the healthcare industry. The two scientific founders attracted to the company the initial team of scientists with a broad base in scientific academic research (see exhibits A4.1, A4.2). Initial funding of $6 million came from the venture capital firms of J.H. Whitney & Co., Greylock Management Corp., and Venrock Associates, as well as individual investors, including William Paley of CBS. Second and third rounds of financing in 1982 and 1983 raised a further $45 million, and the company went public in May 1986, raising an additional $85 million with the initial public offering (see exhibit A4.3).

By year end 1985, GI had 234 employees, of whom 162 were in R&D, including 60 with PhDs. The company occupied 125,000

Exhibit A4.1 Genetics Institute Inc.: Management and backgrounds

---

Gabriel Schmergel, President and Chief Executive Officer, formerly President-International at Baxter Travenol Laboratories; elected President of the Industrial Biotechnical Association in October 1985

RESEARCH

Dr Robert Kamen, Vice President of Research, formerly Director of the Transcription Laboratory at the Imperial Cancer Research Fund Laboratory

Dr Leonard Lerman, Director of Diagnostics, formerly Professor and Chairman of Biological Sciences at State University of New York at Albany

DEVELOPMENT

Brett Schmidli, Vice-President of Process Development, formerly Department Head of Chemical Manufacturing at Eli Lilly & Co.

PATENTS

Bruce Eisen, Vice-President–Chief Patent Counsel, formerly Director of US Patents at Schering–Plough

MARKETING AND BUSINESS DEVELOPMENT

Gustav Christensen, Vice-President of Marketing & Business Development, formerly Vice-President of Fenwal Laboratories, a Division of Baxter Travenol Laboratories

Tuan Ha-Ngoc, Director of Marketing, formerly Director of Drug Delivery Systems, Travenol Laboratories, a Division of Baxter Travenol Laboratories

FINANCE

Garen Bohlin, Vice-President of Finance and Treasurer, formerly partner at Arthur Anderson & Co.

OPERATIONS

Thomas Crowdis, Vice-President of Operations, formerly CEO of the Emerson Hospital, Concord, Massachusetts

TOKYO OFFICE

Kuni Yamamoto, Director of Tokyo Branch Office, formerly President of Travenol Laboratories-Japan

---

Scientific Board
Golde (UCLA)
Kamen (Genetics Institute)
Lerman (Genetics Institute)
Maniatis (Harvard)
Ptashne (Harvard)

Board of Directors
Evnin (Venrock)
Gregory (Greylock)
Jocobs (Jacobs Engineering)
Maniatis (Harvard – Founder)
Paley (Founder/Chairman – CBS)
Ptashne (Harvard – Founder)
Schmergel (Genetics Institute)
Schmidt (J.H. Whitney)

President and CEO
Schmergel

Patents/Intellectual Property
Eisen

Process Development
Schmidli

Operations
Crowdis

Research
Kamen
Lerman

Finance
Bohlin

Marketing/Business Development
Christensen
Ha-Ngoc
|
Tokyo Office
Yamamoto

Microbial Fermentation

Cell Culture

Biochemical Engineering

Pilot Plant

Large-scale Biochemistry

Research Planning

Project management

Cell Biology — *Analytical Biochemistry*

Molecular Cloning

Core Technologies

Gene Expression

Applied Agriculture

Enzymology

Protein Sequencing

Peptide Sequencing

DNA Synthesis

DNA Sequencing

Monoclonal Antibodies

Immunoassays

Animal Studies

Bacteria

Yeast

Mammalian Cells

Insect Cells

Exhibit A4.2

Exhibit A4.3 Genetics Institute Inc.: Equity financing and stock ownership

---

- $135 million-plus in equity raised through three rounds of private financing and company's initial public offering

- No single investor owns in excess of 10 percent of voting stock of company
  - Key venture capital investors
  - J.H. Whitney & Co.
  - Venrock Associates
  - Greylock Management
  - William S. Paley (Founder/Chairman – CBS)

- Key Corporate investors
  - Allied–Signal
  - Baxter Travenol Laboratories
  - Jacobs Engineering
  - Sandoz

---

square feet of facilities in Cambridge, Mass., encompassing state-of-the-art R&D laboratories and a pilot production plant designed to manufacture a limited level of products for clinical trial needs only. Plans were under way to expand significantly the existing process development and pilot/clinical manufacturing groups in the company as well as pilot/clinical production capacity in general. GI had no internal capability to conduct human clinical trials and no sales organization at this time. With $64 million in assets and $33 million in working capital, the company reported operating expenditures of $22 million in 1985, one-third of which was devoted to self-funded proprietary research (see exhibit A4.4).

Biotechnology

Biotechnology entails the use of living micro-organisms or cultured tissue cells for the production of biological substances. This forms the basis of genetically engineered products. The purpose of genetic engineering is to harness the ability of cells to secrete desired substances. All cells, from the simplest bacterium to the most complex human cell, contain genes, made up of deoxyribonucleic acid (DNA), which constitutes the blueprint or instruc-

Exhibit A4.4 Genetics Institute Inc.: Summary of operating revenues and expenses for the years ended November 30, 1984, 1985 ($)

	1985	1984
Operating revenues:		
Sponsored research	17,058,630	9,565,602
Operating expenses:		
Research and development	19,391,095	11,715,510
General and administrative	2,907,648	2,490,420
Total operating expenses	22,298,743	14,205,930
Loss from operations:	(5,240,113)	(4,640,328)
Other income, net:	3,508,554	4,705,576
Net (loss) income:	(1,731,559)	65,248

Consolidated balance sheets as of November 30, 1984, 1985 ($)

	1985	1984
ASSETS		
Current assets:		
Cash and cash equivalents	343,938	354,545
Interest-bearing investments, at cost		
which approximates market	31,975,874	40,130,784
Funds held in escrow	–	2,597,097
Accounts receivable	2,166,413	1,291,200
Unbilled services	1,456,640	753,567
Accrued interest receivable	917,899	1,113,052
Other current assets	783,806	558,860
Total current assets	37,644,570	46,799,105
Investment in United AgriSeeds, Inc.	7,988,300	7,990,00

Exhibit A4.4 Continued

For the Years Ended November 30	1985	1984
Property and equipment, at cost:		
Equipment, furniture and fixtures	15,130,042	9,534,101
Leasehold improvements	6,477,848	1,690,225
Less-accumulated depreciation	(3,456,096)	(1,623,799)
Net property and equipment	18,151,794	9,600,527
Other assets	299,918	416,134
	64,084,582	64,805,766
LIABILITIES AND STOCKHOLDERS' EQUITY		
Current liabilities:		
Obligations under capital leases	2,672,254	1,239,310
Accounts payable	322,685	205,994
Accrued expenses	1,248,414	1,128,285
Construction progress payments payable	–	3,031,415
Total current liabilities	4,243,353	5,605,004
Long term debt:		
Obligations under capital leases	8,544,933	6,124,662
Bank notes payable	189,765	374,950
Total long-term debt	8,734,698	6,499,612
Total liabilities	12,978,051	12,104,616

Exhibit A4.4 Continued

For the Years Ended November 30	1985	1984
Stockholders' equity:		
Capital stock		
Preferred stock, par value $100:		
authorized 80,000 shares: issued and outstanding 60,000 shares	6,000,000	6,000,000
Convertible preferred, par value $1-		
Series A – authorized, issued and outstanding 505,000 shares	505,000	505,000
Series B – authorized, issued and outstanding 286,337 shares	286,337	286,337
Series C – authorized, issued and outstanding 600,000 shares	600,000	600,000
Common stock, par value $.01:		
authorized 10,000,000 shares: issued and outstanding 2,886,826 shares and 2,887,509 shares in 1985 and 1984 respectively	28,869	28,876
Additional paid in capital	47,698,630	47,561,683
Accumulated deficit	(4,012,305)	(2,280,746)
Total stockholders' equity	51,106,531	52,701,150
	$64,084,582	$64,805,766

tions of how a cell functions. Recombinant DNA technology isolates fragments of DNA from separate sources and splices them together to form a new functional unit.

The production of genetically engineered pharmaceuticals starts with the insertion of new genes into living cells, which in turn become tiny factories, producing a desired substance according to the cell's new genetic instructions. These substances or proteins can be grown and harvested in sufficient quantitites to be used in the treatment of diseases and disorders. Insulin, a protein used to treat diabetes, was the initial example of such a successfully developed drug. The choice of cell is crucial. Bacteria, yeast and insect culture cells are appropriate for the production of simple proteins, but the cells of mammals, such as mice and hamsters, are necessary for some of the more complex proteins found in humans. A mammalian cell process requires more costly technology, a much larger production facility, and different scientific and manufacturing expertise. GI had determined that this process would be optimum for the development of its most promising therapeutic protein products and had substantial experience in the scale-up and production of clinical trial quantities of proteins in this environment.

In keeping with a philosophy of developing a broad capability, GI offered a range of very widely applicable and interrelated technologies, including expertise in mammalian, bacterial, yeast and insect cell processes to produce recombinant proteins (see exhibit A4.5). A number of distinct phases were involved in the development of a recombinant DNA product. This included discovery, cloning, expression or cell production, and the scaling-up of a process from the laboratory to the pilot plant and commercial manufacturing level (see exhibits A4.6 and A4.7). The scale-up for a mammalian cell process entailed going from 10 liter tanks in the lab to 1,000 liter volume in a pilot plant and up to 10,000 liter tanks at the commercial plant level.

By mid-1985, GI was engaged in twenty R&D programs, and the company's four most advanced healthcare products had been developed in collaboration with corporate sponsors on a funded research basis. GI would receive downstream royalties on eventual commercial sales (see exhibit A4.8). Tissue Plasminogen Activator (tPA), a protein to dissolve blood clots, used in the treatment of heart attacks, had been licensed to Wellcome Biotechnology, Ltd. Granulocyte Monocyte Colony Stimulating Factor (GM–CSF), for treating certain blood cell disorders, was licensed to Sandoz Ltd., and Erythropoietin (EPO), a protein to treat chronic anemia had been licensed to Chugai Pharmaceutical and Boehringer Mannheim GmbH. These products were expected to enter clinical trials in 1986, while Factor VIII, a protein for the treatment of hemophilia, licensed to Baxter Travenol, was expected to be ready for clinical trials a year later (see exhibit A4.8). A program to develop DNA-based diagnostic kits for certain infectious diseases had been licensed to the Henley Group (formerly part of Allied–Signal). While some products were licensed, others were kept in-house. For example, GI's proprietary research and development primarily involved the development of bone growth factors for use in orthopedic and periodontal surgery; various

Exhibit A4.5 Genetics Institute's range of technology capabilities

---

Cell biology
- Bioassay of regulatory molecules
- Animal cell cultures
- Insect cell culture
- Plant cell culture
- Fluorescence-activated cell sorting

Biochemistry
- Protein chemistry
- Protein microsequencing
- Carbohydrate analysis
- Peptide synthesis
- Protein purification
- Enzymology

Molecular biology
- Molecular cloning
- DNA synthesis
- DNA sequencing
- Site-directed mutagenesis

Gene expression
- Bacteria
- Yeast
- Mammalian cells
- Insect cells

Immunology
- Monoclonal antibodies
- Polyclonal antibodies
- Immunoassays
- Immunoaffinity purification

Process development
- Fermentation
- Large-scale cell culture
- Protein purification
- Protein characterization

Commercial scale-up
- Biochemical engineering
- Pilot production for clinical use

Source: Genetics Institute Annual Report, 1985

Exhibit A4.6 Genetics Institute Inc.: Product development costs

Phase of development	Cost ($ million)	Time frame (years)
Project idea to cloning	1–5	1–5
Expression to pilot plant	2–4	1½
Clinical trials (Including production of clinical trial materials)	10–30	2–4

additional blood cell growth factors beyond GM–CSF and EPA, and a second-generation tPA program.

GI was also active in the agricultural products area. In 1984, the company took the major step of acquiring a one-third interest in United AgriSeeds, Inc., the tenth largest supplier of agricultural seeds in the US with a view to developing improved strains of hybrid corn seed. Research was being conducted with biological insecticides for agricultural use, and in the area of industrial biocatalysis work was being done to develop enzymes for the enhancement of certain industrial processes.

Following a conservative financial strategy, GI management initially sought to utilize equity capital for strategic investment as opposed to operations. By licensing out rights to products on a contract research basis, the company set out to build sophisticated, extensive capabilities with someone else providing the capital and assuming the financial risk. By thus preserving GI's equity capital, the interest earned could be used to self-fund valuable proprietary research. "I like to take a big leap, but I also like to provide a safety net," was how Gabriel Schmergel described this basic philosophy.

Initially preoccupied with economic survival in a highly competitive and volatile industry, by 1982 the fledgling company's perspective began to change, according to the CEO. "It was felt that as an R&D boutique licensing out products, GI's ultimate valuation would top out at a moderate level offering only limited financial rewards. To keep building value for the investors and our employees, it became apparent that we had to engage in downstream activities," he explained. "Licensing could be very unsatisfying, especially for our scientists, whose emotional bond to their projects made it difficult to hand them over to large companies," he added. Cultural clashes were inevitable. Decision-

Exhibit A4.7 Genetics Institute Inc.: Development of new medicine

---

The search for new substances of value for the prevention and treatment of disease and for the relief of symptoms is usually a difficult, complex and lengthy process. During the initial *research phase*, desired objectives are often not achievable and have to be modified.

When the initial research objectives have been attained and a substance has been identified with the required biological activity, a phase of *pre-clinical evaluation* follows in which the details of its biological action, tests in various species relating to its safety and optimal methods of manufacture are studied. This phase rarely takes less than two years, and often much longer. Many substances fail to survive such rigorous evaluation. Those that do are studied in man.

The phase of *early clinical trials* establishes how the substance is metabolized in man, whether it has the desired therapeutic effect in patients and whether it is safe when given in an optimal manner. This phase again rarely takes less than two years and in many cases the substance does not achieve the desired effect or is poorly tolerated.

A substance which passes this stage enters the final and often the most expensive phase, that of *full product development*. During this phase further extensive safety evaluations are carried out and processes for the manufacture and quality control of the substance and its formulations are developed. In addition, extended clinical trials are carried out in a much wider range of patients, often in a number of territories, comparing the new product with existing treatments.

When these activities are complete, and if the full product development phase has produced satisfactory results, comprehensive dossiers of information on the product's safety, efficacy and quality are submitted to regulatory authorities for marketing authorization. The time taken to obtain such authorization in particular countries varies, but generally takes from six months to four years from the date of application, depending upon the degree of control exercised by the regulatory authority, the efficiency of its review procedure and the nature of the product.

Source: Wellcome PLC, Offering Memorandum, January 29, 1986

Exhibit A4.8 Genetics Institute Inc.: Key R&D activities (licensing status)

Human healthcare
- Tissue Plasminogen Activator (Wellcome)
- Factor VIII (Baxter Travenol
- Erythropoietin (Chugai and Boehringer Mannheim)
- Colony Stimulating Factor/GM–CSF (Sandoz)
- Human Diagnostics/DNA Probes (Allied/Henley)
- Blood Cell Growth Factors (proprietary)
- Bone Growth Factors (proprietary)
- Several second-generation products (proprietary)

Agriculture
- Corn seed improvement (United AgriSeeds)
- Biological insecticide for Heliothis (proprietary)
- Other crop improvement areas and biological insecticides (proprietary)

Industrial Biocatalysis
- Unannounced projects (Gist–Brocades, Chemie Linz, Arizona Chemical)
- Other process technology with potential application in food processing and personal care industries (proprietary)

---

making could be slow in a large, diverse corporation, whereas decisions at GI were made quickly. "Besides, the more licensing you do, the more widespread your technology transfer and leakage," he pointed out. "Licensing might be a comfortable existence in the short and medium term, but ultimately forward integration held more appeal for the aggressive and hard-driving GI staff."

Weighing the Options

In an industry characterized by uncertainty and high risk, timing was critical in a decision to build a manufacturing plant. A minimum of three to four years was normally required for FDA approval of a product, but for some of GI's proteins due to enter clinical trials in mid 1986, there was a possibility of earlier approval. A fast-track approval could be as short as two years, underscoring the need for commercial manufacturing capacity by early 1989. The possibility also highlighted the twofold risk inherent in this decision. "To be too early and have a fully-staffed plant standing idle would be very costly, but on the other hand not to have a plant ready to supply the market would mean a huge opportunity cost," explained Gustav Christensen.

"In the biotechnology business, one of the difficulties of strategic and operational planning is the number of variables that have to be taken into account," commented Chief Financial Officer Garen Bohlin. "This includes technical variables as to whether you can develop and economically produce the product; regulatory issues relating to clinical testing, and complex patent situations, each of which can change numerous times during the course of a project. Biotechnology is not like some of our more traditional industries where there is a more predictable product development cycle," he added.

"Faced with the need to scale-up from a laboratory process to commercial manufacturing, GI could have taken an interim step of only expanding its pilot plant facilities, thereby extending slightly the time horizon until a full-scale plant was needed. But this would have been a stopgap measure at best, and the need for volume manufacturing capacity would still have to be addressed," Gustav Christensen noted.

By early 1985, three clean manufacturing options had been identified; GI could build its own plant, thereby retaining total control, but risking considerable financial exposure; enter an agreement for outside manufacture of its products with one of its client companies; or form a joint venture with a major pharmaceutical manufacturer. The choice was essentially between a stand-alone plant and a joint venture, according to CEO Gabriel Schmergel (see exhibit A4.9). "Going it alone would have meant a smaller plant," he said, while total outside manufacturing was considered too risky, since most of the large pharmaceutical companies at the time lacked the necessary expertise and capability in mammalian cell technology. Also this would have meant abandonment of the forward integration strategy.

After extensive modeling and analysis, a consensus was reached that a joint venture was the best option, providing an opportunity to combine products and technologies in addition to spreading the financial risk. "Product assurance and economies of scale were the key criteria and weighed more heavily than the financial aspects in the decision," Garen Bohlin noted. A joint venture was seen as a way of bridging the disadvantage of size relative to GI's strongest competitor in the industry, the California-based

Exhibit A4.9 Genetics Institute Inc.: Commercial manufacturing alternatives, quantitative considerations ($ million)

Capital requirements and financing	Wellcome joint venture	Stand-alone facility
Capital investment	25	16
Financing		
Cash	10–12[a,b]	6–7[b]
Debt	18–20[a,c]	11–12

[a]GI share is 50 percent of total joint venture requirement.
[b]Includes cash required to finance plant start-up costs.
[c]Debt financing done by joint venture rather than joint venture partners.

Cost inputs used in financial models

- capital investment and depreciation lives (fixed assumptions)
- financing vehicles and rates (fixed assumptions)
- operating costs (fully absorbed into product costs)
  - fixed costs – G&A, depreciation, taxes/insurance (fixed assumptions)
  - variable – Media/serum supplies (varies directly with product output and yields)
  - semivariable – labor, utilities (fixed minimum plus variable element that corresponds to plant utilization)
- inflationary cost increases offset by productivity gains

Financial model construct and variables

- projections made over period of fifteen years (three years of design and construction and twelve years of operation)
- scenarios established in both joint venture and stand-alone environments in following areas:
  - transfer pricing to outside GI partners of material produced (three levels for each GI product)
  - manufacturing productivity/yield rates (three levels for each GI product)
  - Risk factor discount on manufacturing profits to recognize technical, regulatory, and other risks of getting products to market (two levels of 30 percent and 50 percent)
- internal rates of return and net present values calculated for each environment (joint venture and stand-alone) for the eighteen-model scenarios presented below

Exhibit 4.9 Continued

Manufacturing profits discounted 30 percent

	#1	#2	#3
Productivity level			
#1	×	×	×
#2	×	×	×
#3	×	×	×

Manufacturing profits discounted 50 percent

	#1	#2	#3
Productivity level			
#1	×	×	×
#2	×	×	×
#3	×	×	×

- individual unit costs of products manufactured in joint venture environment under the various model scenarios were generally 30–50 percent of comparable costs of producing product in the stand-alone environment
- net present values in joint ventures environment under the various scenarios generally ranged from 1.5 to 3.0 times net present values in the stand-alone environment

---

Genentech (see exhibit A4.10). "A joint venture offered substantial economies of scale, in terms of both capital commitment and operating costs. As an example, a manufacturing plant with twice the capacity would require only one and a half times the capital cost," he added.

The GI team were mindful of the potential disadvantages. "Joint ventures take a tremendous amount of effort to make them work, and conflicting priorities can present a problem," Gustav Christensen said. "We had to be sensitive to the reaction of our clients to such a move. How would they feel about the possibility of technology leakage by having their products manufactured by one of their competitors?" Given the complex and inherently ambiguous nature of client relationships within the biotechnology industry, this was not viewed as a major problem, but had to be

Exhibit A4.10 Leading US biotechnology companies (recombinant DNA-based), December 1984 ($ million)

Name	Revenues	Expenses	Income before taxes	Assets	Cash	Emp./PhD	Market value, Dec. 31, 1984	Founded
Genentech	70	67	3	150	32	674/128	490	1976
Cetus	68	67	1	134	88	610/100[c]	193	1971
GENETICS INSTITUTE	14	14	0.1	65	41	197/50	[a]	1980
Enzo Biochem	5	3	2	23	21	51/23[c]	130	1977
Biogen	31	44	(12)	110	72	376/n.a.	102	1978
Genex	35	42	(7)	44	5	264/51	68	1977
Amgen	9	17	(8)	49	25	133/49[c]	53	1980
Advanced Genetics	1	8	(7)	10	4	87/28	46	1979
Molecular Genetics	9	10	(1)	33	26	124/28	45	1979
Collaborative Research	10	13	(4)	27	19	131/20	41	1981
BioTechnica (BTI)	1	6	(4)	7	<1	86/31	34[b]	1981
Chiron	7	9	(2)	21	15	108/n.a.	33	1981
Immunex	4	6	(2)	17	12	87/28	33[b]	1981
Integrated Genetics	5	8	(3)	23	18	127/n.a.	30	1981
California Biotech	8	8	(0.1)	17	11	85/33	28	1981

[a]Private company. Approximate rank if company were publicly held.
[b]Market value as of March 31, 1985.
[c]Mid-1984 figures; end-year figures not available.
Sources: Wall Street Journal, annual reports, consultants' reports. Table taken from HBS case "Genetics Institute enters the seed business", by Associates Fellow Michael Kennedy, under the supervision of Professor Ray A. Goldberg, 1985.

carefully handled none the less. An affiliation with a leading pharmaceutical giant entailed a certain lack of control and the danger of the smaller company being absorbed and eclipsed by the larger partner. "A pharmaceutical company with worldwide manufacturing operations would have so many more alternatives to fall back on. If it proved beneficial at some point to manufacture these products in another plant, or another country, a company with that level of resources and financial muscle could do so," noted Garen Bohlin.

By mid-1985, GI management had reached the decision that, on balance, a joint venture was the best option, providing the lowest cost products and the greatest opportunity to capture some of the end profit. The process of sorting out potential corporate partners was initiated, with a view to presenting a proposal to the board at the upcoming December meeting.

Selecting a Corporate Partner

As only FDA-approved products would be manufactured by the joint venture, the stage of readiness of products would be crucial. GI's most advanced product was tPA, the enzyme to dissolve blood clots, due to enter clinical trials in 1986. (The San Francisco-based Genentech was acknowledged as the furthest along in the making and testing of tPA, and was close to being granted a patent in the UK.) A mammalian cell system suitable for the production of tPA in commercial quantities had been developed at the laboratory level, under sponsorship from Baxter Travenol. As GI's product line was geared to the development of proteins using a mammalian process as opposed to a bacterial process, "it was critical to find a joint venture partner with expertise in large-scale manufacturing and a track record in that area," noted Gustav Christensen.

This led GI to the British-based pharmaceutical giant, Well-come, who had acquired the rights to tPA from Baxter Travenol in mid-1984, and were scheduled to take the product into clinical trials. "Whereas some companies had a cell culture capability in the development of vaccines, but not with protein projects, Wellcome was the only company worldwide with expertise in both areas, largely on account of work done on interferon, which incorporated both capabilities," Christensen explained. Person-ality fit was also a major factor in the choice of a corporate partner, and "the technical staff and management teams in both companies felt that they could co-exist," he added. Wellcome's financial substance met all of GI's criteria for a partner "as strong or stronger financially." Furthermore, it was vital to minimize product competition in any joint venture, and given the state of readiness of both companies' products, a link-up with Wellcome would satisfy that need.

Wellcome Biotechnology

Wellcome was a major international research-based pharmaceutical group, engaged in the research, development, and manufacture of human and animal healthcare products. Established in London in 1880, Wellcome's origins went back more than one hundred years. Employing 18,000 people, the company operated worldwide, including a strong presence in North America through its subsidiary, Burroughs Wellcome. In 1985, North American operations accounted for more than 40 percent of the group's sales and approximately 60 percent of profits. Wellcome reported revenues of £1,004 million in 1985, with R&D expenditures amounting to £122 million, representing 12.2 percent of revenues (see exhibits A4.11 and A4.12).

Human healthcare products accounted for approximately 82 percent of sales. Wellcome held a leading position in a number of product areas, including topical anti-infectives, anti-gout preparations, anti-virals, muscle relaxants and in the over-the-counter market in the US for cough and cold preparations, with Actifed and Sudafed the market leaders in the antihistamine/decongestant category. The company had a distinguished history of innovation in the development of new drugs. Among Wellcome's early achievements was the large-scale manufacture in the UK of a product for the treatment of diphtheria in 1895. Manufacture of insulin began in 1922, and in the early 1980s Wellcome led the way in the anti-viral field with the discovery of acyclovir, an active ingredient effective against herpes, marketed under the trade name Zovirax.

Wellcome Biotechnology was formed in 1982, engaged primarily in the research and development of therapeutic proteins. In addition to collaboration with Genetics Institute on tPA, Wellcome Biotechnology had licensing agreements with Biogen for the development of a genetically engineered hepatitis B vaccine, and with Sumitomo Chemical Company in Japan for interferon. Wellferon, the company's trade name for interferon, was used to treat a rare form of leukemia. Furthermore, an agreement with the Terry Fox Medical Research Foundation, a biomedical research

Exhibit A4.11 Wellcome PLC – group profit and loss account for the financial year ended August 31, 1985 (£ million)

	1985	1984
Turnover	1,003.6	806.4
Operating costs	(873.5)	(706.4)
Trading profit	130.1	100.0
Share of profits of related companies	1.0	0.3
Net interest payable and similar items	(9.4)	(11.3)
Profit on ordinary activities before taxation	121.7	89.0
Taxation on profit on ordinary activities	(56.9)	(41.0)
Profit on ordinary activities after taxation	64.8	48.0
Minority interests in losses/(profits)	3.9	(0.7)
Extraordinary loss on divestment of interest in Indian subsidiary	–	(1.7)
Profit for the financial year distributions to the Wellcome Trust	68.7	45.6
Amount payable under deeds of covenant	(23.3)	(17.0)
Dividend	(0.5)	–
Profit retained for the financial year	44.9	28.6

Source: Wellcome Annual Report, 1985

center at the University of British Columbia in Vancouver, Canada, gave Wellcome the rights to products developed by the center.

Wellcome's expertise in mammalian cell technology was the result of a major strategic decision in the early 1980s, according to Bill Castell, managing director of Wellcome Biotechnology. "With the landmark 'cloning' of alpha interferon in 1981, the

Exhibit A4.12 Wellcome PLC balance sheet, 1985 (£ million)

| | Group | | Parent company | |
	1985	1984	1985	1984
Fixed assets				
Tangible assets	352.7	321.1	149.7	140.3
Investments	4.1	4.9	79.0	22.4
	356.8	326.0	228.7	162.7
Net current assets				
Stocks	181.9	160.6	63.1	61.0
Debtors	198.9	189.6	103.2	90.8
Investments	134.1	108.7	56.9	66.3
Cash at bank and in hand	19.7	15.4	5.4	3.0
	534.6	474.3	228.6	221.1
Creditors – amounts falling due one year or less				
Loans and overdrafts	(61.0)	(51.5)	(16.6)	(21.1)
Other creditors	(148.4)	(122.4)	(43.5)	(48.5)
	325.2	300.4	168.5	151.5
Total assets less current liabilities	682.0	626.4	397.2	314.2
Creditors – amounts falling due after one year				
Loans	(164.6)	(167.0)	(84.3)	(89.4)
Other creditors	(4.6)	(5.2)	(24.6)	(52.2)
Provisions for liabilities charges	(36.5)	(29.6)	(11.7)	(6.9)
Minority interests	(37.7)	(4.0)	–	–
Total net assets	438.6	420.6	276.6	165.7
Capital and reserves				
Called up share capital	100.0	100.0	100.0	100.0
Revaluation reserve	39.5	40.0	–	–
Other reserves	12.7	16.7	–	–
Related companies' reserves	0.3	0.6	–	–
Profit and loss account	286.1	263.3	176.6	65.7
Shareholders' funds	438.6	420.6	276.6	165.7

Source: Wellcome Annual Report, 1985

entire biotechnology industry was interested in developing large-scale expression capability. It was thought that cloning would automatically go into a bacteria process, but with its 20-year history of work with interferon in a mammalian cell culture, Wellcome was faced with the decision of which way to go. We decided to stay with the mammalian cell process, which in fact turned out to be a very good decision, since it emerged as a far superior process for protein production," he said.

By the end of 1982, Wellcome had begun to realize that the mammalian cell process being used for interferon had other applications, and the company set out to explore links with emerging R&D companies. The relationship with Genetics Institute evolved over a two- to three-year period. An initial link in 1982 with a target piece of work in the insulin area led to the purchase of the rights to GI's tPA in 1984 from Baxter Travenol. "It was apparent that process technology would be key to the development of tPA, and Wellcome had a major advantage with the mammalian cell process," noted Castell. "We were confident that with Wellcome's proven process technology linked with Genetics Institute's technical expertise, we had a better chance of remaining state-of-the-art," he added.

From Wellcome's perspective, a joint venture represented a deliberate policy to link up with one of the emerging US biotechnology companies and gain a foothold in the North American scene. "At first we were looking for a technical link, not an equity link," Castell explained. "We were particularly impressed with GI's ties to Harvard, and with Gabriel Schmergel's business acumen and managerial abilities. GI's strength of focus was also a plus. For a diverse pharmaceutical company such as Wellcome, vigorous in a number of areas, an association with a group such as GI, with its narrower area of focus could be very valuable, enabling us to build a framework that would increase our chances of success in the biotechnology market," he said.

From GI's standpoint, in addition to benefiting from Wellcome's expertise in mammalian process technology, GI would gain access to the pharmaceutical company's superior operating experience in contamination control. "The joint venture was a chance to combine old proven technology with some new advances in process controls and downstream purification methods," Christensen explained.

The Proposed Joint Venture Agreement

Under the proposed agreement, both companies would contribute equally to the building and start-up of a $30 million, 100,000-square-foot plant. The new venture would start production with two products, tPA and Wellferon, and would rank as one of the world's largest biotechnology manufacturing facilities.

The proposed venture would be a totally independent manufacturing company with separate employees. Both parties would have equal representation on the board, and would be equally responsible for financing any additional capacity in the future. No marketing strategy or sales organization was required as the joint venture would serve essentially as a captive manufacturing operation for GI and Wellcome. Escape clauses were built in to cover certain bail-out situations.

The proposed agreement allowed for a pooling of general manufacturing process technologies. The final draft focused on three technologies involved in the biotechnology production.

- Manufacturing process technology – generic to the manufacture of a biotechnology product on a commercial scale, including plant design, vessel design, modes of filtration, and support systems. Both parties would agree to contribute this technology on a nonexclusive, royalty-free basis.
- General product technology – the various generic factors used in the development and scale-up of a process to reproduce a given protein, for example, gene splicing, cloning, and expression. These factors varied depending on whether a mammalian cell, bacterial or yeast-based process was used. Licenses could be granted on a nonexclusive, royalty-bearing basis, by agreement between the two companies under certain conditions.
- Product-specific technology – the specific DNA sequence coding for the product protein, and other product-specific proprietary data relating to the product which Wellcome or Genetics Institute were free to disclose because of third-party arrangements. Such data could include proprietary purification techniques in respect to which a "Chinese wall" would be maintained.

In the biotechnology industry, purification techniques could impact the development of new products or the cost of production for liter products. This included the composition of the medium for growing cells; density of cell lines; and purification steps. For example, in some instances, the composition of the medium could vary considerably, and so could the cost. The choice of medium could have a substantial impact on the final cost of a product. The output of cell lines varied, and a more efficient cell line could give a company a competitive edge. Purification determined how much product was ultimately recovered and ranged from a two-step to a ten-step process depending on the specific protein. Although the various purification steps were common knowledge, finding the optimal sequence of combination for a given protein was proprietary and product-specific. The trick was to come up with the best combination for growing a high density of cells in the lowest cost medium.

Location of the proposd plant was an issue, and was viewed as a potential deal breaker from GI's perspective. The Cambridge-based firm was determined to hold the line on locating the facility somewhere in New England, even though Wellcome's North American operation was headquartered in North Carolina. This was seen as vital, both from the point of view of recruiting technical personnel and to ensure GI's position as an equal partner in the venture. This and many other issues remained to be resolved in late 1985 and early 1986. GI's management knew that there were still barriers to be broken down in both companies. The joint venture would not be a given sell to either board.

Originally conceived on a Cape Cod beach in early September 1984, by GI's Gustav Christensen and Wellcome's Bill Castell, "the project died at least three times before a consensus was reached," said Christensen. "Both companies looked at this several times over, and several times said 'no'," Bill Castell agreed.

After such protracted discussion, analysis and scrutiny, the GI team was confident that the volume of debate would ensure a greater likelihood of success for the project. All that remained was to convince the board.

5
Human Resource Management

Introduction

The growing diversity of strategic alliances has important implications for the management of human resources. In fact, the management of people and competencies in multicultural and multinational settings is likely to have a large impact on the overall, long-term operations and effectiveness of these alliances, along with their parent firms.

There is a great deal of general advice available for selecting the people to be involved in a strategic alliance. The success of a strategic alliance is, indeed, shaped by individuals, and choosing people for key positions is a vital step in alliance planning. In addition to suitable technical abilities, Lewis (1990), for instance, identifies nine characteristics strategic alliance management should have: negotiation skills, flexibility, humility, risk acceptance, repair skills, integrity, sensibility, patience, and curiosity. Although this type of laundry list of characteristics provides guidance in the selection of people, it is difficult to see that these traits are required only for people involved in strategic alliances – wouldn't everyone like to possess such characteristics?[1]

Two major types of parental characteristics influence human resource management processes as related to strategic alliances (Zeira and Shenkar 1990). First, a number of interactive features tie the parents and the alliance together; the number of parents, equity participation, objectives, resource dependency, and contractural arrangements. Second, there are more specific attributes of each parent firm which exist regardless of the alliance; industry size, reputation, and personnel policies. All of these characteristics can strongly influence various organizational personnel processes for each type of employee group dealing with the strategic alliance. A framework for such an analysis is presented in exhibit 5.1. It should be noted that this framework assumes a full-blown joint venture or a project-based joint venture type of strategic alliance (exhibit 1.4) which is international in scope. It is useful to view the characteristics of the parents as independent variables strongly influencing the two other dimensions in exhibit 5.1. Thus, we can investigate how each employee group and/or management process is affected by different parent characteristics.

It is clear that the human resource is a strategic resource that should be managed in an explicit, pro-active manner. People represent core competencies which need to be identified and cultivated.[2] In the following we use the term "human resources"

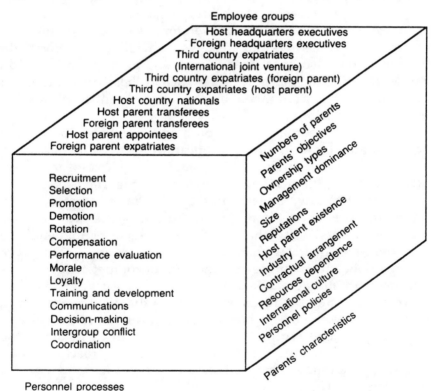

Exhibit 5.1 Human resource management issues in strategic alliances.

to mean the actual people involved and the competencies they represent. Although it cannot be allocated and generated in a way exactly like the financial resources of a corporation, the human resource can still be considered along similar lines. Just as when it comes to financial management, the management of human resources is an integral part of strategic management. Without the development of human resources and core competencies as a strategic resource within a strategic alliance, it will be difficult to secure the long-term strategic future of the cooperative effort, even though financial resources and returns might be adequate for now. Human resource management considerations play a pivotal role in the development of strategic alliances.

Strategic alliances arise through various types of interactions between the partners. These interaction processes are of two principal types: exchange and adaptation (Håkansson 1982). First, exchange processes can be of a social or a business nature, or concern information only. Therefore, we need to be clear regarding in what ways and areas we are willing to interact with the partner(s). Also, what is the width and depth of information we can reveal to the partner? Issues such as these have important implications for a number of the above-mentioned human resource dimensions.

The second important type of partner interaction concerns the potential adaptation and/or modification needed in connection with establishing a strategic alliance. This may involve manufacturing routines, financial procedures, or managerial processes. It is important to have a clear strategy of what areas to adapt to the partner's wishes. Similarly, how much of the input are we prepared to modify so that we do not lose our independence and identity? Again, we can see that issues such as these have strong implications for the management of competencies in connection with strategic alliance.

We have decided to focus on six issues that we have found to be particularly crucial for management of human resources and core competencies within strategic alliances. In this chapter the manner in which each of these issues can be approached in the context of the four strategic alliance archetypes (exhibit 1.4) will be discussed. The six issues are:

- assignment of managers to strategic alliances: who should be assigned where
- the human resource transferability issue: who controls a particular manager
- the trade-off in time-spending between operating and strategic tasks among various managers involved in the strategic alliance
- judgment calls regarding the performance of the human resource in the established strategic alliance: how to avoid biases
- human resource loyalty issues: the strategic alliance versus parent
- individual managers' career planning issues: how they can achieve career progression through strategic alliance assignments

Assignment of People

A difficult issue in the assignment of managers to a strategic alliance is the identification of the best person for each job. How will the required numbers and the skill mix of employees of the strategic alliance be determined? Who is responsible for future demands of people and competencies? From what labor markets will new employees be recruited?

Managers dealing with the strategic alliances will usually be assigned by the partners. Often they will have worked for one of them beforehand. Various partners' perceptions of the types of human skills and talents needed may, in fact, differ. Some partners may have unrealistic biases regarding the quality of the managerial capabilities being assigned, and some may not wish to assign their best people because they want to keep them in their own organizations. The assigned managers may be competent as individuals, but unable to work together in a cooperative context due to cultural differences, communication problems, and so on. These are only a few of the issues that could influence the staffing of a strategic alliance.

In an ad hoc pool type of strategic alliance there is no one common organization, in the classical sense, to be staffed jointly. Instead, there are separately staffed organizational modules which are provided by each of the partners under their largely individual jurisdictions. Appropriate staffing is still important because there must be compatibility between managers from the different organizations. Managers allocated to this type of organization must, above all, be able to communicate the key concepts of their task roles contributed to the project. Equally importantly, each member must be able to understand the unique features of the other members' task packages so as to "translate" them into integrated, project-based opportunities. The creation of compatible organizational entities is of major importance to the ad hoc pool strategic alliance.

When assigning managers to the consortium type of strategic alliance, one must remember that there will also be separate complementary organizational entities which must interact. The partners must assign staff capable of providing sufficient training and assistance for the adequate transfer of know-how, and competent managers must be assigned to the venture by the parents. It is a danger that one of the partners might be tempted to assign second-stringers, thereby creating another potential source of friction.

For project-based joint ventures, with more or less permanently complementary roles by the parents, assigning human resources to the project is accomplished according to the following three minimum criteria. First, assigned human resources must reflect the necessary specialized skills that each partner has agreed to contribute to the strategic alliance. These skills must be of adequate quality; thus, second- or third-stringers should not be assigned to the project. Second, the managers assigned must be sufficiently compatible in style to communicate and work together in the strategic alliance. This requires team-work and cooperation across functions, not isolation within each specialized camp. Third, the assigned managers must have the ability to provide adequate feedback to their respective parent organizations, preparing the ground for continuous support for unforseen backup activities within a reasonable amount of time.

The assignment of critical management resources to the full-blown joint venture also requires that management commitments be made for long periods of time. Usually, the joint venture organization will attract people, after some time, from sources outside the parent organizations. In the meantime, the assigned managerial resources must have relevant capabilities and must be of adequate quality. The overall blend of these human resources should also have a cultural dimension which allows the development of an effective ongoing concern. The Showa–Packard case study at the end of this chapter illustrates this challenge. The difference in relative strategic position of the strategic alliance to each of the partners makes it possible that some firms might assign relatively weak management resources.

In summary, the assignment of relevant management resources to various strategic alliances is critical, but in different ways. For instance, with less formalized strategic alliance organizations, such as an hoc pool strategic alliance, the critical management assignment issue is employing people who can communicate and interact with one another effectively in such settings. In the more formal full-blown joint venture, the parents' role in the assignment of human resources may become less of an issue over time, because the jointly-owned organization gradually brings in necessary human resources on its own, as in an independent business.

Transferability of People

By definition, a resource is strategic only if it can be freely transferred from one application to another, or divested from an established, already successful strategy and diverted to an emerging strategy to be built for the future. People are not robots, and in order for them to be strategically transferable from one work application to another, care and understanding must be used. In the present context this implies that parents must be able to transfer human resources to and/or from the strategic alliance, and they might also be transferred within the strategic alliance from old to new job applications. In the latter case, the human resource has direct strategic value to the strategic alliance itself.

The transferred people have strategic value to the parent organization, owing to the parent's discretionary power to transfer them back. Therefore, it must be ascertained whether the strategic alliance and/or a particular parent has discretionary decision-making powers when it comes to managerial reassignments and within which strategic context these powers are used. This can be applied to all of the four archetypal settings of exhibit 1.4.

The partners in an ad hoc pool will typically maintain their own organizational capabilities within the cooperative network.

In this situation, the human resource transfer issues center on how each partner provides human resources on loan to the pool. An example is technical specialists being temporarily assigned to a product development project. The transfer of these people/ competencies is temporary and is controlled by the parents. The parent also controls which type of assignment the manager in question will go to after the ad hoc venture is completed. Of course, the people who do not have sufficient alternative applications may be dismissed after the project is terminated. It often seems to be the case, in fact, that too many people are let go when a particular strategic alliance is over. This creates a stop–go human resource management approach which sooner or later deprives parent organizations of important competencies. It should be noted that a parent organization will keep its own interests in mind when consenting to reassign some of its key people on loan. Therefore, it may at times be difficult for the parent to justify loaning managers, even though the competitive network as a whole might clearly benefit. Half-heartedness or paranoia regarding these types of assignments can, in the long run, hamper the successful development of the strategic alliance.

A similar situation exists for a consortium type of strategic alliance. One partner may transfer people temporarily to another partner for training and technical assistance, provided that the first partner has sufficient human resources available, and that they can retrieve this resource.

The transfer of key people in a project-based joint venture type of strategic alliance is slightly different. The parent organizations will in principle be obligated to make available the relevant managerial resources. Each partner must, also, however, have available sufficient additional human resources to cover its own independent needs. Given the nature of this type of strategic alliance, each parent organization should put particular emphasis on developing the capability to retrieve people; these competencies may have significant strategic value in future organizational contexts.

Some transfer of human resources among partners may at times be necessary. For instance, a parent firm may provide human resources on loan to the alliance, such as the aforementioned technical specialists. A parent firm may also loan human resources to another parent firm to strengthen its market understanding and to ensure that the output package remains relevant and adapted to market realities.

In a full-blown joint venture, the issue is whether or not a parent organization is willing to transfer critical human resources to the new business venture. These people would normally be assigned to the alliance for a long period of time, perhaps for their entire remaining working career. The parents may have to transfer people on a net basis during the initial phase and they will not necessarily be returned.

Human resource management decisions will gradually be handled by the joint venture organization itself. Within this strategic alliance, human resources will have to be regenerated and developed and reallocated to new jobs, as in an independent business organization. Given the opportunity, however, the parent organizations should attempt to welcome back relevant personnel from the joint venture. One should avoid automatically releasing them so that they do not "accidentally" end up with competing organizations.

Managers' Time-spending Patterns

It is worthwhile to keep in mind that the implementation of a strategic alliance requires the expenditure of efforts in the present, in order to achieve payoffs in the future. This typically results in an immediate lessening of operating results, however, owing to the diversion of resources for strategic use.

It must be ascertained where in a strategic alliance the people and competencies reside which have the responsibility, capability, and capacity to carry out the development of further strategic moves. In other words, how does the strategic alliance, on its own or together with the parent partners, meet the challenge of tackling both operating and strategic tasks on a parallel, ongoing basis? There are different considerations regarding the role of human resources in the trade-offs between operating and strategic challenges in each of the four archetypes.

In the less fully developed ad hoc pool strategic alliance, the strategic tasks are carried out by the partners on behalf of the strategic alliance. It is, therefore, particularly important in this type of alliance that the parent organizations are explicitly willing to spend resources in a coordinated fashion to facilitate strategic development.

A common understanding and a clear division of labor between the managers of the participating organizations must be apparent with respect to the time allotted to strategic tasks, for instance the further development of the technical base for the project cooperation and additional marketing efforts. The premise behind this is that future projects might result as a consequence of such coordinated strategy developments. If no future potential cooperation is contemplated, then the issue of setting aside resources to build strategic strengths will be largely irrelevant. Usually, these tasks will involve specific hands-on cooperation between the various pool organizations, sometimes in the form of task forces. The managers assigned to such groups must have the time, energy, and motivation to contribute actively to strategic development work, using some of the time normally spent in their own organizations for strategy development or operating tasks.

In a consortium, strategic development tends to take place independently within the organizations. Each organization must provide the relevant human resource capacity for strategic self-renewal. This involves the same type of cooperation as in ad hoc pool strategic alliances.

Relatively few free-standing strategic development tasks will be carried out within the project-based joint venture, because it is created to take advantage of a strategic opportunity based on a pooling of the partner organizations' strategic capabilities. To some extent there will be independent adaptation and strategic self-renewal by each parent to ensure that they set aside sufficient human resources to maintain unique capabilities. This splitting up of the responsibilities to adapt, with strategic development tasks being carried out by the partners alone, may not be enough, however. Common adaptive strategic efforts may have to be carried out by the strategic alliance itself.

The full-blown joint venture faces a situation that is in many ways parallel to any independent business organization, in that it must be able to draw sufficient human resources from its own operations to develop its own strategy further. If the joint venture is too thinly staffed, strategic development will suffer, and an eventual lack of self-renewal and decreasing strategic focus will result. The challenge, similar to that of any type of business organization, is to allot sufficient organizational energy and time for the pursuit of business self-renewal and further strategic development. As we have noted, this must always be done in parallel with the other operating tasks. Parent organizations must not exercise so much near-term pressure for operating results that the strategic alliance is left with insufficient resources for its staffing and strategic self-renewal.

Full-blown joint ventures execute independent judgment regarding how much resources to spend on the implementation of business strategies on their own. The strategic alliance has to carry out a set of operating duties simultaneously with its development of new strategies. Sufficient human resources will have to be earmarked for strategic development as well as for operating tasks.

Avoidance of Judgment Biases

People assigned to strategic alliances must be able to satisfy the skill requirements of the value-added chain in carrying out the functional activities for which each partner is responsible. The importance of choosing appropriate people for assignment to specific tasks has been emphasized previously. The challenge is how to judge managers in terms of how well they carry out their assignments once the initial assignment of executives has been made.

In an ad hoc pool, the bulk of the judgments regarding managerial competencies in carrying out jobs will primarily be done by each partner on its own. The partners must be able to judge performance in order to develop a relevant way to execute their team roles. Although the partners will have to make such judgments largely on their own, in some instances it is not uncommon for the partners also to make joint judgments regarding team effectiveness and contribution towards making the strategic alliance work.

In a consortium each partner will also have to make human resource performance judgments and considerations largely on its own, as in ad hoc pools.

Judgments on performance and competency issues are also

critical in the project-based joint venture. In this instance, however, the partners must cooperate in assessing the performance of one another's functional specialists. Given that each partner may feel that it is solely responsible for making the human performance judgments that fall within its given sphere of competence, biases could occur, with a partner looking too favorably upon the performance of managers from its own organization. This could result in the inadvertent build-up of second-string functional specialists who cannot perform as effectively within the cooperative network as is desirable. For this reason, such judgments should be dealt with by all of the partners in cooperation. In these situations, it may be appropriate to use joint performance review committees to make judgments and give feedback. The purpose, of course, is to be as free as possible from individual partner culture biases.

Judgments on people's performance and competency must also be kept strictly in mind in the full-blown joint venture. Joint ventures have failed because they have been inappropriately staffed, owing, in part, to the lack of cooperation between myopic, biased parent organizations. In some instances, partners may have intended to get rid of some managers by unloading them on the strategic alliance. Whatever the case, it is imperative that the jointly-owned strategic alliance establishes a thorough human resource performance review, so that ameliorating actions can be taken with regard to less than adequate performance within the organizational setting.

Management Loyalty Issues

Managers may at times find themselves in conflict between loyalty to the parent organization and loyalty to the strategic alliance organization to which they are assigned. These loyalty conflicts may be difficult to manage and must be considered an integral part of the human resource management task within a strategic alliance.

Divided loyalty issues are usually minimal in ad hoc pools. Here, each partner's employees will, of course, be loyal to their respective parent organizations. There may be, however, occasional raiding of good managers within this type of strategic alliance. A partner may easily notice outstanding talents, given the typically close cooperation within such arrangements, and some managers may transfer between various partners. This may cause stress within the network; the partners usually do well not to raid one another's talents.

For the consortium, loyalty division similarly is not a major issue. Technical advisers on loan from one partner will usually remain loyal to the other. If a technical adviser remains in an assigned advisory capacity for too long, however, loyalty will tend to diminish. Therefore, to avoid such defections, it may make sense to rotate key technical advisers on a regular, scheduled basis.

Loyalty issues may more often become problematic, however, in a project-based joint venture. Each employee is ordinarily on loan from the parent organization and usually expects to return to the parent after some time. At the same time he or she must be loyal to the temporary assignment if it is to succeed. This sometimes involves having to take positions which may go against an original parent organization's wishes. Professional integrity and judgment are the key in implementing such assignments.

Problems that may create conflicts most typically arise around transfer pricing and other pricing issues relating to each party's inputs. In this context, the employees must be loyal to the strategic alliance organization as a practice of professional management conduct. The parent organization must have enough maturity and cultural tolerance to understand that these types of conflicts are almost inevitable. They must not punish former employees who have been involved in divided loyalty conflicts. A mature approach on the part of the parents is necessary to prevent the development of a feeling of paranoia among key employees on such assignments.

Assigned managers and specialists tend to be loyal to the full-blown joint venture, and generally can expect to stay with the strategic alliance for a long period of time. In fact, they rarely return to their old parent organization at all. If a conflict arises, they will typically find it natural to side with the joint venture.

In multinational settings, there can be, at times, problems when a native from a parent firm moves to a strategic alliance based in another country. Despite the reassignment, the employee may often be perceived as still being associated with the parent organization. The loyalty issue can then become difficult and stressful for the executive. A similar situation arises when national loyalty concerns conflict with loyalty to the strategic alliance's business when it pursues global strategies that may be at odds with strict national interests.

Career and Benefits Planning

Individual executives must be motivated to perform their assigned strategic tasks within the strategic alliance. To achieve this, a feeling of future career relevance and a sense of job security is a must. Assignment to a strategic alliance may make one's future career appear uncertain. An employee may wonder what types of jobs will be waiting, if any, after the assignment is over. They might fear that others who remain in the parent organization will be assigned to interesting new jobs on a fast-track basis, while they are forgotten in the strategic alliance assignment.

Steps must be taken to ameliorate employees' feelings of being forgotten by the parent after having been assigned to the alliance. Fast-track, up-and-coming executives may feel that the joint venture assignment is a side-track, that they are out of sight and out of mind, and that this assignment will actually impair the further development of their career. To counteract such misperceptions, parent organizations must offer career planning, and they must inform up-and-coming talents of potential assignments that might be available after the strategic alliance. There must be, of course, a certain degree of formality in the career-planning system to make it credible. A clear-cut career planning approach can counter the ambiguity and riskiness frequently associated with joint venture assignments.

Strategic alliance assignments may also require relocation, which can affect quality of living in general. This is often expensive, may be disturbing for the family, may require a change of housing, and so on. Individual employees' economic and emotional discomforts must be minimized in this respect. In a strategic alliance setting, the split decision-making roles among the parents make this issue an important consideration. Executives must be able to maintain the employee benefits they would have accrued in the parent organization. They should not feel that they are losing salary, retirement benefits, bonus eligibility, fringe benefits, and so on; they should be able to draw on these benefits after temporarily leaving for the alliance.

One partner may feel that the other's benefits are too high, thus wanting an executive from the other partner's organization to take a cut in benefits. Even though harmonizations among the benefit levels of the two partners in the strategic alliance may have many positive sides, for example the avoidance of creating an expatriate class, it is still questionable to let a particular executive experience personal setbacks or cuts. How these career planning and benefits issues apply to each of the four archetypes will be considered next.

Within the ad hoc pool, the individual executive's career outlook and incentives will have to be closely aligned with the administrative procedures of each parent organization. The temporary nature of this strategic alliance may present a problem for individuals who desire to grow, unless their parent organization demonstrates a sensitivity to this by offering stimulating opportunities for further individual growth. The parent may, for instance, give the executive the opportunity to transfer to a meaningful new job within the partner's organizations or to another strategic alliance assignment. In addition, the compartmentalization of jobs into free-standing temporary organization assignments should not engender a lack of willingness to implement career planning within the overall system. This overall view must override the somewhat narrower temporary organizational focus.

In a consortium, the partners must motivate their employees to support the implementation of the consortium agreement. This can be facilitated by implementing a career development plan within the consortium. The consortium organization must similarly ensure that it motivates the people from the parent firms to approach these jobs without fearing that they are being exploited or side-tracked. The managers must not feel that they are out in the cold and have reached an organizational dead end. Systematic job rotation schemes must be utilized for these managers.

In the project-based joint venture, the executive must have a strong feeling of job security. These strategic projects often involve temporary assignments which might engender uncertainty and anxiety in the employees as to what type of jobs they will go to next. Many of them will have to find entirely new jobs outside the present organizational network. The temporary nature of these assignments must not cause so much anxiety and perceived loss of job security that the employees become dysfunctional. Career planning is essential here so that employees know what they are coming back to.

Career planning for employees in the full-blown joint venture should be developed within the organization itself. Here too, employees should be given the opportunity to return to the parent organization if they so wish, to avoid the fear of stagnating within the joint venture organization or of being deprived of promotional opportunities elsewhere in one of the parent organizations. However, employees must decide quickly whether they want to stake out their career in the parent or in the alliance. It is important to be explicit regarding preference and expectation for the broader or narrower career tracks.

Summary

Within an ad hoc pool strategic alliance executives can see their assignment as, generally, quite short-term with clearly defined tasks. Their long-term career planning should not be part of the strategic alliance but linked to how the parent sees executives' jobs in the strategic alliance as part of a string of activities that the individual carries out at the parent level in general. The performance measurement to assess the goodness of the job done will be whether the executive can get his/her share delivered to create the intended output measure for the pool.

For the consortium strategic alliance the same types of considerations apply. Here, however, a larger number of executives will be involved. Individuals tend to build up success patterns in the eyes of the parent through how well they have adapted to carrying out roles of various types in successive consortia assignments. Flexibility, sensitivity to various cultural settings, ability to adapt to new colleagues, etc., become critical in this case. Ordinarily this situation can be found in project teams within exploration activities in oil companies, large engineering consulting firms assigned to various construction projects, large R&D development consortia, etc.

For project-based joint ventures, individuals tend to be judged on their ability to carry out a shoe-string role in such an alliance over time, typically alone or associated only with a few colleagues from the parent organization. This type of human resource management is quite similar to sending diplomats out to far territories to act on their own and calls for the ability to get things done without much supervision and demand for additional support and input from the parent. These types of executives tend to be quite entrepreneurial and develop a lot of general skills, but frequently become quite difficult to bring back to the parent organization later on.

For the executives in the full-blown joint venture organization, the issue is squarely one of being assessed on how well the strategic alliance as a whole functions. Here the key is for the executive to be measured on this and not on some split loyalty expectations relative to the parent organization. Normal human resource management procedures apply here.

In conclusion, the human resource management function will, at times, differ quite dramatically in strategic alliance contexts compared to that of the better-known, wholly-owned corporate settings. Further, the human resource function may differ dramatically among different types of strategic alliances, such as between the four types of alliances which have been discussed in this chapter. In an ad hoc pool type of cooperative venture, the human resource management function will largely be carried out by each partner in a compartmentalized manner, and largely on behalf of its own organizational entities. However, the strategic human resource management functions must be coordinated. The establishment of a common communication style can be a major positive determinant to success. This can be enhanced by allowing consultation among the parents regarding the handling of such issues as dealing with biases in human resource assessments, allowing for broader career opportunities, and so on.

Quite separate human resource management arrangements among the partners will have to be made in the consortium type of strategic alliances. Here, the human resource management groups of all parties must find ways to cooperate to a certain extent but, above all, in the assignment of managers to the consortium.

The human resource function will probably also, to some extent, be dealt with independently by each parent in the project-based joint venture with permanently complementary roles by the parents. In this setting there must, however, be solid coordination between the various human resource management functions of the parents so that a common organizational approach can be established which is functioning with the necessary compatibility among members' styles. A separate parallel human resource management function may have to be established within the strategic alliance itself, complementing the parents' human resource management capabilities.

Finally, regarding the full-blown joint venture, a strong, fully-fledged human resource management function will have to be established within the venture itself. It must find ways to work closely with each parent, particularly during the initial stages of cooperation. The human resource function within the joint venture should also gradually encourage the development of new human resource capabilities which can enhance the strategic progress of the joint venture.

Overall, the human resource management function within all types of strategic alliances must attempt to undertake two types of tasks. First, it must attempt to assign and motivate people in appropriate ways, so that the value creation within the strategic alliance will proceed as well as possible. To create such an arrangement requires particular attention to job skills, compatibility of styles, communication compatibility, and so on. Second, human resources will have to be managed strategically in order to sustain and enhance their competencies. This means that people will have to be allocated with a view not only to the needs of the strategic alliance activity but also to potential repatriation to a parent or to a new joint project, to be used later in other contexts for other strategic purposes. As such, the strategic alliance must be seen as a vehicle to produce not only financial rewards but also various competencies which can be used later in other strategic settings.

Appendix
Showa–Packard[1]

When Richard Johnson, President of the International Division of Packard Foods, Inc., got on a JAL flight from Kennedy Airport to Tokyo, he was still undecided as to how best he could approach several delicate issues with the Japanese company which was a joint-venture partner. He planned to make good use of the gruelling sixteen-hour flight to Tokyo to formulate his policy. In many ways, he considered this trip of vital importance. For one thing, the nature of the problems to be discussed was such that they were likely to affect the long-term relationship between the Packard Company and the Japanese partner in the management of their joint venture in Japan. Moreover, this was his first trip to Japan in the capacity of the President of the International Division and he was anxious to make a good impression and to begin to build a personal relationship with senior executives of the Japanese firm.

Mr Johnson had assumed the position of President several months previously. He was forty-two years old and was considered to be one of the most promising senior executives in the company. He graduated from a well-known eastern business school in 1959. After two years of military service, he entered a prominent consulting firm. In 1964, he joined the marketing group of Packard Foods, Inc. Prior to this promotion to the presidency of the International Division, he had served as Managing Director of Packard's wholly-owned subsidiary in the UK.

Packard was a major manufacturer of breakfast cereals, canned products, instant coffee, frozen foods, and pet foods. The company's total sales for 1978 were roughly $1.5 billion and it had fifteen manufacturing subsidiaries and twenty sales subsidiaries throughout the world. International operations, including exporting, accounted for roughly 25 percent of the company's total sales. International sales had been growing at a rapid rate during the previous decade and the company's top management felt that this represented a major thrust for future growth.

The company, after about two years of difficult and often frustrating negotiations, was successful in establishing a joint venture in Japan with Showa Foods, a leading Japanese foods manufacturer. The arrangement was formalized in the summer of 1977 and the venture went into operation in the spring of the following year.

Prior to the establishment of this joint venture, Packard had had limited export operations in Japan through a major trading company, but the company's management recognized that in order to capitalize on the rapidly growing Japanese market for processed foods, the changing diet pattern, and the emerging mass market, more extensive local presence was essential. By the mid-1970s, the company began to receive a number of inquiries from major Japanese corporations concerning licensing as well as the possibility of establishing a joint manufacturing venture.

Showa was one of the companies that approached Packard initially for licensing. It appeared to be an attractive potential partner. Showa Foods, Inc. had been a major producer of canned fish. In the late 1960s the company began an active program of diversification into new food products. The company successively entered into new product fields, including ketchup, mayonnaise, salad dressing, and a number of other lines. The company had established a reputation for high quality, and its brands were well established. Moreover, the company had built one of the most effective distribution systems in the industry, using a myriad of wholesalers and small retailers.

In the mid-1970s, Showa began to seek still more new products. It was particularly interested in breakfast cereal, artificial coffee cream, canned soup, frozen foods, and pet foods. The company's management felt that these products would be a field for major growth. The management, after some investigation, concluded that the quickest and most efficient way to achieve entry into these product lines was through either licensing or a joint venture with a leading American company. The Showa management felt that the timing was of particular importance, since its major competitiors were also considering a similar move. Showa's expression of interest to Packard was indeed timely, since the latter company, having enjoyed considerable success in Europe, had become increasingly interested in Japan as the only untapped major market. Showa was at first interested in a licensing arrangement, but Packard, anxious to establish a permanent presence in Japan, wished to establish a joint manufacturing venture.

The negotiations concerning this joint venture were difficult in part because it was the first experience of the kind for both companies. Packard had had virtually no prior experience in Japan, and for Showa this was the first joint venture with a foreign company, although it had engaged in licensing agreements with several American and European firms.

The ownership of the joint venture was equally divided between the two companies. In addition to the predetermined level of cash contribution, the agreement stipulated that Packard was to provide technology and the Japanese partner was to make available part of the plant facilities. The joint venture was at first to produce and market breakfast cereal and instant coffe, and later was to introduce pet foods and frozen foods. The products were to be marketed under the joint brands of Packard and Showa. The agreement also stipulated that both companies would have equal representation on the Board of Directors, with four persons each, and that Showa would provide the entire personnel for the joint venture from top management down to production workers. Such a practice is quite common among foreign joint ventures in Japan since, given the almost total lack of mobility of personnel between large corporations, recruiting would represent a major, often almost insurmountable, problem for foreign companies. The companies also agreed that the Japanese partner would nominate the President of the joint venture, subject to approval of the Board, and the American company would nominate a person for the position of Executive Vice-President. Packard agreed to supply, for the time being, a technical director on a full-time basis.

Packard had four members on the Board: Mr Johnson, Mr Harper (Packard's nomination for Executive Vice-President of the joint venture), and the President and Executive Vice-President of Packard Foods, Inc. Representing the Japanese company were the President and Executive-Vice President of Showa, and two senior executives of the joint venture, namely, the President and Vice-President for Finance.

By the spring of 1979 the operations were well under way. Production began and a reasonably effective sales organization had been built. Although the operating plans were progressing reasonably well, Mr Johnson had become quite concerned over several issues that had come to his attention during the previous two months. The first and perhaps the most urgent of these was the selection of a new President for the joint venture.

The first President had died suddenly about three months before at the age of 64. He had been Managing Director of the parent company and had been the chief representative in Showa's negotiations with Packard. When the joint venture was established it appeared only natural for him to assume the presidency; Packard management had no objection.

About a month after his death, Showa, in accordance with the agreement, nominated Mr Kenzo Tanaka as the new President. Mr Johnson, when he head Mr Tanaka's qualifications, concluded he was not suitable for the presidency of the joint venture. He became even more disturbed when he received further information about how he was selected from Jack Harper, the Executive Vice-President of the joint venture and one of Packard's representatives on the Board.

Mr Tanaka had joined Showa forty years previously upon graduating from Tokyo University. He had held a variety of positions in the Showa company, but during the previous fifteen years, he had served almost exclusively in staff functions. He had been manager of Administrative Services at the company's major plant, Manager of the General Affairs Department at the corporate headquarters, and Personnel Director. When he was promoted to that position, he was admitted to the company's Board of Directors. When he later became Managing Director, his responsibility was expanded to include overseeing several service-oriented staff departments, including personnel, industrial relations, administrative services and the legal department.

Mr Johnson was concerned that Mr Tanaka had had virtually no line experience, and could not understand why Showa would propose such a person for the presidency of the joint venture, particularly when it was at a critical stage of development.

Even more disturbing to Mr Johnson was the manner in which Mr Tanaka was selected. This first came to Mr Johnson's attention when he received a letter from Mr Harper, which included the following description.

> By now you have undoubtedly examined the background information forwarded to you regarding Mr Tanaka, nominated by our Japanese partner for the presidency of the joint venture.
>
> I have subsequently learned the manner in which Mr Tanaka was chosen for the position, which I am sure would be of great interest to you. I must point out at the outset that what I am going to describe, though shocking by our standard, is quite commonplace among Japanese corporations; in fact, it is well-accepted.
>
> Before describing the specific practice, I must give you a brief background of the Japanese personnel system. As you know, the major companies follow the so-called lifetime employment where all managerial personnel are recruited directly from universities, and they remain with the company until they reach their compulsory retirement age which is typically around 57. Career advancement in the Japanese system comes slowly, primarily by seniority. Advancement to middle management is well placed, highly predictable and virtually assured for every college graduate. Competence and performance become important as they reach upper middle management and top management. Obviously, not everyone will be promoted automatically beyond middle management, but whatever the degree to which competence and qualifications are con-

sidered in career advancement, chronological age is the single most important factor.

A select few within the ranks of upper-middle management will be promoted to top management positions, that is, they will be given memberships on the Board of Directors. In large Japanese companies, the Board typically consists exclusively of full-time operating executives. Showa's Board is no exception. Moreover, there is a clearcut hierarchy among the members. The Showa Board consists of Chairman of the Board, President, Executive Vice-President, three Managing Directors, five ordinary directors, and two statutory auditors.

Typically, ordinary directors have specific operating responsibility such as head of a staff department, a plant or a division. Managing Directors are comparable to our group Vice-Presidents. Each will have two or three functional or staff groups or product divisions reporting to them. Japanese commercial law stipulates that the members are to be elected by stockholders for a two-year term. Obviously, under the system described, the members are designated by the Chairman of the Board or the President and serve at their pleasure. Stockholders have very little voice in the actual selection of the Board Members. Thus, in some cases it is quite conceivable that Board membership is considered as a regard for many years of faithful and loyal service.

As you are well aware, a Japanese corporation is well known for its paternalistic practices in return for lifetime service, and they do assume obligation, particularly for those in middle management or above, even after they reach their compulsory retirement age, not just during their working careers. Appropriate positions are generally found for them in the company's subsidiaries, related firms, or major suppliers where they can occupy positions commensurate to their last position in the parent corporation for several more years.

A similar practice applies to the Board members. Though there is no compulsory retirement age for Board members, the average tenure for board membership is usually around six years. This is particularly true for those who are ordinary or managing directors. Directorships being highly coveted positions, there must be regular turnover to allow others to be promoted to Board membership. As a result, all but a fortunate few who are earmarked as heir apparent to the chairmanship, presidency or executive vice-presidency, must be "retired." Since most of these men are in their later 50s or early 60s, they do not yet wish to retire. Moreover, even among major Japanese corporations, the compensation for top management positions is quite low compared with the American standard and, pension plans being still quite inadequate, they will need respectable positions with a reasonable income upon leaving the company. Thus, it is a common practice among Japanese corporations to transfer senior executives of the parent company to the chairmanship or presidency of the company's subsidiaries or affiliated companies. Typically, these men will serve in these positions for several years before they retire. Showa had a dozen subsidiaries and you might be interested in knowing that every top management position is held by those who have retired from the parent corporation. Such a system is well routinized.

Our friend, Mr Tanaka, is clearly not the caliber that would qualify for further advancement in the parent company, and his position must be vacated for another person. Showa's top management must have decided that the presidency of the joint venture was the appropriate position for him to "retire" into. This is the circumstance under which Mr Tanaka has been nominated for our consideration.

Mr Harper's letter then went on to discuss other matters.

When he had read this letter, Mr Johnson instructed Mr Harper to indicate to the Showa management that Mr Tanaka was not acceptable. Not only did Mr Johnson feel that Mr Tanaka lacked the qualifications and experience for the presidency, but he resented the fact that Showa was using the joint venture as a haven to accommodate a retired executive. It would be justifiable for Showa to use one of its wholly-owned subsidiaries for that purpose, for understandably Mr Tanaka had been a loyal, effective employee who had made significant contributions to Showa, but there was no reason why the joint venture should take him on. On the contrary, the joint venture needed dynamic leadership to establish a viable market position.

In his response to Mr Harper, Mr Johnson suggested as President another person, Mr Shigeru Abe, Marketing Manager of the joint venture. Mr Abe was 50 years old and had been transferred to the joint venture from Showa where he had held a number of key marketing positions, including Regional Sales Manager, and Assistant Marketing Director. Shortly after he was appointed to the latter position, Mr Abe was sent to Packard headquarters to become acquainted with the company's marketing operations. He spent roughly three months in the US, during which time Mr Johnson met him. Though he had not gone beyond a casual acquaintance, Mr Johnson was much impressed by Mr Abe. He appeared to be dynamic, highly motivated, and pragmatic, qualities which Mr Johnson admired. Moreover, Mr Abe had a reasonable command of English. While communication was not easy, at least it was possible to have conversations on substantive matters. From what Mr Johnson was able to gather, Mr Abe impressed everyone he saw favorably and gained the confidence of not only the International Division staff but those in the corporate marketing group as well as sales executives in the field.

Mr Johnson was aware that Mr Abe was a little too young to be acceptable to Showa, but he felt that it was critical to press for his appointment for two reasons. First, he was far from convinced of the wisdom of adopting Japanese managerial practices blindly in the joint venture. Some of the Japanese executives he met in New York had told him of the pitfalls and weaknesses of Japanese management practices. He was disturbed over the fact that, as he was becoming familiar with the joint venture, he was finding that in every critical aspect such as organization structure, personnel practices and decision making, the company was managed as though it were a Japanese company. Mr Harper had had little success in introducing American practices. Mr Johnson had noticed in the past that the joint venture had been consistently slow in making decisions because it engaged in a typical Japanese group-oriented and consensus-based process. He also learned that a control and reporting system was virtually nonexistent, and felt that Packard's sophisticated planning and control system should be introduced. It had proved successful in the company's wholly-owned European subsidiaries, and there seemed to be no reason why such a system could not improve the operating efficiency of the joint venture. He recalled from his British experience that the American management practices, if judiciously applied, could give American subsidiaries abroad a significant competitive advantage over local firms.

Secondly, Mr Johnson felt that the rejection of Mr Tanaka and appointment of Mr Abe might be important as a demonstration to the Japanese partner that Showa–Packard, Ltd., was indeed a fifty-fifty joint venture and not a microcosm of the Japanese parent company. He was also concerned that Packard had lost the initiative in the management of the joint venture. This move would help Packard gain stronger influence over the management of the joint venture.

Showa's reaction to Mr Johnson's proposal was swift; they rejected it totally. Showa management were polite, but made it clear that they considered Mr Johnson unfair in judging Mr Tanaka's suitability for the presidency without even having met him. They requested Mr Harper to assure Mr Johnson that their company, as half owner, indeed had an important stake in the joint venture and certainly would not have recommended Mr Tanaka unless it had been convinced of his qualifications. Showa management also told Mr Johnson, in no uncertain terms through Mr Harper, that the selection of Mr Abe was totally unacceptable because in the Japanese corporate system such a promotion was unheard of, and would be detrimental not only to the joint venture but to Mr Abe himself, who was believed to have a promising future in the company.

Another related issue which concerned Mr Johnson was the effectiveness of Mr Harper as Executive Vice-President. Mr Johnson appreciated the difficulties, but began to question Mr Harper's qualifications for his position and his ability to work with Japanese top management. Mr Johnson had no concrete evidence but nevertheless had formed a definite impression of ineffectiveness in the last two or three months through correspondence and from two visits Mr Harper made to the home office. During the last visit, for example, Mr Harper had complained of his inability to integrate himself with the Japanese top management team. He indicated that he felt he was still very much an outsider to the company, not only because he was a foreigner, but also because the Japanese executives, having come from the parent company, had known each other and in many cases had worked together for at least twenty years. He also indicated that none of the executives spoke English well enough to achieve effective communication beyond the most rudimentary level and that his Japanese was too limited to be of practical use. In fact, his secretary, hired specifically for him, was the only one with whom he could communicate easily. He also expressed frustration over the fact that his functions were very ill defined and his experience and competence were not really being well utilized by the Japanese.

Mr Johnson discovered after he assumed the presidency that Mr Harper had been chosen for this assignment ostensibly for his knowledge of Japan. Mr Harper graduated from a small Midwestern college in 1943 and when he was inducted into the Army he was sent to the Japanese language school where he underwent a year's full-time, intensive language program. He was among the first language officers to go to Japan with the Occupation in the fall of 1945. He spent a year in the Counter Intelligence unit in Yokohama. Upon returning home, he joined Packard as a management trainee. Much of the ensuing years he spent in the field. In 1968 he became Assistant District Sales Manager in three Western states, California, Oregon, and Washington. When the company began to search for a candidate for Executive Vice-President for the new joint venture, Mr Harper's name came up quite accidentally. Reportedly, when Mr Albert Gardner, Mr Johnson's predecessor, mentioned the problem to Mr George Vance, corporate Vice-President for Marketing, in a casual conversation, the latter recommended Mr Harper. Mr Harper had worked under Mr Vance in the field in the early 1960s, and Mr Vance had known his background. Mr Gardner called Mr Harper into New

York to meet with him and explore the latter's interest in assuming the new position. Mr Gardner felt that Mr Harper would be an excellent choice because of his age (57 years), his experience in sales and his previous language training. Mr Harper, although somewhat ambivalent about the new opportunity at first, soon became persuaded that this would represent a major challenge and opportunity. He was sure that his advancement opportunity in the company was limited if he stayed on in his present position. Moreover, he thought it would be pleasant to get back to Japan after some twenty-five years. The fact that his children had all grown up made the move less complicated. He was still able to carry on a simple conversation in Japanese and believed that with some effort he might be able to regain his language competence.

Mr Johnson was wondering by what means he could find out how effective Mr Harper was in working with Japanese management and how the Japanese regarded him. Mr Johnson was also considering, if Mr Harper had to be replaced, what qualifications would be required of another person to be effective in this unfamiliar environment.

PART IV
Contextual Issues

6
Culture, Management Approach, and Performance

Introduction

In the previous chapters we argued for the importance of a thorough formation process. However, several issues were left unanswered regarding the relationships between the strategic intent of the parent firm, the management approach to forming the strategic alliance that the parties took, and the subsequent performance of the strategic alliance. Clearly, no exact answers or rules exist regarding such relationships – one can never know exactly when to do what. Still, we shall outline some broad guidelines on what types of approaches seem to make general sense and under what circumstances.

This chapter consists of two sections. In the first section we discuss how managerial competencies interplay during the strategic alliance formation process. We specifically consider what might happen when the firms have distinctly different strategic intents for forming strategic alliances. In this section, we assume that the parties involved are relatively similar from a cultural point of view, and we draw on examples from Swedish–Norwegian strategic alliances as illustrations.

In the second section we discuss how management approaches to the formation of strategic alliances are shaped by both the strategic intent behind an alliance and the underlying national differences. We draw on an example from Japanese–US strategic alliances to illustrate this point. In the first section we assume that cultural differences between Swedish and Norwegian management teams play little or no role, owing to cultural similarities between the two countries. In the US–Japan case this assumption is clearly not true.[1]

Similar Cultural Settings

Researchers have pointed out that differences in strategic settings lead to a need to tailor particular business practices to a given context (Gupta and Govindarajan 1984; Lorange 1980; Lorange and Vancil 1976). Chakravarthy and Lorange (1990) argue that strategic intent should determine how management processes are tailored. Firms put together different competence mixes in the management teams involved in forming the alliance which are dependent on strategic intents, cultural biases, and other factors. Such competence mixes might differ in terms of political, entrepreneurial, and/or analytical competencies.

A primary competence may be an ability by the parties to deal with a broader set of stakeholder management issues, reflecting an ability to have a *political competence*. For instance, a party may use a stakeholder, such as an outside venture capitalist organization, as a source of professional competence in cooperative venturing, and this may provide additional momentum to various steps in the formation process.

An *entrepreneurial competence* aims at reflecting the competence within the organization to bring together qualified and motivated people who can support the particular venture idea. Given the many human resource management aspects of cooperative venturing, such willingness may be determined by how individuals on various organizational levels view themselves relative to the venture. As discussed in Chapter 2, without internal organizational commitment and entrepreneurial drive, it is hard to see how strategic alliances can be made to work in an effective mode.

An *analytical competence* reflects the ability in the company to carry out relevant types of strategic analyses and investigations. This demonstrates an overall internal capability to thoroughly gather and process relevant information, which serves as a basis for subsequent decisions in the formation process. As discussed in Chapter 2, a lack of analytical drive means there is an inadequate basis for making important decisions when establishing a strategic alliance.

The combined effect of these competencies is the core of the formation process. If put together in a relevant mix this core should positively effect performance. If a relevant mix of core competencies does not exist, the performance of the alliance could suffer.

Measuring the performance of the strategic alliance is not only a question of producing tangible benefits such as profits.[2] Strategic alliances are established for a number of purposes, such as joint product development or other development efforts (Hergert and Morris 1988). Often the short-term goal may not be only to increase profits *per se*. Rather, the main purpose of a strategic alliance might be to learn from the other partner how to get a complex task done. When this learning is accomplished, the sign of success could very well be the termination of the strategic alliance. Therefore, to measure the success of a strategic alliance based on life-length is not always correct – a short-lived strategic alliance may indeed be successful, once its purpose is achieved.[3]

There might, of course, be a virtually infinite number of other factors that influence the parent companies' assessment of the strategic alliance's outcome. Factors stemming from other sources, such as economic changes, governmental interaction, shifts in demand, new technologies, substitute products, owner-ship changes, management turnover, general goodness of a decision, and so on, could have a decisive impact on the alliance. The ability of the strategic alliance to adapt to such new circumstances will also strengthen the chance of successful performance.

Different strategic intents can impact the competence mix of the management teams. This was illustrated in a study of Swedish and Norwegian firms who were forming such alliances (Lorange and Roos 1990). The formation process in the Swedish firms was generally characterized by a strong entrepreneurial drive behind the strategic alliance, which, in turn, stimulated both strong political considerations and thorough analytical efforts. The analytical efforts were, in themselves, given further momentum by influences from political considerations. The overall picture was that the managerial activities during the formation process reflected a particular strategic intent regarding what the firms wanted to get out of the strategic alliance – namely to expand the home market into Norway. Such strategic decisions require thorough market analysis, good political sense and a strong entrepreneurial drive.

The Norwegian firms' management approach during the formation process, on the other hand, showed very little analytical emphasis. This may be quite understandable, given what seemed to be the overriding strategic intent of what these firms wanted to get out of the alliance; namely to "piggy back" on the international strength of a partner. The strategic analysis was, basically, already done by the partner!

Given the strong cultural similarities between Norway and Sweden, the differences in management approaches cannot be easily explained by cultural or national differences. They more than likely stem from differences in the firms' strategic intents. The previous example, which is based on a large, empirical study of 67 parent firms' strategic alliances, underscores how strategic intent plays a key role in how firms go about managerially handling the formation process.

Different Cultural Settings

A fundamental question in this section is: what is the relative importance of cultural versus strategic intent differences in shaping the strategic alliance formation process? Or, from a managerial point of view, how much attention should be paid to tailoring one's approach to the cultural factor, to the strategic intent factor, or to both of these?

In our examples, we consider the empirical evidence from the examination of 26 parent firms of strategic alliances, with three potentially separate types of strategic intents (Lorange and Roos 1990). The first group of alliances which exercise a certain strategic intent consists of US firms entering the Japanese market. Such firms have a typical entry strategy with the objective focused on how to build the business in Japan. We expect relatively heavy emphasis on generating sales and building market share, as contrasted with expecting immediate profits. The strategic intent of these firms is to gain a beachhead to expand into the Japanese market by selecting appropriate local Japanese partners (Root 1984).

The second group of alliances, with yet again separate intents, occurs where Japanese firms enter the US market. Many of the objectives of the Japanese entrants are, of course, similar to those of the US entrants into the Japanese market. However, given the openness of the US market, in contrast to the Japanese, there is relatively less emphasis on gaining know-how insights through the partner when it comes to local market or political factors. Rather, the local US partners to the Japanese entrants will probably have complementary product lines, helping the Japanese to save time and gain rapid access (Fifield, Hanada, and Pucik 1989). Thus, we see slightly different strategic intents.

The third group of strategic alliances, exercising a third type of strategic intent, is that formed by Japanese domestic partners together with US firms entering the Japanese market. These firms have entirely different strategic intents when promoting their strategic alliances and gain certain benefits from allowing a foreign partner access to their domestic market. In exchange, they look for technologies, proprietary products, and/or process know-hows as benefits for admitting the foreign partner (Abegglen 1984).

This set of examples suggests that it is difficult to understand the differences in the formation process patterns based solely on nationality distinctions alone or, alternatively, based on strategic intent differences alone. We recommend a contingency-based analysis, which incorporates both of these dimensions. Both strategic intent and cross cultural differences play important roles in shaping the managerial process of forming strategic alliances. We feel that a unilateral emphasis on cross-cultural differences, as seen between Japanese and US practices (Athos and Pascale 1981; Ouchi 1981) is a too narrow approach when it comes to strategic alliance formation processes. Nor does a unilateral approach towards tailoring formation processes to settings with different strategic intents seem to be valid (Chakravarthy and Lorange 1990).

The Importance of Strategic Intent Differences

In our study, both US and Japanese firms who were attempting to enter the Japanese or US foreign markets, respectively, had quite similar strategic intents. They took quite similar approaches regarding the influence of design issues that fell within the following four categories; relative objectives, strategic plan development, staffing, and experience.

The *relative objectives* of the strategic alliance were increased sales, increased market share, and increased profit. Increased sales was expected to be heavily emphasized by all three classes of firms. However, this objective was perceived to be more important for the Japanese domestic partners relative to the US firms. This might stem from their anticipation of receiving products and technologies that could boost their domestic sales. Similarly, market share improvement was seen as important for the two other classes of firms, that is, US firms entering Japan and Japanese firms entering the US.

Regarding profit, our example illustrates that the US partner firms did not see increased profits as a major objective relative to increased market share and sales. They recognized, perhaps, that it takes time and a balanced approach when establishing and expanding a beach-head in Japan. The Japanese firms in our example, on the other hand, look at increased profits as a very pronounced objective. This underscores the point that Japanese firms seem to make this type of strategic move to enhance their profits. Thus far, the differences we have seen indicate that strategic intent, rather than cultural settings, influences the managerial approach to forming strategic alliances.

A *strategic plan* is the way firms assess the realism of objectives, the partners' capabilities, the reactions from stockholders, and the control issues. Both US and Japanese entry firms' strategy places heavy emphasis on assessing the partner's distribution network and the availability of human resources relative to the Japanese domestic partner respondents. These issues are, of course, naturally particularly critical in entry strategy contexts. However, both the Japanese entry and domestic firms put heavy emphasis on the assessment of the (US) partner's technology.

This was typically much more important for the Japanese, again given their strategic intents.

The *staffing* issue deals with which of the partner firms assign various key personnel to the strategic alliance. Japanese and US entry firms both heavily emphasize letting their local partner assign the President of the strategic alliance. On the other hand, the entering firms tended to assign the second-in-command themselves. Strategic intent, again, plays a relatively heavy role, in that the entry partner wants to benefit from the strength of the local partner, while the local partner still wants to be in charge.

The degree of improved capability that a partner receives from the strategic alliance is called the *experience* issue. This relates to product development, manufacturing, marketing, and service, as well as to a better understanding of quality and the political dimension of cooperation. Domestic Japanese partners seemed to feel that they derive a lot of useful experience from product development and the improved manufacturing capabilities of their US partner. At first, this could be seen as somewhat contrary to what we expect, in that the Japanese are generally viewed as world leaders in terms of manufacturing capability. It should be kept in mind, however, that the US entrants that the Japanese firms wanted to let in as partners in their home market typically represented new technologies, frequently combined with proprietary manufacturing processes. Here, again the importance of strategic intent is prevalent.

The Importance of Cross-cultural Differences

Formation process issues involved in strategic alliances are also influenced by cross-cultural differences. In our example, we see how these differences can have impacts within the following areas; negotiations, strategic plans, and performance.

When it comes to the *negotiation* issue, concerns that often arise are that the negotiations take too much time and that the partner pushes too much. US firms tended to feel that negotiations with the Japanese often took too long. The Japanese firms typically experienced little notion of too much time passing, and they often felt that their US partner pushed them during the negotiations. This indicates that cross-cultural differences might be specially critical when it comes to time expenditures. For foreign firms negotiating a strategic alliance with the Japanese, it is particularly important to pay attention to the early warning steps built into the formation process model that were laid out in Chapter 2. If these are not heeded, there is a definite risk of wasting time by pursuing negotiations that will never lead to results.

As to the *strategic plan*, US entry strategists typically paid little attention to competitors' reactions while Japanese entry strategists paid more attention to this issue. This may be related to cultural differences in that the Japanese are very good at assessing competitor reactions. As a matter of fact, there is an interesting difference between Japanese and US entry strategists (as well as the Japanese domestic partners) with regard to concerns for public reactions in the host country. Japanese firms entering the US placed heavy emphasis on these reactions, while the US entrants and the Japanese domestic firms placed little or no emphasis on them. This is another example of an area where cross-cultural differences play a role.

When looking at the *performance* issue, we consider how well the objectives of the strategic alliance are fulfilled. For instance, there is much more satisfaction for the US entry strategists compared to the Japanese entry strategists regarding sales volume. This same pattern is true for market share, pointing towards the role of cross-cultural factors, in that US firms tended to be happy with the better results they achieve through their strategic alliances, while the Japanese firms typically were much less patient regarding what they consider satisfactory growth and were always striving for more.

Summary

The managerial approach, in terms of staffing and emphasis, during the formation process must, as we have seen, reflect the firm's strategic intent regarding what a firm wants to get out of a strategic alliance. If the purpose of the alliance, for instance, is to expand geographical operations, the management team should include a balance of people covering a mixture of entrepreneurial, analytical, and political competencies, and it should focus on understanding the business plan behind the venture. On the other hand, if the purpose is more to hook up with a winning partner, the management team should reflect more unilaterally an entrepreneurial and political competence. There is then little need to carry out extensive strategic analyses, given that a firm banks on the strategy of the partner.

A firm contemplating a strategic alliance must carefully consider the human resource aspects of putting together an appropriate team of people who are assigned to the formation/ negotiation tasks. This must be done in such a way that the team reflects the particular strategic intent that the strategic alliance is meant to meet. Differences in strategic intent leads to fundamentally different managerial processes for forming strategic alliances. One must be careful not to propose approaches that have general validity in all cases. Rather, it is more appropriate to develop approaches to strategic alliance formation that are tailormade to the particular circumstances stemming from the strategic intents at hand.

In general, strategic intent is more important than cross-cultural managerial differences when shaping the strategic alliance formation process. Tailoring a strategic alliance formation process should primarily be driven by the strategic intents of the partners and should not to be overshadowed by differences in the cultural settings in which they are located. We may, indeed, see the emergence of global management practices that do not differ much between professionally run firms, whether they are located in Japan, in the US, or elsewhere.

Cross-cultural sensitivity will, of course, always be an important issue, and will undoubtedly always play a role in a strategic alliance formation process. This is true for achieving a political stakeholder consensus platform and for selling in the alliance concept in the organizations involved. Still, such cultural differences should not be allowed to overshadow the importance of keeping one's strategic intent in mind. Cross-cultural management must support strategic intent, not hinder it.

Appendix
Fuji Xerox[1]

The interview was over. Now it was Motohiko Tsuchiya's turn to ask the questions: "Sometimes the people in Rochester are hard to work with when we are working on a product similar to one they are working on," the director of copier development and manufacturing for Fuji Xerox said. "Do you have any suggestions for how we can cooperate better?"

The interviewer took a piece of paper and wrote two numbers: 17,000 and 12,100, with an arrow pointing down, the Xerox employment trend in its hometown. "Some people there think you are costing them as many jobs as the rest of the Japanese competition."

"I know that," Tsuchiya said. "I understand that. That attitude is fine if there were no Canon. But there is. Why don't they want to do what's best for the company?"

The history of Fuji Xerox in a sentence. A marketing subsidiary that sold American-made equipment in Japan becomes an expert design and manufacturing company that wants the unhindered ability to sell Japanese-made equipment in the United States and around the world. And this makes Fuji Xerox both a partner and a competitor of Xerox Corporation.

Rank Xerox workers in Europe may speak different languages, but there is no question they pledge their allegiance to the Star-Spangled Banner. Xerox owns 51 percent of Rank Xerox and gets two-thirds of the profits, but Fuji Xerox is a fifty-fifty joint venture between Fuji Film and Rank Xerox. No one in the United States tells Fuji Xerox what to do. Its 15,000 workers still first salute Hi-no-Maru, the Rising Sun of Japan.

This independence, frankly, saved Xerox in the low end of the copier market. Xerox would not have a competitive machine today at 30 cpm or slower if Fuji Xerox had not ignored the desires of Xerox corporate headquarters at Stamford and pressed ahead with developing its own products. On the other hand, this independence has caused the two companies to waste millions of dollars on developing similar products, and has led to frustration on both sides of the Pacific. Some Fuji Xerox workers think their American partner is hindering their growth and the development of their own world markets. Some Xerox workers, especially in the Rochester engineering and manufacturing community, fear Fuji Xerox as much as Canon and Ricoh. The more successful Fuji Xerox is at developing its own products, the greater is the threat that it will take even more work away from the United States.

"I think the relationship between the two companies is excellent," David Kearns (Xerox chief executive) says. "It is probably one of the best partnerships that exists between a Japanese and an American company, but it is not without difficulty. There is competition. The problem is never going to go away. One of the strengths of Fuji Xerox is its independence, but it is also touch. It's tough to manage."

"Fuji Xerox is in a unique and difficult position," agrees Jeff Kennard, the Xerox liaison between Tokyo and Stamford. "They're Japanese so they know what has to be done to be successful. But they are also part of Xerox Group so they have to be good corporate citizens."

Fuji Xerox is indeed one of the most successful joint ventures in Japanese business history. In two decades it has grown from a strictly sales organization into a completely self-sufficient high-technology company with annual revenues exceeding $1.5 billion, more than half the size of its Japanese parent, Fuji Photo Film. Net profit exceeds $60 million. More than $1 billion of Fuji Xerox revenues comes from the copier business, ranking it just behind Canon and Ricoh and just ahead of Kodak and IBM on a world-wide basis for plain paper copiers. From 1975 to 1985, Fuji Xerox had the best year-over-year compound growth record in the entire Xerox Group; sales and profits both quadrupled in that span. President Yotaro "Tony" Kobayashi has set an even tougher target for the future. He wanted revenues and profits to quadruple again by 1990.

In image-conscious Japan, Fuji Xerox is proud of the Xerox name. Atop its headquarters building in Tokyo is a huge neon sign that says "Xerox" not "Fuji Xerox." Fuji Xerox workers are quick to point out that their company has a better reputation, and much more renown, in Japan than Rank Xerox does in Europe. But as the American company began to experience its earnings difficulties in the early 1980s, that age began to fade. Fuji Xerox employees in Tokyo actually felt as if the poor performance of Xerox Corporation was hurting them. The earnings stories were in the Japanese press as soon as they were in the American. Fuji Xerox began to slide in the rankings of the most-admired Japanese companies and began to have some difficulty recruiting new

employees. When Xerox sold its headquarters building in Stamford in early 1985 as part of its strategy to increase return on
assets, there was particular concern in Tokyo. Japanese companies
don't sell assets.

Xerox Corporation has not developed a successful low-end
copier since the 3100, which was introduced in 1973. Fuji Xerox
has been supplying low-end machines to the rest of the Xerox
world since 1977 – the same year Fuji Xerox spent $500,000 for a
McKinsey & Co. study when the executives at Stamford were
actually considering abandoning the low end. McKinsey told Fuji
Xerox: "You've got to be there. Change your distribution system
and find a way to stay in that market." Since then Fuji Xerox has
moved into the design of mid-volume machines with the 3500
and 5870, which sells in the US as the 1055, and is helping
significantly on the design of the 1075 replacement product.

The basic reason for Fuji Xerox's desire to be independent is
best summarized by Yoichi Ogawa, general manager of Fuji
Xerox's corporate research labs: "Our market should be protected
by ourselves," he says. The problems arise because the feeling is
mutual among many Xerox workers in the US. What's good for
the company as a whole may not be good for particular segments
of it. Understanding that dilemma is understanding Fuji Xerox.

An example: from 1980 to the beginning of 1985, Fuji Xerox
shipped 800,000 small copiers to the United States and Europe in
the form of kits. Fuji Xerox refers to these as "knockdown" or
"KD" units. It's almost used as a disparaging term. Fuji Xerox
would rather supply completed machines. Instead, half of the kits
were assembled in Webster and the other half in Mitcheldean,
England. The main reason was to save American and British jobs.

Decisions such as that, made because of labor and community
relations half a world away, make Fuji Xerox think its own growth
is being stunted. It can operate on its own in south-east Asia,
where it is licensed, but if it wants to sell in the United States or
Europe, it still has to go through Xerox channels. Canon is
exporting 80 percent of its production; Fuji Xerox only 20 percent,
lowest among the Japanese copier makers. Until it can become as
export-conscious as other Japanese companies, Fuji Xerox won't
grow as fast. "We have to develop *dantotsu*, or super-products so
Xerox Corporation will import more Fuji Xerox products," says
Tadashi Kobayashi, the manager of competitive analysis. "It's a
real sore point."

No one understands that dilemma of internal competition better
than Bill Glavin. It's his job to coordinate the activities of Fuji

Xerox with the rest of Xerox Group. Glavin called a summit meeting between the copier development groups of the two companies in November 1984. Xerox was wasting too much money in duplicative development programs. Xerox Corporation spent about $600 million a year on R&D, $400 million of that on reprographics. Fuji Xerox spent $100 million a year on R&D, $60 million on reprographics.

"That was an important milestone in our future," Glavin says. "We finally turned our partnership into an advantage, not a disadvantage. The first disadvantage has been both of us spending money to develop a product for the same segment of the market. The second disadvantage is that because we don't use one product worldwide, we're not getting the manufacturing volumes we would like."

Glavin and Kobayashi were joined at the summit by Tsuchiya, Wayland Hicks, and their top managers.

"I started the conference off by telling everybody that others are trying to find out how to make deals with the Japanese and here we've been working with somebody for 22 years. Why the hell can't we make it work better?" Glavin said. "I mean Canon and Kodak got together because they didn't have the other guy's products. You couldn't have made a better match; they're not going to have duplicate products. Here we are working with somebody for twenty-two years and we don't manage that."

The duplication of effort began in 1976 when Fuji Xerox initiated the 3500 project. It was a declaration of independence. It came after a series of copiers – code-named SAM, Moses, Mohawk, Elf, Peter Paul & Mary – on which Fuji Xerox was depending were canceled by Rochester. One after another they expired, all the while Fuji Xerox's market share in Japan was declining. Kennard remembers that when Tony Kobayashi was told about the death of Moses, the Fuji Xerox boss was also asked to stop work on the 3500. "Tony refused," Kennard says. "He said, 'As long as I am running this company I can no longer be totally dependent on you for developing products. We are going to have to develop our own.'"

Glavin remembers the reaction in Rochester:

It was the first big machine they had designed and the engineering community in the US said, "Absolutely no way is Fuji Xerox going to do what they say they are going to do. They just can't make it. They don't know how to make machines. It will be a disaster." So the rest of Xerox Group went down the path of the 1045, a similar machine. If we were to look back now, that would be another decision which we would say was wrong, but at that time it would not have been wrong because Fuji Xerox had never built a machine in that class. It required a tremendous amount of help from the United States, which we gave them. The machine was successful and it was the beginning of a whole family of products. You can find a heritage of the 1055 coming from that 3500. When they started to show what they could do, they sprouted their own wings, so to speak, and started to go off designing their own machines.

That led us down the path of a lot of duplication of products. They have products we don't have and we have products they don't have, in the same market segment. They do not develop products with new technologies. They take a technology from a product that has already been used and matured in the US or in Europe and add to it technologies from other machines, but they do not develop their own new technologies. When you do that, you can make a new machine quicker and for less cost. So every time Wayland sits down with them and says let's do this product, they'll come up with one that's better than his because he's trying to put in new technologies. And they say, well, we can do it in two years. Well, he can't. It takes him three years. We kept getting ourselves further and further apart.

The competition has been healthy; we both have learned a lot. But after our summit conference we now have a number of operating and management principles that say we will no longer diverse ourselves through product families. Anytime Wayland and the Fuji Xerox product planners cannot come up with one common product worldwide, they cannot advance any further without my personal approval.

A low-volume copier code-named Benkei, which means warrior, is a good example of the manufacturing volumes Glavin referred to. The product, designed and manufactured by Fuji Xerox, was announced in Japan in October, 1984 (the 3870) and in the United States in early 1985 (the 1025). Glavin said Fuji Xerox planned to sell 60,000, but because the two companies coordinated the development, they planned to sell 180,000 units worldwide the first twelve months. The 1025, by the way, was the first machine Xerox assembled in China, through its joint venture there. Other Fuji Xerox–Xerox summits on copiers and the systems business have been held regularly since.

The Japanese photographer was almost ready to take the picture. Then he stopped. Something was wrong with the rug in front of the Fuji Xerox board of directors.

"Well, will you look at that," one of the Americans on the board cracked. "He even has to comb ..."

Tony Kobayashi interrupted. "It's that attention to detail that makes Japan great," he said.

Almost every day in the Japanese newspapers you can read the phrases, "before the war" or "after the war." That's how they measure time. For a Japanese businessman, however, it's "before the oil shock" or "after the oil shock." That's when their world changed. The Fuji Xerox profit chart is typical of many Japanese companies. Since 1966, there have been only two down years for profit, 1970 and 1974. The first was the so-called Nixon shock, when gold-backing was removed from the dollar and it was allowed to float against world currencies. The second was the oil shock. That's when Fuji Xerox and many Japanese companies discovered they could never do business the same way again.

"Before the oil shock, Fuji Xerox enjoyed a monopolistic position in PPC," says Toneo Noda, the managing director for finance and overseas operations. "After the oil shock, even though the world had changed, our thinking was still like a monopoly."

Or, as Atsushi Hirai, managing director for quality control, says: "We were spoiled by overconfidence. We had deaf ears to customer complaints. Xerox copiers were excellent in performance, but they were too costly."

The answer for Tony Kobayashi, then a vice-president, was a total commitment to quality. He headed the so-called New Xerox movement in 1976, which became the pattern for David Kearns's Leadership Through Quality at Xerox Corporation. "Fuji Xerox through the 1960s and up through 1971–2 was not only a glamorous company but also hard working," Kobayashi says. "Having come from Fuji Photo Film I knew Fuji Xerox was different. We had a different attitude. But while we were working hard, we were really missing something: the real customer requirements. There had been some feeling among customers that our prices were too high. Could we make it cheaper? Our feeling was that we were offering the best. The best can command the highest price. What's wrong with that?"

After the oil shock, Fuji Xerox tried to raise prices twice in ten months, 9 percent in January 1974 and 10 percent in November 1974. The first time the other Japanese copier companies followed. The second time they didn't. It put an end to the American way of raising prices when costs went up. "The oil shock made our customers much more acutely aware of the cost," Kobayashi says. "They turned to less costly alternatives as a short-term solution. To their surprise, and certainly to ours, many of those customers decided to stay with those machines. The quality wasn't that bad. In 1973, 1974 and 1975, the company had been used to high levels of expenses and profits. We came to the conclusion that unless some really drastic and fundamental changes occurred, the company was going to sink very quickly. We really thought it was a question of survival. In the US, the dangers were still a couple of years off. People have to feel and face the reality before they change. That was the beginning of our TQC (total quality control). In a sense, the New Xerox movement means continually renewing, almost forever. I think we have come a long way, but our friends have also come a very long way. Very."

Kobayashi is fond of quoting Joe Wilson. Near the beginning of a book Kobayashi published to commemorate the first twenty years of Fuji Xerox is a reprint of Wilson's favorite poem, Robert Frost's "The Road Not Taken." Kobayashi still quotes that poem. "The road not taken is a sense of challenge," he says. "Joe Wilson would say if there is a choice, choose the more challenging. Joe Wilson was the most important single individual in the Xerox world. He always emphasized the importance of excellence. He had the long term in mind, but he was also very realistic. He was a very tough man to demand the best out of the short term as well. It is that combination of idealism and realism that is the key to TQC today. It is something we had before. It is something we had forgotten."

The similarities in Wilson and Kobayashi go beyond philosophy: Wilson earned a degree at Harvard Business School; Kobayashi was born in London and earned a business degree at Wharton. Wilson was deeply involved in community affairs in Rochester; Kobayashi serves on more than twenty outside commissions and advisory boards. The fathers of both men were leaders of their respective companies – Joseph R. Wilson was president of Haloid Company, Setsutaro Kobayashi was president of Fuji Photo Film and the first president of Fuji Xerox when it was established in 1962. Some Xerox workers, on both sides of the Pacific, even ask: Can Tony Kobayashi ever become CEO of Xerox Corporation? It is used more as a compliment to his ability than as a statement of high probability. A Japanese running an American *Fortune 500* company? However, it illustrates the high regard people have for Kobayashi and the spirit of Joe Wilson.

Jeff Kennard was in Japan during the year leading up to winning the Deming Prize for quality control in 1980. "It was an incredible ordeal," he says. "Wives were writing Tony at home – very un-Japanese – saying 'My children haven't seen their father in two months.' After we won the award, Tony wrote everyone and said, 'Now we have to earn it. The real work and sacrifice is only just beginning.'"

Warriors of Japan have always sacrificed.

For the first ten years of its existence, Fuji Xerox was strictly a marketing organization. It took what Xerox had to offer and did the best it could with the products in the Japanese market. Sometimes it was painfully obvious that these Fuji Xerox machines from America weren't designed with the Japanese in mind. When the Xerox 7000 arrived in Japan, for instance, secretaries had to stand on a box to reach the print button. It had been designed with the taller American secretary in mind. Today, in some offices around Japan, you can still see a small wooden platform nudged up against the 7000.

The machines were manufactured at facilities owned by Fuji Film. Those factories were taken over by Fuji Xerox in April 1971 after long negotiations and strong urging by Peter McColough and Joe Wilson, and it was the first step towards independence. Even before the transfer of the plants, Fuji Film had begun design work on a brand new copier, the 2200. It was based on the Xerox 660, but smaller and had a moving platen. Yoichi Ogawa, currently general manager of corporate research at Fuji Xerox, was in charge of the 2200 project, which began in 1967. With a staff of six, he was able to develop a breadboard prototype within a year. After that it went to Fuji Film's Iwatski plant where thirty engineers worked on it. When it was introduced in 1972, it was the world's smallest PPC.

Toshio Arima, now manager of corporate planning at Fuji Xerox, went to Rochester to convince Xerox to take the 2200. "We laid it out in front of them," he said. "We said a Konishiroku machine is coming, a Ricoh machine is coming. But they didn't believe it. For some internal reasons we didn't understand, they said 'no' to us." So Arima went ahead with plans of his own for the 2200 in Japan. It was the best low-end machine available at the time. Had Xerox taken it, he thinks it could have forestalled the Japanese invasion of the US.

One of the reasons the United States didn't take the 2200 was the moving platen. Xerox engineers, reared on such fixed optics machines as the 914, didn't think a moving platen was what customers in the US wanted. The NIH – not invented here – syndrome was hard at work. The engineers in the US couldn't believe this Japanese company could develop machines as good as theirs.

Glavin thinks the 2200 decision set the tone toward Fuji Xerox for most of the 1970s. The machine was the subject of the first copier/duplicator meeting he attended in Rochester. He had just left Xerox Data Systems (the old SDS) and was still living in California. He ran planning and finance in Rochester. After a six-month study, the copier management group made a presentation to Peter McColough on what Xerox ought to do in the low end of the market. Following normal meeting procedure, an overview of the meeting was quickly given, including the top recommendation take the 2200 from Fuji Xerox. "The answer is unacceptable," Glavin remembers McColough saying. "We are not going to buy a machine from Japan. The meeting was scheduled for three hours but it stopped in five minutes," Glavin said. "The group said, 'Well, if that's the answer, we haven't got the right position here today.' They walked out. The reason I remember the meeting so distinctly was that I walked out of there – I had never been involved with the Xerox management group – and I went to Ray Hay, my boss, and I said, 'Ray, how in the hell could you have a team of guys that are experts working six months on something and the old man just said, look, we aren't going to buy anything from Japan? You mean to tell me that nobody knew that?'"

Others at Xerox also remember that meeting, but McColough doesn't.

Glavin agrees with Arima that Xerox could have stalled the entire Japanese copier invasion of the United States by taking the 2200. Other industry observers make the same argument, but the idea seems unlikely. Savin and Ricoh were well into the development of the 750 by that time, and no one could have stopped Paul Charlap from his appointed duty. Even Glavin's boss, Kearns, disagrees: "I have never bought that thesis."

On the other hand, while the 2200 wouldn't have stopped the Japanese, it may have slowed them down. Rank Xerox proved that with the 2202, which was a speeded-up version of the 2200. The US finally took a Fuji Xerox machine in 1979, the 2300. It was so successful that in 1980, 700 tons of machines had to be airlifted to the US, in addition to regular ocean shipments. With the 2300, Fuji Xerox started to regain market share in Japan.

Yuji Okano is a public relations specialist for Fuji Xerox based in Tokyo. He is in his late thirties. He usually awakes at 6.30 a.m. so he can catch the 7.30 train for the one-and-a-half-hour commute to the office. He doesn't return home until 12.30 the next morning.

"When do you sleep?" he was asked.

"Saturdays," he said.

Okano is married and has two small children.

Quality control was practiced at Fuji Film, which won the Deming Prize in 1956. When Fuji Xerox became a manufacturing company, it instituted its own statistical quality control measures for production under the guidance of Professor Tetsuichi Asaka of the University of Tokyo. This was the beginning of quality control (QC) circles. Kobayashi's New Xerox movement took those activities company-wide, and today there are more than 1,780 active QC circles at Fuji Xerox.

The first goal of the New Xerox movement was to design and build a copier in half the time and at half the cost of previous machines. The Fuji Xerox 3500 accomplished that. Code-named Ace, it was the 914 of Fuji Xerox and showed that they were capable of operating and thriving in the post-oil shock business environment. Teams of Xerox engineers traveled to Japan to study the project and composed long reports that said the 3500 would never meet its cost, schedule, or reliability targets. They were a little right and a lot wrong. Original specifications called for a 60-cpm machine; Ace came in at 40 cpm. The goal was to complete the machine in two years; it took twenty-six months. It also exceeded its cost target somewhat, but only fifty-two people worked on it and the total development cost was only $8 million. "The 3500 was a damn good machine," David Kearns says. "Fuji Xerox learned a great deal doing that."

Kearns first visited Japan and Fuji Xerox in 1975. He has since made the trip more than twenty-five times. His first impression was: "How is Fuji Xerox ever going to be successful? They were basically taking equipment designed in the US and making changes to it for their market. What that did was bring the product to market later and at a higher cost against their competitors over there, who I realized even then had lower costs, although I didn't realize how much lower. I encouraged them to begin to develop some products of their own, which they wanted to do." Kearns, at that time, didn't have the responsibility for product development in the US, so he wasn't concerned about competition between the two groups. "When I first saw the Ace machine, I applauded," he says. "I really was impressed. There were a number of people at Stamford who thought that was not a good thing to do."

After success with the 3500, Tony Kobayashi challenged the workers at Fuji Xerox to win the Deming Prize. The workers accepted his challenge. People would actually punch out after their shifts and then go back and work another eight hours without punching in again because they didn't want to charge the company for the time. TQC was expanded to vendors and to subsidiary companies. Xerox coporation is continuing that same strategy today with its vendors around the world.

Product development is now one of Fuji Xerox's strengths. It spends 8.5 percent of revenues on R&D in addition to a 3 percent technology royalty to Xerox Corporation. The key to that strength in copier development lies in the closeness and cooperation between the designers and manufacturing, not in automation. In fact, the Fuji Xerox Ebina plant was one of the last of the Japanese copier facilities to automate its materials handling in mid-1985. During a tour of the facilities in early 1985, Sharp, Canon, and Ricoh were far advanced. For instance, at one station in Ebina, a worker visually inspected the parts packages on a conveyor and decided where to route them. At Canon and Ricoh, and even Webster, that function is performed automatically by a light sensor reading a bar code. Ebina's top priorities are automating parts handling and then moving into automated production. The goal was to complete automation by 1987.

The major advantage at Ebina, however, is that the design engineers are down the hall from the manufacturing floor. If there is a problem, it gets solved quickly. The design community at Ricoh and Canon are off-site from manufacturing. In Europe, mid-volume Xerox copiers are designed at Welwyn Garden City in England and manufactured across the English Channel at Venray. Even in Webster, the designers are located in a different building from manufacturing. "Sometimes even a walk down the hall is too far when you have a problem," says Yoichi Oshima, manager of product planning and program management at Ebina. Shortly after Oshima began his current job he moved his office down the hall to a site just off the main manufacturing floor.

Oshima works for Motohiko Tsuchiya, the Wayland Hicks of Fuji Xerox. Tsuchiya headed the New Xerox movement, reporting directly to Tony Kobayashi. He echoes Kobayashi's philosophy on the never-ending process. "QC training is elementary school," Tsuchiya says. "Many people felt good about winning the Deming Prize, but our work was just beginning."

Kearn's comments recalling when he first talked to Kobayashi about total quality control sound oddly similar. "I did not understand the real meaning," he says. "I almost went back to school. When they talked about total quality control they meant running their company in a very different way. I really didn't understand that then. As I understood more of what they were doing, and as others within the company did, I think that became an important motivator, a real knowledge base for change at Xerox."

The Fuji Xerox product development system is patterned after Xerox corporation's low-, mid-, and high-volume business units, which were set up in 1981. Fuji Xerox established low-volume and mid-to-high volume units in 1982. In 1983, they were combined under Tsuchiya. For each product, a team is assembled that remains together from concept to launch. Service technicians are brought in during the early stages of a project to test their reactions to new machines. This helps designers to understand better the service requirements of a machine. Typical development time for a so-called clean sheet product is two to three years. A derivative product can be pushed out much more quickly. About sixty engineers are involved on a typical project, and about six months before mainline production begins, many key assembly-line workers are used to make prototypes. These workers are shifted back to the mainline and their experience helps the factory reach full production faster. The whole idea is to shift more responsibility to the manufacturing line. "You are manufacturing the machine so you should develop how you want to do it," Tsuchiya tells his production people. "Come to the model shop and develop your concept."

In one hallway near the engineering area is a bulletin board for the employees. In January, 1985, it was covered with photographs of the engineers at a year-end party. Funny hats, costumes, and bottles of Kirin beer were everywhere.

"What's the purpose of those photographs?" Oshima was asked.

"Forget 1984," he said. "This is new year with new challenges."

Fuji Xerox has never had a strike. Ask the question, and managers get a puzzled look on their face. They don't know what a labor dispute is. Fuji Xerox has never had a lawsuit filed against it by employees alleging discrimination, or by customers, competitors, or the government. Oh, there have been some minor disputes involving a traffic accident with a company vehicle. But those have been settled quickly. In 1986 Fuji Xerox had only eight people on its corporate legal staff, five of them lawyers. In comparison, Xerox Corporation had sixty-eight lawyers in the United States, not including Crum and Forster; another thirty-five outside the country, not counting Japan. Fuji Xerox legal workers aren't even lawyers in the traditional, American sense. They have gone to law school, but they haven't taken a bar exam. They handle contracts, but they don't advise senior management on legal matters, a major part of a corporate lawyer's job in the United States.

Fuji Xerox also doesn't have any female managers. "So far, women haven't stayed long enough to qualify for managerial positions," explains Kazuhiko Ijichi, manager of personnel. "Some females are project leaders, but no managers. We are prepared to promote women in the future. We expect that." At Fuji Xerox, as at many Japanese companies, it is thought that workers' overall level of ability cannot be accurately assessed until they are well into the thirties.

The Ebina factory, located about 30 miles west of Tokyo next to Atsugi City, the site of Ricoh's main plant, accounts for 60 percent of all Fuji Xerox production. It employs 3,500 people, about 1,100 of those part-time. Full-time workers throughout Fuji Xerox are guaranteed jobs until age 55–60. In 1986 the average wage for production workers was about $12,000 a year, which included bonuses. (Every Fuji Xerox worker gets an annual bonus; for most it is equal to about six months' regular pay.) That's 10 percent higher than the average wage at Canon and about 20 percent higher than the average wage at Ricoh's Atsugi plant. While only about 11 percent of the full-time employees are women, they make up the majority of contract workers or part-timers. The plant has seven of its own buses and hires eighteen more to help transport the workers to company-owned dorms or other housing. There are no Xerox dorms in Rochester.

About four hundred workers live in bachelor dorms, for which they pay less than $40 a month. "It's a steal," says Kazu Sugiyama, who was product manager for the 1055 and lived in the United States for three years while helping prepare the 1075 for the Japanese market. Another 1,000 workers with families live in contract housing, subsidized by Fuji Xerox. Most Fuji Xerox workers are eligible, after three years with the company, for a company loan with which to buy a home.

At Ebina, all the workers dress in blue uniforms and wear blue hats. In one section of the plant a huge chart lists the names of every worker. Next to each name are colored dots, a different color for each month of the year; each dot represents a suggestion that worker has made. The average worker makes two hundred suggestions a year; the highest total is 1,700. Many of the suggestions deal with new tools or alterations in the workers' work stations that will help them be more productive. Most of the suggestions are implemented.

Ebina has 124 main vendors, 57 percent of whom are located within thirty miles of the plant; not one is outside Japan. Typical parts inventory is five working days, which will be reduced to two and a half by 1987. Lead time for production was six months in 1982. By 1986 it was two months. When a brand new machine model is introduced it starts down the regular production line at the rate of fifty a day. It will take about a month or a thousand machines to reach full production. Because the designers work so closely with manufacturing, there are very few design changes once mass production begins – an average of twenty per machine and that's usually within the first month. The company's goal is to solve all problems during the preproduction stage. If problems occur on the main line, a massive effort is needed to correct them. Production capacity at Ebina is much like Venray: about two hundred mid-volume console models a day.

The setting was surreal. The music was Japanese, but it had an odd quality about it, almost as if someone was playing *The Star Spangled Banner* on a sitar. The curtain across the stage was embroidered with a large peacock. The people in the audience were dressed in three-piece suits. Tony Kobayashi walked on to the stage and said good morning. In unison, the crowd responded. Kobayashi talked about the theme for the day. On the cover of the program were two pyramids and four camels lumbering across the desert. The pyramids were built over a long period of time by thousands of people. Camels walk slowly but they make steady progress, like the story of the tortoise and the hare. Kobayashi talked about the accomplishments of the company, but at one point said, "I feel like being skeptical." When he finished, two young workers in suits took the stage and acted as cheerleaders to get the crowd warmed up. On cue, 450 people stood. Tony Kobayashi, and other members of his board of directors, all sang the QC Circle Song:

> With beaming smiles exchanged
> Friends gather with bright spirits
> Ah, these friends talk about
> New dreams of quality control
> And strive with goals well in mind
> QC Circle filled with light
>
> With morale constantly growing
> The days assume the pure mission
> Ah, these days are beautiful
> Prosperous enterprises bloom as flowers

They strive for the ideal of tomorrow
QC Circle filled with aspiration

By communicating well with each other
The path is chosen with proper measure
Ah, that path means happiness
Further growth of Japanese culture
Powerfully and affluently
QC Circle filled with future

Welcome to the Xerox Circle Convention

Fuji Xerox has been regaining market share, on both a unit and a copy volume basis, in Japan, just as Xerox has in both the United States and Europe. Most people in the industry concede that Japan is the toughest copier market in the world. No one releases exact figures for domestic placements or copy volume, but Fuji Xerox calculates that during 1985 it had 50 percent of the copy volume in Japan, while Ricoh had 20 percent and Canon 10 percent. In terms of unit placements, Ricoh led with 35 percent, Canon had 21 percent, and Fuji Xerox 20 percent, up slightly from the year before. The reason for the disparity in shares is the same as in the US: Fuji Xerox is strongest in the larger, higher-volume machines that produce most of the copy volume. That's also where most of the profits are, 80 percent in the case of Fuji Xerox. Ricoh is stronger in the smaller machines, and Canon is stronger in the United States than in Japan.

Fuji Xerox divides Japan into three markets: big cities, medium-level business establishments, and rural areas. It's similar to Xerox Corporation's approach in the United States. Fuji Xerox has five sales channels:

- Direct sales: 54 branches, 206 locations, 2,500 salesmen.
- Sales subsidiaries: 29 marketing subsidiaries set up as joint ventures, 51 percent owned by Fuji Xerox – some of these are with Suntory, a major distillery in Japan – with more than 1,500 salesmen.
- Dealers: some sell two or three kinds of products, and since in Japan many companies want exclusive dealers, this is a rather unique approach. Fuji Xerox had 500 dealers at the end of 1985 and set a goal of 1,000 by 1988.
- So-called push channels: sales agents go out and kick a door and say hello.
- So-called pull channels: this is storefront business; Fuji Xerox has four stores in Japan on an experimental basis.

Ricoh's direct sales force, by contrast, is limited to national major accounts such as the central government and has more than four thousand dealers in Japan. Canon uses only dealers, roughly 800 in Japan, for its NP copiers; for its personal copiers, Canon has roughly three thousand outlets, including stationery, camera, department, and discount stores.

About 30 percent of all Fuji Xerox establishments are concentrated in the Tokyo and Osaka areas. This represents more than 60 percent of the market value of the products sold. "If we want to conquer Japan we must conquer Tokyo and Osaka," says Haruhiko Yoshida, manager of the marketing planning department. In the 350 miles between Tokyo and Osaka are two-thirds of Japan's 120 million people – that equals 75 percent of the country's buying power. Obviously, winning the Tokyo–Osaka market is a must if you want a high market share.

Fuji Xerox is convinced Xerox Corporation will have to adopt a similar aggressive dealer strategy. The problem is not just having a good, low-volume, low-cost copier product, but also having a strong distribution network that can move those machines in large numbers and at low cost. "We need the dealers from two viewpoints," Yoshida says. "Market share and profitability. In PPCs the mid- and high-volume areas are almost mature, almost saturated. So if we want to install our product we have to replace Canon and Ricoh. Some customers don't buy a brand, they buy from a particular dealer because he is a friend. We have switched our strategy to forge a better relationship with dealers. If we succeed in our dealer operation it will be good know-how for Xerox Corporation in the future."

One area in which Fuji Xerox had great success was stopping IBM from becoming a major factor in copiers in Japan. The giant computer maker had serious designs on the Japanese copier market shortly after it launched its first plain paper copier in the United States in 1971. Fuji Xerox, however, stopped the attack dead. Today, there are fewer than a hundred IBM copiers in all of Japan. This despite the fact that IBM Japan, at almost $4 billion a year in revenues, is one of Japan's biggest companies. In order to do this, Fuji Xerox identified every IBM trial site or account in Japan. It then got a Xerox machine on the site, even if it had to put it in for free. It also developed a new machine on short-notice, a speeded-up 2400. Fuji Xerox then gave special pricing against IBM. The strategy worked. Today, IBM is no factor in the Japanese copier market.

Fuji Xerox also has operating companies in Korea, Taiwan, the Philippines, Indonesia, and Thailand. Those markets, however, account for less than 5 percent of the company's total revenue. A sore point is the fact that in other areas in which Fuji Xerox would normally consider its territory – Singapore, Australia, New Zealand, and China – it has to export through Rank Xerox because that company holds the territorial rights. At one time, Fuji Xerox products even had to be first shipped to London where they were reshipped to Australia or Singapore. It doesn't happen any more, but Rank Xerox still attaches its own mark-up to the products. "Since virtually all of our competitors are Japanese, that mark-up puts us at a price disadvantage in those areas," Yoshida says.

During a tour of the new Fuji Xerox training center at Tsukahara, near the base of Mount Fuji, we passed a courtyard that had a highly polished metal cone in the middle. "Remember that," Yoshiaki Nagai, a senior technical trainer, said. "I'll explain later." We passed to more courtyards – one had a tree, the other a stone statue. "Rember that," Nagai said after each one. Later he explained: "In Japan, when we do things we think in terms of three things: mind, technique, and body. The stone is our mind, the tree our body, and the cone our technology or technique, always progressing to the top."

In the US, workers jump from company to company to gain new experiences. In Japan, they move from job to job within the same company. Many of those changes would be considered lateral moves in the United States and not promotions. In Japan, however, they are considered important for training and learning. About one percent of Fuji Xerox revenues are spent on education and training. Hirosuke Yoshina, manager of the management development and training department, believes each employee should spend about 5 percent of his or her working time in some educational activity. "Otherwise the company can't expect to improve its employees."

The Tsukahara training center was completed in October 1984 at a cost of $8 million. It has more than 2,000 Xerox office machines on site for use in training service employees. It has two video studios, one two stories high, that can simulate a small office environment for interpersonal relations training. In 1984, more than six thousand people were trained at Tsukahara. The shortest stay was two days, the longest 53, for a basic training program required of all new employees.

About twenty Fuji Xerox instructors teach English to 350

employees a year. Anyone who would have contact with Xerox Corporation must learn English. The American parent company does not have a similar program for the Japanese language.

On the floor of the Suzuka Fuji Xerox factory in Suzuka City, near Nagoya, are eleven injection molding machines, making everything from small plastic copier parts to rubber rollers. There isn't a human within 50 feet; the machines run 24 hours a day, automatically. The raw materials are automatically supplied and the finished parts are automatically picked up by unmanned dorries. The parts are shipped the same day they are manufactured. Even the dies for the different parts are changed automatically.

Suzuka Fuji Xerox is one of five subsidiary companies of Fuji Xerox. Companies establish subsidiaries to take advantage of a more favorable location or wage situation, a common practice in Japan. The subsidiaries aren't bound by the same labor agreements as the parent company. Suzuka makes parts for copiers as well as printed circuit boards for Toshiba personal computers, parts for home appliances and automobiles, and even a practice putting machine for Matsushita. It has just begun to market its products around the world, including the US. The plant has 13 shaft-making machines which are operated the same way as the injection molding machines. They run 24 hours a day and only three or four workers are needed each shift. The same computer that controls the delivery of raw materials and the shipment of finished parts also handles customer billing. Most of the suppliers of the raw materials used in the plant are an hour away in Nagoya. Typical inventory levels of raw materials are two to three days and some electronic components can be stocked for up to a month, depending upon shortages in the semiconductor industry.

Each machine in the $20 million plant, which was completed in December 1982, is labeled with its cost and the operator's name. "That's so each worker knows the investment we have in him," says Hiro Matsumoto, managing director of Suzuka Fuji Xerox. The plant won a factory automation prize from the *Japan Economic Journal* (the same prize won by Ricoh's Atsugi plant in 1984) just eleven months after it opened. Because it is so advanced, the plant is popular for tours. In its first two years of operation, more than two hundred Xerox Corporation personnel went through Suzuka and more than four thousand Japanese customers. "We are very glad to have many visitors because after a while they will be our customers," Matsumoto says. "If a prospect comes to our plant, there is a 95 percent chance he will do business with Suzuka. He will be that impressed."

In 1984, Xerox Corporation bought one percent – $500,000 – of Suzuka's production. In 1985, that was doubled to $1 million. Matsushita buys some parts from Suzuka that eventually wind up in copier components it supplies to Canon and Ricoh, but Canon and Ricoh have not yet contacted Suzuka directly. "We wish they would," says president Chuji Kurihara. "We'll sell to anybody."

In 1978, Jim O'Neill, then in charge of copier development and manufacturing for Xerox, was in Japan to review a proposed laser printer based on the 3500. O'Neill, who previously had worked at Ford, had a reputation for asking questions that could always be answered by numbers.

"How many people worked on this project?" he asked the five young Fuji Xerox engineers making the presentation.

"We did," they said.

"How long did it take you?" O'Neill asked.

"Six months," they said.

"I'm not even going to ask you my third question," O'Neill said. "The cost is insignificant."

Kearns doesn't discount the complaints Fuji Xerox has about being stifled, about not being able to sell enough of its products around the world, but he says Wayland Hicks and Bob Adams have similar discussions with Rank Xerox and Dwight Ryan. Everybody wants the marketing groups to take more of their product.

"Fuji Xerox has been good for Xerox," Kearns says. "We make good money [about a third of Fuji Xerox profits go to the United States]. We have gotten good products from them. I do think we have to be careful inside the company not to build up Fuji Xerox bigger and better than it is. There are a lot of things they do better in Webster than they do at Fuji Xerox. And there are things they are still doing better at Fuji Xerox than we are. But I tell you, we're gaining on them. And we're going to catch them. I hear statements from the Japanese, even Fuji Xerox, today they sound like Americans twenty years ago. You talk about Singapore or Korea and they say, 'No, they don't have the quality, they don't have the infrastructure, they don't have the trade experience, they don't have the education.' It's kind of interesting."

7
Common Obstacles

Introduction

In the previous chapters we discussed how to form strategic alliances with the primary focus on achieving a strategic alliance that would be consistent with a firm's strategic intent through an appropriate management process. In this chapter we discuss a set of practical challenges that stem from implementing strategic alliances. Because most strategic alliances are demanding and difficult to pull off in their own right, it is particularly important to take these challenges seriously. Otherwise, an organization might unnecessarily load the dice against success. In particular, organizations must understand the challenges in the context of specific strategic intents, so that they can act appropriately to enhance the chances of successful execution.

A caveat regarding failure of strategic alliances must be made, however. Some authors argue that the failure rates of such alliances may be no higher than those of internal corporate ventures: "The thrust of that literature [on strategic alliances], perhaps unwittingly, seems to overemphasize the problems of running international joint ventures. There is, however, no hard evidence that their failure rate exceeds the normal corporate failure for comparative single-owner ventures" (Contractor and Lorange 1988).

It is undoubtedly hard to make new business activities take off under any circumstances, and we must be careful not to overemphasize arguments for strategic alliance failures, even though many examples of devastating failures can be found in the literature. There are also many examples of strategic alliances working out as intended. It is always inherently difficult and a major challenge to develop a new business.

We now discuss seven major challenges to the successful implementation of strategic alliances that, in our experience, can play a key role in the difference between success and failure:

- how to overcome reluctance to give up autonomy over one's own strategic resources
- how to achieve operating momentum
- how to deal with the need to maintain focus on the external environment, i.e., the competition and customers, rather than on internal friction points
- how to avoid unnecessary politicking
- how to maintain organizational energy to continue cooperation over time
- how to increase one's willingness to learn
- how to keep particular individuals from becoming bottlenecks in the strategic alliances

Overcoming Reluctance to Give Up Autonomy

One fundamental challenge to strategic alliances, and from many points of view a major disadvantage, is that a partner must give up some autonomy over its own strategic resources. The partner is therefore no longer as free to decide how to use its strategic resources. Further, the other partner will now have gained joint access to, or co-ownership of, strategic resources that otherwise might have been solely owned. There is always the threat that the other partner may subsequently use this knowledge and insight in a non-cooperative way. Hence, it is easy to understand that many enter into strategic alliances with a great deal of apprehension.

Finally, since the strategic resources generated through a strategic alliance may not belong solely to any one of the partners, they can no longer be used exclusively by one firm for building new strategic positions. These limitations on one's discretion over strategic resources may be particularly problematic when dealing with core technological know-hows and/or core markets.

For instance, could it happen that an alliance we form with a partner who has superior products and technology ends up giving the other firm access to our markets? In other words, this traditional type of joint venture, where the partner's upstream strengths are combined with one's own downstream strengths, might give them access to our previously fully controlled market contacts. "Our" customers might now, with our help, be exposed to the partner's products! It would probably have taken the partner a long time to achieve this alone. We have given up autonomy over our moves in the market place, and these will now have to be coordinated with the partner. On the other hand, the partner gives up its unique technology, which undoubtedly would have taken a long time for us to develop on our own. In other words, both parties get short-term gains from this strategic alliance. In the long term, however, the question is whether any partner has learned enough from the other that they may be tempted to break the cooperation and get out on their own. Both partners must assess the possibility of such a scenario.

In strategic alliances that aim to gain scale and/or scope advantages, potential gains result from building interdependencies between the partners' technologies, manufacturing and/or market-oriented activities. This cooperation assumes, however, that both parties continue to contribute fully in the future – to do their share – in order to maintain the scale and/or scope advantage. What happens if one party is no longer able to maintain its unique input of excellence? What happens if one of the parties falls on to economic hard times and/or reprioritizes its strategic intents so that the necessary resources are no longer provided to support the strategic alliance? The potential disadvantages stemming from changes in the strategic priorities and circumstances of one of the partners might be a definite minus when it comes to strategic alliances. This type of problem is illustrated in the Swed–Nor Partner case in the Appendix to this Chapter.

Strategic alliances represent a demanding way of working for both parents' management teams, requiring a lot of top management's time and energy, and one should keep in mind that this is probably the most scarce strategic resource of all. To enter into a strategic alliance can represent a loss of opportunity in the sense that one's management might have better spent its efforts on developing wholly-owned businesses requiring relatively less managerial inputs relative to outputs. Excessive expense of management's time must definitely be factored in as a prospective disadvantage. This underscores the point that strategic alliances are typically best suited in situations where both parties have a long-term commitment. In dealing with this challenge it is essential reiterate the need to prioritize, to keep in mind that "strategic management means making choices."

Achieving Operating Momentum

A second challenge to a strategic alliance is to get going operationally. Analogous to the necessity of thorough post-acquisition integrative efforts (Haspeslagh 1988), it is crucial that the formation team transfer its energy and enthusiasm into becoming the implementation team. Individuals in the parent firm and in the strategic alliance organization must move to get things done! In this context, early success in the business is, of course, very helpful.

One of the difficult issues when it comes to maintaining momentum has to do with the fact that the formation process very often tends to be energy-consuming, and it requires quite intense cooperation and inputs from many key executives. When the contract is finally signed one can easily risk the follow-on "let-down syndrome" in that there simply is not enough drive, self-generating momentum, and urgency left to pick up on the less glorious day-to-day follow-through that now ensues. This can be a particularly serious issue if the resource availability question, introduced in Chapter 1, is not paid attention to: this means that each partner must assign resources to stand behind the permutational steps that have been agreed on. Needless to say, realism regarding resource assignment is essential. For instance, while both partners may agree that the strategic alliance should have enough resources to be able to adapt readily to new opportunities and changing circumstances, it may be that, *de facto*, so little resources of sufficient quantity are being assigned that little or no adaptation can taken place. This means that the strategic alliance may *de facto* be of the ad hoc project type or project-based joint venture type when indeed it was meant to be implemented as a consortium or full-blown strategic alliance.

The business plan which should be an integral part of the final stages of the formation process should keep in mind that there will be a day after the signing ceremony, and the focus should also be on such issues as who is supposed to do what, and at which point in time. The spelling out of the various strategic programs to be carried out in the strategic alliance, and the assignments of responsibilities to each of the partners for their various segments of the strategic program efforts is crucial here.

It is essential to insist on prioritizing activities within the early stages of the strategic alliance. A guiding principle is to develop the organization's self-confidence by selecting achievable targets during the early phases. In the early phase, it is also important to rely on individuals known to be doers, experienced persons who are familiar with getting relatively unstructured work done. Early success is thus a critical factor for gaining and maintaining operating momentum. The opposite side of the spectrum can be found when it takes many more resources and more time and effort than planned to get to the various targets that are being contemplated. During such periods of strain it can easily happen that a particular partner loses its commitment, thus hampering the operating momentum.

Maintaining Focus on the Environment

A third challenge is maintaining the external focus: the purpose of the alliance is a means to an end, not the end *per se*. Value is created through successful business transactions with customers by being better than the competition! Too often, managers tend to view the strategic alliance as being a set of cooperation problems. This easily leads to spending excessive time on internal discussions regarding management of the alliance. While various parts of the network organizations spend their time discussing the organization, the competitors move ahead.

The strategic plan for the alliance should have a heavy emphasis on the customers. This includes developing target lists and milestone plans for how to reach particular customers. For example, what does it take to bring each of them into the network of active clients? Specific responsibilities relative to each client may be assigned to individuals, but it is particularly important to be clear regarding how the strategic alliance's management team should work vis-à-vis its external environment. It might also be useful to practice "benchmarking" (Jacobson and Hillkirk 1986) relative to major competitors to further articulate what it takes to win the customers.

A particular challenge when it comes to maintaining an environmental focus has to do with the fact that since a strategic alliance involves cooperation among several partners who each carry out their complementary aspects of the value creation process, it will be hard for each given partner to get a complete picture of how the business operation of the strategic alliance is doing, such as it would get if this was a wholly-owned operation where it would experience the full range of issues facing a business. Thus, it is important that the parties get together and share in their experiences regarding how their particular cooperation around a business concept is progressing, so that each party can get a full and complete picture of what is going on. One party may, for instance, have a closer tie to the market-related issues and the customer, while the other party may be more closely focused on technological, product development, and manufacturing issues. Needless to say, neither of these functions can succeed on its own without cross-fertilization from the other. Also, partitioning these functions could mean a debarkation from a healthy environmental focus.

Avoiding Politicking

A fourth, and related, challenge is avoiding politics in the working of the strategic alliance. It is important first to achieve a measure of early success in the business, then the parties can address how potential imbalances in the partners' roles should be adjusted to a new optimal win–win situation.

We have already pointed out how the avoidance of politicking can be achieved. Our discussion here summarizes the three types of concerns that we have raised.

First, it is critical during the formation process that senior stakeholders are all involved and are committed to the strategic alliance. This needs to be followed up with a broad internalization of the concepts that strategic alliances are to be built on so that there is understanding within each participating organization. Only then can a basis of trust and understanding be created with a focus on the positive values that are needed to succeed. Only then, too, can fear of the unknown be minimized.

Second, the issue of human resource management in strategic alliances is, of course, critical as a factor for conquering politics (discussed in Chapter 5). The crux of this issue is that each participating executive must feel satisfied that their own personal career plans, their own incentives and their own development needs are taken care of. Given, in particular, the uncertainty in seeing the end point of a strategic alliance, no matter what type of alliance we are talking about, it is essential that the human resource planning provides a safety net for the individual. The feeling of being safe and feeling confident that the strategic alliance activities coincide with the executive's own personal goals is a major factor in minimizing the risk of politicking.

Third, the strategic planning process, as outlined in Chapter 4, provides a basis for minimizing politicking. Here the roles of the various stakeholders will be laid out, calling for a codification of tasks and mutual expectations. This should ideally narrow down the areas of ambiguity, i.e., the grey zones in the pattern of cooperation between the parties. Thus, a good strategic plan settles potential politicking issues at the planning stage, making politicking unnecessary.

The management team of the strategic alliance might well remind itself of the proverbs "don't count your chickens before they're hatched" and "a bird in the hand is worth two in the bush." A sense of maturity is critical so that managers can focus on running the business, on creating value, and on achieving the upside, rather than on maneuvering. One should avoid politicking regarding how to split a gain which is not yet created.

Maintaining Organizational Energy to Cooperate Over Time

We have outlined in Chapter 3 that a strategic alliance never, or seldom, represents a stable entity in itself; it is virtually always an organization in transition from its present form to something else. It goes without saying that organizational momentum needs to be maintained throughout an evolution. This means that not only must the members of the cooperative venture perform and be committed to the strategic alliance at a given point in time, with the result, if successful, that they will all be satisfied with the way the strategic alliance is working at that phase, but also that the participants must be able to be open for new challenges, to embrace changes and to modify the way of operating in light of the evolutionary momentum that the strategic alliance may be facing. Thus, strong operating momentum among the participating firms and their executives at one point in time, coupled with excellent performance, may indeed be an entrapment when it comes to maintaining the ability to change and innovate, i.e., to create strong performance during subsequent evolutionary stages.

We are here, again stressing the importance of the resource-based viewpoint that we introduced in Chapter 1. It may well be that there is enough human capital and complementary resources available for a strategic alliance to succeed in a static sense. Still, the resources available to handle the evolutionary trajectory that may be desirable may not be available. Thus, intentional over-staffing by each of the partners may be necessary to provide for maintenance of the dynamic momentum of the alliance. It goes without saying that if no further dynamic changes are intended then this argument is not valid.

Issues of organizational fatigue, which need to be handled through linkage with the human resource management process described in Chapter 5, must, of course, be faced here. It is hard to see how the dynamic momentum can continue unless a well articulated human resource management process is in place, with sensitivity to the evolutionary pressures being addressed.

Needless to say, the investment in human capital to maintain the momentum does need to focus on having the necessary breadth of management resources available, an issue which can be particularly hard given the partial focus of each of the parent partners. Needless to say too, the maintenance of organizational momentum is easier to achieve if there is no temporary dip in this momentum at any point in time. Ongoing, relatively small successes on a regular basis, rather than large successes and large crises, is the way to manage dynamically.

Increasing the Willingness to Learn

A sixth challenge is developing and/or increasing one's willingness to learn from the partner. A good example of this is General Motors and Toyota in their NUMMI joint venture. General Motors had a major strategic intent of learning how Toyota's famous manufacturing and operations management processes function; Toyota wanted to learn how to deal with US parts suppliers and subcontractors. When the intent to learn is relatively clear, the organization's openness and aptitude regarding such learning will probably also be greater. Another aspect of this is keeping up with the partner. The US-based aircraft manufacturer Fairchild's role in its strategic alliance with SAAB illustrates this issue. To some extent, the commercial commuter aircraft business was somewhat peripheral to Fairchild, leading to a relatively less intensive learning process on its part to stay at the technology frontier. The US firm was therefore not able to deliver vital state-of-the-art wing and tail components for aircraft which were assembled in Sweden.

Learning was uneven among the partners, and they were unable to help each other to bring the overall organizational competence up to even consistency. Instead, stress and finger-pointing prevented mutual learning. Subsequently, SAAB bought Fairchild's share of the venture.

Several steps can be taken to achieve the fullest learning effects. First, a careful articulation of the intended learning purposes is useful, so as to make this often overlooked issue explicit. Second, the willingness to follow control processes is critical. Deviations from plans, as detected through strategic control, have more of a control significance than a learning significance. It is important to take the time to analyze why things really went differently than expected and to contemplate how to build on these new experiences (Argyris and Schon 1978). The strategic alliance should be seen as a laboratory, or a positive experiment, and the benefits from this become clear only through systematic follow-up and learning.

Active involvement from several people in the organization is also crucial. There can often be too much of a tendency to isolate the strategic alliance activities to only a handful of people in the organization, and to keep those people assigned to the alliance over a considerable period of time. While there might be compelling reasons for this, such as creating unique experiences in cooperative work, developing stable interpersonal contacts, and so on, it is equally important to rotate people to achieve the broader learning effects. Assignment to strategic alliances should also be motivated from a human resource management development point of view and seen as an opportunity to build new important learning insights.

Most of all, an organization must mobilize its willingness to learn. This is perhaps one of the most critical features often found in Japanese corporations and may be the reason why they tend to get so much out of strategic alliances relative to many of their Western partners, who at times appear to be too laid back (Hamel and Prahalad 1989; Reich and Mankin 1986).

Avoiding "Bottleneck" Dependence

A seventh challenge is avoiding being too dependent on certain individuals. This risk is illustrated by Tecator–AME, a joint venture between two relatively small automotive electronics components manufacturing firms, one from Sweden and one from Norway (Lorange and Roos 1987). The project leader in one of the partner firms was extremely important in implementing the project due to his unique technological skills, as well as his strong commitment. When this individual suddenly died, the alliance began to deteriorate. The speed of implementation was also clearly hampered by the fact that the project leader in Tecator changed several times during formation and implementation. On the other hand, the positive benefits from having continuity in these matters is illustrated by the quite successful joint venture between VIAK and Terotech (1987). Here a broad and stable contingent of central executives was involved from both sides.

It is important to institute the human resource management function before assigning executives to strategic alliances. And the systematic rotation of managers is essential to avoid too much dependence on specific individuals who after some time may become irreplaceable, and to achieve broader organizational learning. A manager in a leading strategic alliance position should be required to train back-up managers in critical tasks and, above all, to introduce his new colleagues to important contacts in the partner firm. Development of contacts should not be seen as a personal ownership issue, but rather as an investment that the particular partner organization makes which must be shared by several members of the organization. Needless to say, this will be hard to achieve unless firms work explicitly at such an issue.

Particular managers may be so fond of their strategic alliance that they more or less unconsciously reject the participation and involvement of other members of the organization. One large strategic alliance between a Brazilian and a Norwegian partner, for instance, fell on hard times owing to the fact that the chief financial officer of the Norwegian firm, the senior officer responsible for the alliance on his side, saw the alliance activities as a "fringe benefit" which gave him the opportunity to run an operation in addition to his financial officer duties. This alliance thus became a fiefdom of his, allowing him to enjoy the satisfaction of being a chief executive officer. The problem was, however, that no understanding was built up regarding the needs of the strategic alliance within his own company and neither was any commitment established in his own company to provide for the continuing support to the alliance after this chief financial officer retired.

Senior management must be careful not to shelter the strategic alliance from the mainstream of their own organization. Too often, particular members of senior management may be the bottleneck by managing the strategic alliance as a personal activity on the side. It is senior management's responsibility to ensure that no one be allowed to monopolize the management of the strategic alliance.

Maintaining Core Competence

As we discussed earlier, the importance of having a strong black box is that it will create a sense of the latent threat of damage to one's partner if it decides to break the rules of the strategic alliance. This makes it easier to cooperate while maintaining bargaining strength. The black box concept can also become a potential threat to the evolution of the strategic alliance itself unless it is being managed, as we shall see in the following paragraphs. We discuss this in terms of the three-phased generic evolutionary model outlined in exhibit 3.1.

During the Phase I evolutionary stage of a shared strategic alliance, it is of critical importance to have a clear black box delineation. This provides the basis for establishing a sense of balance and complementarity in the cooperative efforts.

If both partners insist on maintaining a static hold on their black boxes as time goes on, it may become difficult for the strategic alliance to evolve towards a Phase II setting. For the now relatively passive partner to give up some of its black box at this point, it is vital that it gets the necessary guarantees on expected returns which are deemed appropriate. Further, it is critical that the now more passive partner is satisfied that what is given up cannot be considered as part of its core technology and/or core market. The partner needs to maintain some control over the latter to be able to build for the future. The evolutionary dynamics of a partner's own technological and/or market developments will be an important issue in assessing the loosening of control of the black box, and thereby contribute to the strategic alliance's evolution.

In a Phase III situation, both partners will have to give up parts of their black boxes. This again implies that none of the partners sees the activities of the strategic alliance as potentially infringing on its core technology and/or core market positions for the future. This brings us back to the fundamental assessment of delineating a strategic role for the alliance which is not in conflict with the specific business strategies of each parent. If the strategic alliance is positioned within the same core technology/core market arena as one or both partners, it will be much harder to see how the strategic alliance can evolve meaningfully.

Again, we see a need for the partners to develop a future-oriented, pro-active view on the black box issue. This should already be assessed at the time of entering into the strategic alliance so that one is willing to give up part of one's unique know-how as time goes on, provided of course that the cooperation evolves as expected. To gradually loosen one's secretive grip is a key management issue which affects the long-term success of the strategic alliance.

Summary

In this chapter, we have pointed out several challenges to implementing strategic alliances. Many of these challenges are quite easy to handle, others are more subtle. Explicit awareness of these issues, recognition of the benefits of mastering them, and intent to capture these benefits are, however, key determinants for success. To avoid unnecessary pitfalls, these issues should be kept closely in mind by keeping checklists and/or by providing progress audits. Strategic alliances are sufficiently difficult to operate successfully as they are. The challenge should not be made harder by falling into traps which easily could have been handled before they became problems.

It is important to note that the various issues raised in this chapter can all be traced back to what we have discussed earlier in the book, i.e., none of them will probably be encountered if a proper formation process has been followed, if a proper understanding of the evolutionary challenges and pressures has been developed, and if a thorough planning of human resource activities have been provided for. In this light, the issues raised in this chapter can be seen as indicators that something is going wrong owing to the lack of good practices regarding the formation, management and evolution of strategic alliances earlier on and along the lines that we have proposed.

A caveat should, of course, be provided at this point. We have argued throughout the book that proper management practices relating to strategic alliances will be a major determinant for ultimate strategic success. This is, of course, a necessary but not sufficient in itself condition for success. The basic match between the strategic alliance and its environment, its positioning relative to customers and competitors, the endurance of its technological base, etc. will be critical. Thus, even the best managed strategic alliance can never succeed if the strategy it pursues turns out to be wrong. Paradoxically, a poorly executed strategic alliance can still be a success if the alliance happens to stumble on to a surprisingly robust strategic concept.

Appendix
Swedpartner–Norpartner[1]

Introduction

This case illustrates the strategic alliance between the Swedish company, Swedpartner AB, and the Norwegian company, Norpartner A/S, in the garden equipment industry.[2] The strategic alliance included product development, licensed manufacturing, marketing of common product line in Norway and Sweden, and future plans for international market development. Both companies had a strong market position in their home countries. Since the products were complementary, the basic idea of the strategic alliance was to pool resources and arrive at a common product line to be sold in Sweden and Norway.

Today, the strategic alliance is terminated. Swedpartner has been sold to the major Swedish competitor in the industry and, after it went bankrupt, Norpartner has been taken over by another Norwegian firm. For a complete actor and event summary, see exhibit A7.5 at the end of the case study.

The Swedish Partner: Swedpartner AB

Swedpartner was established in 1952 in a small town in southern Sweden. Until 1983, the firm was a typical family company but from 1984, the company was owned by Swedconcern AB. Swedconcern, which has an over-the-counter listing on the Stockholm Stock Exchange, is a holding company for some hundred autonomous medium-sized companies. Swedpartner's operations involved production and sales of a range of park products. The company had approximately 35 percent of the total market in Sweden in all product segments. In 1987, Swedpartner had 111 employees, and a turnover of $8 million.

The Norwegian partner: Norpartner A/S

Norpartner was founded in 1942 by the Nor family in the city of Haugesund on the Norwegian west coast. Until mid-1988, the company was owned by the Nor family. Norpartner's operations were organized in two separate divisions: (1) product development and manufacturing, and (2) market development. Norpart-ner's business was divided into the following segments:

- garden equipment (50% of turnover)
- offshore related mechanical equipment and service (35% of turnover)
- specialized steel equipment (15% of turnover)

A family member was Managing Director of the company and his brother, Mr Nor, was head of the largest business segment – garden equipment. In 1987 the company had 38 employees and a total turnover of $5 million.

Background to the Strategic Alliance

The garden equipment industry in Scandinavia can be characterized as an oligopoly. In 1984, the two major producers on the Swedish market – Swedpartner and Competitor – had a market share of some 40 percent each. Both companies were represented in Europe, but Competitor's export share was 50 percent of a turnover of SEK70 million, while Swedpartner only had about 10 percent of its sales of SEK50 million on the international market.

The situation was slightly different in Norway. For more than thirty years, Norpartner A/S had been more or less the sole manufacturer of garden equipment. It was not until 1968 that a competitor entered the Norwegian market – the Swedish company Competitor, through its agent. Competitor turned out to be successful, since its large system-oriented products were particularly well suited to Norwegian market conditions in the early 1980s and, after a few years, Competitor had achieved a market share of 25 percent. After 1983, Mr Nor worked hard to develop the garden equipment business segment of Norpartner. He established good contact with a German designer, and they developed a new set of wooden garden products that became very attractive on the market. In addition, in order to enhance management competence in the company, the Nor family decided to bring in additional professionals. Two new members of the Board were recruited, one with extensive banking experience and a management consultant specializing in financial control. The latter – Mr Consult – became Chairman of the Board of Directors. In addition, it was decided that instead of recruiting a new financial manager, Mr Consult would complement the acting financial manager.

During a discussion between Mr Nor and Mr Consult, the latter came up with the idea of approaching the venture capitalist, SNI. Mr Consult was acquainted with SNI, and he argued that this was a good way to finance a potential strategic alliance. Mr Nor explained that he thought this was a good idea since he, at that time, was determined to find a partner in Sweden to cooperate with in one way or another. From his long experience, he was quite familiar with all the major companies in the industry. He explained his reason for not contacting Competitor: "Norpartner and Competitor would have represented more than 65 percent of the Norwegian market, and, since I believe in competition, it was unnatural to approach this company. Therefore, we were looking for a more suitable Swedish partner."

In May 1985, Mr Nor read an article about one of the major actors on the Swedish market – Swedpartner AB. In the article, its Managing Director, Mr Swed, expressed his company's ambition to expand both in Sweden and on the international market. Mr Nor explained how he felt about Swedpartner:

> I felt that Swedpartner could be a suitable partner to us for three reasons: (1) It was a well-known fact that Mr Swed had great ambitions for Swedpartner, (2) the company was owned by Swed-concern AB, which was known to emphasize innovations, product development, and exports, and (3) neither of us had been particu-larly successful on the other company's home market. In addition, I was personally willing to work with the project in our company.

Mr Nor decided to send the German designer to a trade fair in Stockholm, where he knew Swedpartner was represented. The purpose was to establish initial contacts with Swedpartner and find out whether they would be interested in a strategic alliance. It turned out that Mr Swed was very interested in Norpartner's new range of garden equipment and therefore approached the designer at the trade fair. He stressed that every time he visited Swedpartner's agent in Norway, he learned about Norpartner's products through their active market development, and "this gave me a very positive impression of Norpartner." He further explained why he was interested in the company: "I also knew that Norpartner was not represented in Sweden at all. Hence, I saw an opening towards a strategic alliance where we could sell each other's products. Surprisingly, the designer said that Norpartner had been discussing the same thing!"

A few weeks after this initial contact, in June 1985, Mr Nor invited Mr Swed to his home town. Both of them said that this was a meeting where "they were to get to know the other party better." According to Mr Nor, this meeting became the embryo of the strategic alliance. Mr Swed said that he quickly developed very good personal contacts with Mr Nor but not with the Chairman of the Board, Mr Consult. It was decided that both parties should analyze the other company's product range and make the strategic alliance idea more tangible at their next meeting.

After the meeting, Mr Consult wrote a letter to Mr Bye at SNI, explaining the oligopolistic nature of the industry and the idea of cooperating with Swedpartner. At Swedpartner, Mr Swed briefed the Board of Directors about his initial discussions with Norpartner.

After a few telephone contacts, the two parties met for the second time in August 1985, this time in Oslo. At this meeting, Mr Swed was informed by Mr Consult that Norpartner considered SNI to be an interesting source of project financing. Mr Swed felt that, even though he could probably obtain project financing from his parent company, and even though he had not heard about SNI, this idea seemed to be an interesting approach to financing a Swedish–Norwegian strategic alliance. Hence, they agreed to form a strategic alliance in line with SNI's intentions.

Strategic Match

The Norpartner team argued for a strategic alliance model that covered:

- market development of each other's product ranges in their respective home markets
- pooling of each party's product development resources
- cooperation regarding international market development.

It was intended that the two latter tasks were to be carried out in a formal fifty-fifty joint venture company. Mr Nor and Mr Consult argued that since the demand in Norway had switched into larger systems, the strategic alliance with Swedpartner would result in twice as large a product range – without an increased capital base. According to Mr Swed, this reasoning was also directly applicable to the Swedish conditions and, thus, did not give rise to any discussions. However, he was not interested in forming a joint venture for the purpose of mutual product development. Instead, he argued that it was better if product development was carried out within each parent company:

> Since I did not know how financially strong Norpartner was, it seemed to be safer if each party could take care of its own share of the product development within each company. Otherwise, there might be problems with allocation of resources, sharing of costs, and division of labor. In addition, it would be easier to know

which party had the formal right to the specific products in case
of a divorce.

After discussions, Mr Nor and Mr Swed agreed that the best
solution would be to pursue a strategic alliance in three steps:

- market development of each other's products in Norway and Sweden.
- coordination of product development
- forming a joint venture company for international market development
  of the common product line

The third step should not, however, be pursued until the first
two steps were successful. Mr Nor realized that a Swedish company was not likely to form a joint market development company
with a Norwegian company without having known the partner
for one or two years.

Both parties agreed that international market development
would be a second phase in the cooperation and should, therefore,
not be considered further in the initial discussions. Mr Swed said
that, even though he was interested in increasing the international
aspects of Swedpartner's operations, Swedpartner did have some
agents in Europe, and it was obvious that Norpartner was most
interested in the international market development.

Strategic Analyses

When it came to assessing the strategic alliance partner, Mr Nor
said that he made some enquiries about Swedconcern. Most of
this information came from SNI and from Swedpartner. He
explained the following: "We found out that Swedpartner was
worth some SEK10–12 million, and that it was a solid company,
and we knew that Swedconcern was known to have profitable
companies. However, I also knew that Swedpartner had difficulties in developing new and competitive products."

In addition, Mr Nor had learned from Mr Swed that Swedconcern viewed Swedpartner as a long-term investment. Mr Swed
said that he did not perform any particular analyses of Norpartner.
He made some inquiries about the company through his former
agent in Norway. He also checked the annual report but felt
that it was very difficult to penetrate the financial situation in
Norpartner's separate divisions. Mr Swed's comment was that
"the strategic alliance was, to a very large extent, based on the
excellent 'personal chemistry' between Mr Nor and myself." At
this stage, they presented the strategic alliance idea to SNI's
Managing Director Mr Atle Bye. He explained his initial feelings:

"The project was certainly unstructured. They were very enthusiastic, but appeared to have limited knowledge about strategic alliances. I suggested that a feasibility study, sponsored 50 percent by SNI, should be carried out. In order to save time, I approved that Mr Consult would carry out this study."

The feasibility study, covering some hundred pages, was presented in September 1985. In addition to an extensive description of the companies, including organizational and ownership structure, the strategic alliance concept and model, each product development project and the potential world-wide market, the budget in exhibit A7.1 was presented. Mr Consult also presented a forecast for product development costs and returns, and costs of international market development in the proposed joint venture (exhibit A7.2).

Mr Swed thought that the feasibility study was a requirement for SNI financing. Mr Consult had explained the SNI procedure to be "initial contact – feasibility study – approval of the loan." Mr Swed was, however, somewhat skeptical about the feasibility report:

> The feasibility study was based on old information that was brushed-up and re-organized. My opinion was that it did not say very much. This made me even more suspicious of Mr Consult's role in Norpartner, and it strengthened my opinion that we should

Exhibit A7.1

	1985/6	1987	1988	Total
Norpartner (thousand NKR)				
Market development	1815	1425	1650	4890
Product development	900	430	100	1430
Other costs	380	550	750	1680
Total	3095	2405	2500	8000
Swedpartner (million SEK)				
Market development	1115	1025	1350	3490
Product development	900	430	100	1430
Other costs	380	550	750	1680
Total	2395	2005	2200	6600

Exhibit A7.2 International market development – costs and revenues (thousand NKR)

	1985	1986	1987	1988
Royalty from sales (15%)		900	1,200	1,950
Total development costs (7 countries)	230	1,100	1,545	1,375
Return	−230	−200	−345	575

Product development costs (thousand NKR)

	1985/6	1987	1988	Total
Product 1	480	360	100	940
Product 2	420	200	100	720
Product 3	175	100		275
Product 4	500	130		630
Product 5	225	75		300
Total	1,800	865	200	2,865

pursue the strategic alliance in each company and not in a joint venture.

Mr Nor knew that the report was somewhat too optimistic:

> The feasibility study was so lengthy that it was difficult to comprehend. However, I think Mr Consult's purpose was to make it very impenetrable, and to enhance the estimated level of sales, etc. The objective was that nobody at SNI would even bother to read it, thereby facilitating a quick decision to sponsor our strategic alliance.

In a second meeting between the parties and Mr Bye, a strategic alliance structure was settled upon (exhibit A7.3).

In a second phase, the parties would focus on international market development, but not until this first phase had shown positive results. Mr Bye explained:

> After one and a half hours of discussions with the parties, we settled for a suitable Swedish–Norwegian strategic alliance model. I felt that they were very pleased with the help I gave them to

Exhibit A7.3

structure their ideas. Even though I knew that both companies were quite weak from a financial perspective, I thought that Norpartner had done something positive about this by hiring Mr Consult – with his broad international experience – as Chief Financial Officer and Chairman of the Board. Swedpartner, on the other hand, was part of the financially sound and well-known Swedconcern company.

Relationship with the Parent Companies

To Swedpartner, the strategic alliance was a natural expansion of its major activities. In 1984, Mr Swed had initiated extensive rehabilitation of the operations, including the renovation of the production plant. As a result, the operating results were quite modest in 1985 and, according to Mr Swed, the company greatly needed to revitalize its product range. Swedpartner would now be able to market Norpartner's attractive range as a complement to its own in Sweden, which would result in both increased revenues and goodwill. Furthermore, the existing agent in Norway had not been particularly successful and as a result of the strategic alliance, sales might improve in Norway through Norpartner. Mr Swed stressed the fact that their largest competitor, Competitor, had a substantial market share in Norway. Hence, the strategic alliance was expected to contribute significantly to Swedpartner's turnover, revenue and future exports.

In 1985 the situation in Norpartner was such that the company had two options for the garden equipment segment – either focus on further product development and hopefully increase sales on the Norwegian market, or initiate extensive international market development in order to increase exports. According to Mr Nor, it was quite obvious that the company could not afford both strategies at that time. He gave four major reasons for entering a strategic alliance with Swedpartner:

- By selling each other's products, the two companies would be one sole distributor with a broad and competitive product line.

- The average sales per customer would probably increase.
- Expansion of the product range would occur with limited additional capital requirements.
- The risk would be shared between the two companies.

The Strategic Alliance and the Project Leaders

When asked how he felt about the strategic alliance, Mr Swed responded that, as a representative of Swedpartner, he considered it important to get into the Norwegian market and to incorporate Norpartner's products into the company's range in Sweden. He also expressed his considerable personal interest in the project: "Even if there was no prestige involved, I desired both the new market and the products that the strategic alliance would result in – it had a high priority on my agenda." As regards his partner in the discussions, Mr Nor, he explained that in spite of different personalities the two of them enjoyed working with each other and that this did not change over time: "I really liked Mr Nor, I thought he was a great optimist."

Mr Swed never achieved personal contacts with Mr Bye at SNI, as Mr Nor had done, "To some extent I felt that I was slightly offside in the contacts with SNI, but I thought that we would develop this over time. However, this never happened."

Mr Nor felt that he had a hard time working with the garden business segment in his own company in the early 1980s. The general feeling on the Board of Directors was that – in spite of a 40 percent market share – profitability was unsatisfactory and, therefore, activities should be terminated. Mr Nor explained the situation as follows: "A Board of Directors must understand the industry – ours did not ... It was difficult to discuss strategy with them, since they were more interested in various financial statements and accounting-based measures."

However, the situation changed when the strategic alliance discussions were initiated. Mr Nor explained that the strategic alliance idea was quite important to him, and that the Board of Directors understood its potential benefits. As a result, Mr Nor increased his efforts in the company. He explained: "It was, of course, marvelous to initiate and implement a strategic alliance like this – I was given both the money and other resources to use in a business segment that I really believed in." Mr Nor also stressed his good personal relationship with his counterpart in Swedpartner, Mr Swed. He felt that Mr Swed was "honest, had an open personality, was ambitious, and did a good job in Swedpartner," and that this did not change over time. According to

Mr Nor, Mr Swed treated the strategic alliance as "his baby." On the other hand, Mr Nor felt that Mr Swed soon developed a poor personal relationship with Norpartner's Chairman of the Board, Mr Consult. Mr Nor felt that this was caused by the somewhat optimistic feasibility study that Mr Consult carried out. Mr Nor also emphasized one fundamental difference between the two companies' management styles: "I immediately felt that the leadership style in Swedpartner was more top-down, compared to ours, but I thought that was perhaps the typical Swedish practice, and then I thought that our style was perhaps a typical Norwegian practice."

Mr Nor tried to establish some operational contacts between the two companies. During a meeting at Swedpartner in September 1985, Mr Nor and the management team in Norpartner met all the key personnel in the company (financial, production, and market development). In spite of a good meeting, personal contacts never developed, and the strategic alliance continued to be, to a large extent, pursued by Mr Nor and Mr Swed.

Venture Capital

The formal application for project financing was sent to SNI in October 1985, and included summaries of the strategic alliance model, project plan, capital requirements and financing plan, and previous years' financial statements from the two companies. (The project plan was based on the feasibility study.) As demonstrated in the feasibility study, the capital requirement for the strategic alliance was NKR8.0 million in Norpartner's case, and SEK6.6 million for Swedpartner.

Mr Bye assigned both a Swedish and a Norwegian consultant to evaluate the SNI application and to recommend whether or not SNI should provide project financing. The SNI consultants' six-page report was presented in November 1985 and included a brief description of the companies, the strategic alliance idea, and the market. It was argued that there was a large market potential in both countries and in the international market. Since the companies had a strong position in their home countries, but had a small export share (less than 10 percent), there was a large potential for increased exports. As a matter of fact, the total market potential in Western Europe was estimated to be SEK150–200 million within five years' time. In addition, the financial aspects of the strategic alliance were discussed. It was argued that since the sales forecast was quite modest, the estimated results from international market development in the seven countries (18 percent return on capital from 1989) might well be exceeded. The consultants also felt that the estimates of the product development costs were acceptable and the pay-back time for these costs was not more than four to five years if sales increased by SEK4–5 million per year. They stressed that SNI financing was particularly important for Norpartner because of the company's weak financial position in the first phase of the strategic alliance. They described the importance of SNI in this cooperation as follows: "If SNI does not grant project financing, there is a risk that the project will be limited to Sweden and Norway only, and that product development will be significantly reduced and delayed."

In the conclusions, the consultants recommended SNI to finance the strategic alliance with a combination of loans and a royalty-based financing: "Because the project is based on a well defined and planned cooperation between two competent companies, the potential return is satisfactory, and the risks are limited. SNI's financing is needed in order to gain Norpartner's whole-hearted contribution."

The consultants stressed that they had not undertaken an assessment of the industrial partners *per se* – only the business concept. However, they remember that they mentally noted that Mr Consult seemed to have an unconventional role in the strategic alliance. As a matter of fact, they initially thought that Mr Consult was hired by SNI, which was not the case. According to the consultants, the feasibility report was undoubtedly adapted to SNI's requirements, which "was always the case for this type of project financing." However, they felt that the project idea was very good: "We all thought that this was an ideal strategic alliance: market development of each other's products, product development and, in the future, international market development." The feasibility report was so inclusive and comprehensive that they "only inspected it and accepted the figures."

Mr Bye noted that the consultants made a positive assessment of the strategic alliance, and that this was the basis for his positive recommendation to the Board of Directors. In addition, he knew that the partners had already, to some extent, started to cooperate and market each other's products. At the end of November 1985, SNI's Board of Directors granted the two companies the amount required, and Mr Bye was given the authoritiy to negotiate whether it should be a loan or a royalty-based financing. The discussions regarding the form of the project financing did not start until April 1986, however. In April and May 1986, Mr Swed wrote two letters to Mr Bye arguing for a royalty-based agreement. After some discussions, Mr Nor and Mr Swed had each signed a royalty-based agreement with SNI by the end of May 1986.

Mr Bye noted that Mr Swed in particular was very anxious for the royalty-based financing. He thought that this was due to pressure from Swedpartner's parent company, Swedconcern, regarding Swedpartner's weak financial position.

The Contract

The strategic alliance agreement between the parties was signed in mid-February 1986. Mr Swed explained that only he and Mr Nor formulated the agreement. In addition to letters and telephone contact, they met twice to discuss the agreement. Mr Swed explained what he felt about these preparations as follows: "It felt great since, in general, everything fitted together. We were both very anxious to protect our companies, but at the same time we wanted to give up some of our secret black boxes, and the agreement was formalized accordingly. The intention was that we should be known as one unit on the market."

Mr Nor also stressed the cooperative objective of the agreement: "Mr Swed presented what I thought was a standard agreement – a type of developed letter-of-intent. It covered a number of major issues regarding the cooperative activities." He further explained that, since the purpose was to extend the strategic alliance in the future, they agreed that it would cause problems if the initial agreement was too formalized and inflexible. He felt that the most important issue was to clarify the sharing of costs.

The two-page strategic alliance agreement covered the following issues:

- range of the agreement
- duration of the agreement
- prices
- terms of payment
- terms of deliveries
- geographical areas
- copying of products
- customer questions
- sales promotion materials
- information
- product development
- export cooperation
- management committee
- termination
- conflicts

Implementation

During the spring and the summer of 1986, product development and market development activities were initiated. Mr Swed explained that market development and sales work had the highest priority. This included printing of Swedpartner–Norpartner common product line catalogues in Swedish, and preparations for various exhibitions. It was not long before Swedpartner sold some of Norpartner's products. However, the typical customer reaction was: "Fantastic products and great design – but too expensive!" As a result, in July 1986 the parties agreed that Swedpartner should start manufacturing some of Norpartner's products under license for the Swedish market. According to Mr Swed, this fitted very well with his plans, since Swedpartner at that time had a significant surplus capacity in its production facilities.

At the same time, the sales of Swedpartner's product line took off in Norway through Norpartner. Norpartner's sales increased from NKR10.5 million to NKR16.5 million from 1986 to 1987. A new local sales office was also established in Oslo, with responsibility for the east Norwegian market.

In early 1986, Swedpartner's parent company, Swedconcern, started to put some pressure on Mr Swed regarding Swedpartner's profitability. According to Mr Swed, the administrators in Swedconcern were worried about the low profitability of Swedpartner. Furthermore, Mr Swed's direct contact, and supervisor, in Swedconcern was replaced. Mr Swed said that the "personal chemistry" between him and the new supervisor did not work at all. He explained how he felt: "The pressure to increase profitability was huge, and it was difficult to get an understanding of what we were doing. I argued for, and pursued, the existing strategy, but that was tough." At the same time, Mr Swed planned to acquire Swedpartner's major rival, Competitor. He was acquainted with the owners of Competitor, and he also knew that they were considering selling the company because of succession problems in the owner family. Mr Swed presented his plans to his parent company and argued that this was a "golden opportunity to structure the industry in Sweden." When Swedconcern initiated negotiations with Competitor in the fall of 1986, without the presence of Mr Swed, they discovered that the owner family had suddenly changed their minds and were not interested in selling the company.

By the end of 1986, the parties had produced three brochures presenting both companies' products and had been represented at several trade fairs in Sweden. In addition, Swedpartner was manufacturing some of Norpartner's products for the Swedish market.

In December 1986, Mr Swed perceived that Competitor was interested in acquiring Swedpartner and, after reporting this at a

Board meeting, the Board of Directors decided to initiate discussions with Competitor. However, Mr Swed was not asked to participate in these discussions at all – his supervisor from Swedconcern headed the negotiations. Mr Swed felt that the situation was very difficult, and as a consequence he applied for a new job: "It was difficult to act as Managing Director when I knew that the company was about to be sold to a competitor, and that we were simultaneously heavily involved with an important strategic alliance with Norpartner. Of course, I could not mention anything about this to the Norwegian team."

In March 1987, Mr Nor and Mr Swed signed a formal licensing agreement that set the rules for Swedpartner's extended manufacture of Norpartner's products. As a matter of fact, Norpartner became, more or less, dependent on Swedpartner's manufacturing capability to manufacture products for marketing in Norway. The six-page licensing agreement was seen by the participants as much more detailed in comparison with the earlier strategic alliance agreement. The licensing agreement had the same duration as the strategic alliance agreement of February 1986. Mr Nor felt that this agreement was very advantageous to both parties:

> The licensing agreement was a good deal for us, since we did not have to make large investments in new production facilities, but it was an even better deal for Swedpartner. The part of the total licensed production in Swedpartner that we were to bring back to Norway was equivalent to almost SEK10 million. This must be compared to Competitor AB's turnover of NKR5 million in Norway – after twenty years of hard work!

It should be noted that the agreement included several clauses covering penalties, delays, and termination of the agreement.

In April 1987, Swedconcern reached an unofficial agreement with Competitor that the latter company would acquire Swedpartner. As a result, Mr Swed was given new directives to suspend a number of employees in Swedpartner. However, he refused to do this since he had planned to use this labor for the licensed production of Norpartner's products that the companies had agreed upon one month earlier. Consequently, he resigned his position at Swedpartner.

For Mr Nor, this was the first indication that something was wrong in Swedpartner. However, since he did not know about the negotiations and subsequent agreement with Competitor, he did not act. Instead, he instantly acquired a new formal project leader in Swedpartner.

Mr Bye responded to Mr Swed's resignation from Swedpartner by calling for a meeting with Mr Nor and the SNI consultants in May 1988. It was concluded that all parties were to aim for a continuation of the strategic alliance.

By the end of June, 1987, a representative of Norpartner visited Swedpartner's new, temporary Managing Director, who was hired by Swedconcern. They agreed to continue the intensive cooperation between the two companies and agreed to meet again in August 1987. Three days later, on July 1 1987, it was announced that Swedpartner had been sold to Competitor.

The New Situation

Mr Nor learned about the acquisition during his vacation in France from one of Norpartner's sales representatives in Norway, who had received the information from Competitor's agent in Norway. Mr Bye was immediately informed by Mr Nor. Neither of them had received any information regarding the acquisition from Competitor or Swedpartner/Swedconcern. When Mr Bye contacted Swedconcern's top management, the deal was confirmed. Both Mr Nor and Mr Bye said that they were very disappointed that Swedconcern could pursue such a sale without notifying the other party – especially since this was a violation of the royalty agreement with SNI.

When Mr Nor and the owners of Competitor contacted each other it was decided that they should meet in August to discuss the strategic alliance between Norpartner and Swedpartner. During this meeting, it became clear that Competitor was not interested in the strategic alliance. Competitor's Managing Director explained how he viewed the new situation:

> First, our opinion was that the previous product development in Swedpartner was useless to us – there were a lot of ideas that were not businesslike. Second, the strategic alliance with Norpartner put us in a competitive situation with our agent in Norway. Consequently, this was of no interest to us. None the less, we would have fulfilled the delivery agreements with Norpartner, i.e., until the end of 1988.

Owing to the subsequent merger of the operations in Sweden in the autumn of 1987, Swedpartner had some production difficulties which resulted in delayed deliveries to Norpartner. This, in turn, resulted in complications for Norpartner in its market development and distribution, which resulted in declining sales income, which affected the company's cash-flow and profitability. In turn, this led to difficulties in fulfilling the financial obligations towards Swedpartner.

When it was evident that Competitor was not going to pursue the strategic alliance in accordance with the original intentions, Mr Bye and the consultant discussed SNI's role. They came to the conclusion that the agreement with SNI must be regarded as having been violated by the Swedish partner. Since the situation in Norpartner was uncertain, SNI stopped further payments on the approved financing in August 1987. It should be noted that Mr Bye and the consultants briefly discussed a temporary stop of further payments to the parties from July 1987, that is, when they learned about the acquisition, but this was very difficult since the agreement had not been officially broken.

When SNI withdrew their project financing to Norpartner, the company's bank became very worried about the company's financial situation. In addition, Competitor was demanding bank guarantees for their deliveries of products made under license from Swedpartner to Norpartner, which further strained Norpartner's financial situation. In spite of a change in management at Norpartner and a significant order reserve, by the end of 1987 the financial situation became worse. In January to March 1988, Norpartner's management first tried to negotiate for an agreement with the creditors, but one of the creditors did not accept the suggested solution. Second, the management tried to increase the company's capital base through equity input from the company's owners and the employees, which did not work out. Third, a subsidized loan from the national Norwegian Industrial Development Fund was applied for, which was not granted. In May 1988, Norpartner went bankrupt.

Today, Norpartner's activities have been taken over by the abovementioned creditor and two production managers in Norpartner.

Outcome

Mr Nor in Norpartner compared the situation with the theoretical "1+1>2" synergy effect of cooperative venturing. He felt that, since the strategic alliance was terminated in this abrupt way, the situation could be characterized as a "1+1=0" situation. Competitor, on the other hand, had acquired its largest competitor in Sweden, and also managed to wreck its largest

competitor in Norway. Hence, this could be characterized as a
"1−1=3" effect.

Mr Swed felt that Competitor's acquisition of Swedpartner was
the second best solution for Swedpartner. Since Competitor was
not interested in either the licensed production or the strategic
alliance as such, the result was disastrous for Norpartner. In
addition, a monopoly situation developed in the garden equipment industry in Scandinavia. He stressed that his resignation
was related to the change of management at Swedconcern: "it
was a matter of honour − Norpartner trusted me and when I was
overruled by my parent company, I did not want to be responsible
for other people's decisions."

Mr Swed's opinion was that nothing in the strategic alliance
agreement could have stopped the acquisition. Mr Nor said that
when the lawyers came in after the acquisition, they labelled the
strategic alliance agreement a letter-of-intent type of contract.

The estimated and achieved total costs for the two companies
as well as the financing obtained from SNI are summarized in
exhibit A7.4.

Competitor's Managing Director was very satisfied with the
acquisition, "since Swedconcern clearly wanted to get rid of
Swedpartner, we had an advantage in the negotiations. Consequently, our bid was not too high ..." He also stressed that the
market's response to the acquisition was very good.

Mr Bye felt that it was too bad that an interesting strategic
alliance failed through this unexpected acquisition. Everything
seemed to work, the personal chemistry, the sales, and the strategic alliance model as such. He realized, however, that the strategic alliance agreement was too general, but "SNI surely cannot
draw up the agreements for them!" Mr Bye argued that it is
necessary to be very careful with the strategic alliance agreements,
and include check points and penalty clauses. He also felt that
this strategic alliance demonstrated how important individual
persons might be for a strategic alliance, and how difficult it can
be to protect oneself, for instance, against a shift in management
and ownership.

Exhibit A7.4 Estimated costs, achieved costs, and SNI financing

		1985/6	1987	1988	Total
Norpartner A/S (Sept., 1985) (thousand NKR)					
Product development	budget	900	430	100	1,430
	outcome	1,200	300		1,500
Market development	budget	1,815	1,425	1,650	4,890
	outcome	1,100	600		1,700
Other costs	budget	380	550	750	1,680
	outcome	100	100		200
Total annual costs	budget	3,095	2,405	2,500	8,000
	outcome	2,400	1,000		3,400
SNI financing	budget	1,550	1,200	1,250	4,000
	outcome	1,200	500		1,700
Swedpartner AB (May 1986) (thousand SEK)					
Product development	budget	900	430	100	1,430
	outcome	600			600
Market development	budget	1,115	1,025	1,350	3,490
	outcome	400			400
Other costs	budget	380	550	750	1,680
	outcome	200			200
Total annual costs	budget	2,395	2,005	2,200	6,600
	outcome	1,200			1,200
SNI financing	budget	1,200	1,000	1,100	3,300
	outcome	600			600

Exhibit A7.5 Actor and event summary

Company	Name	Title
Norpartner A/S	Mr Nor	Project leader
	Mr Consult	Chairman of the Board
Swedpartner AB	Mr Swed	Managing Director 1983–87
Swedconcern AB		
Competitor AB		Managing Director
SNI	Mr Atle Bye	Managing Director Consultants

Event summary

Year	Month	Event
1985	May	Initial contact at a trade fair in Stockholm.
	June	First meeting between the parties.
	August	Second meeting between the parties. Meeting with SNI.
	September	Reporting of the feasibility study.
	October	Application to SNI.
	November	Consultants' report. SNI's Board of Directors decide to grant project financing
1986	May	Royalty agreement between SNI and the two partners.
	December	Swedconcern contacted Competitor AB regarding a potential acquisition of Competitor AB.

Exhibit 7.5 Continued

Event summary

Year	Month	Event
1987	January	Swedconcern contacted Competitor AB regarding a potential sale of Swedpartner to Competitor AB.
	March	Licensing agreement between Swedpartner and Norpartner.
	April	Unofficial agreement between Swedconcern and Competitor AB regarding the sale of Swedpartner. Swedpartner's Managing Director resigned.
	June	Meeting between Norpartner and Swedpartner's new Managing Director.
	July	Announcement of the sale of Swedpartner to Competitor AB.
	August	Competitor AB stated that it was not interested in the cooperative venture.
	September	SNI stopped further payments of the financing granted.
	November	Change in Norpartner's management.
1988	January–March	Negotiations for an agreement with Norpartner's creditors and reconstruction.
	May	Norpartner went into bankruptcy.

8
Emerging Challenges

Introduction

In this chapter we discuss the role of strategic alliances as part of global strategies. Strategic alliances are, of course, an integral part of international business, as we certainly have seen throughout this book. We have not, however, made a clear distinction earlier regarding what type of international strategic settings we are considering. Two types of international strategic settings are: (1) multidomestic, or doing business in several countries as more or less free-standing, country-based strategic entities, but based on some common technology, manufacturing, and/or marketing concept; and (2) global, or coordinating technology, manufacturing, and/or marketing activities among several countries, to achieve scale and/or scope advantages (Porter 1986). In this chapter we will discuss the global strategic setting and see how strategic alliances play an important role in the achievement of this type of potent, ultimate strategy.

It is important to understand, as we shall see, that global strategies are executed via strategic alliances in two fundamentally different ways. Leading firms may wish to pursue a global strategy if they can facilitate the development of a network of links with several local/native firms. Each of these links is on a one-to-one basis, but the total provides the dominant organizing firm with a global network analogous to a franchising network. Typically, it is the superior technology of the dominant partner that holds this network together. A second approach is for several prospective partners, with relatively equal and/or complementary strengths, to combine in a shared way in order to form a common global network with a strategy based on gives and takes from several firms.

In the previous chapter we discussed how strategic alliances evolve over time towards more or less free-standing entities. The two archetypes of global strategic alliances, dominant or shared, also follow evolutionary processes. In the first evolutionary phase, strategic alliances between multinational firms are often dominated by one partner. However, some of these alliances gradually evolve into more shared cooperation between two or several equal partners. The main reason for this is to gain political credibility in several key markets – a task hard to do through one company's dominance.

We shall not discuss the underlying reasons behind global firms or global alliances *per se*, except to underscore that striving to gain competitive advantage through scale and/or scope considerations may ultimately lead to one partner going global, particularly if one or more competitors have succeeded in doing so. A need to pay attention to local adaptation needs is often a dampening effect on gaining competitive advantage. This stems from political and/or consumer preferences. These issues have been abundantly discussed by other authors.[1]

Dominant and Shared Strategic Alliances

In a dominant global strategic alliance one partner is the distinct driving force behind the cooperative strategy in question, and each local partner is merely a participant with this firm in its particular country arena. The organizing partner may dominate the alliance in several ways. It may have a sustained relative advantage over its prospective partner(s) in terms of any part of the value chain (Porter 1985) by possessing a strong technology and/or a strong brand name, for example. This may result in specific scale and/or scope advantages on a global basis.

Coca Cola, with its protected secret syrup ingredients and its strong global brand and image, is clearly dominating its franchise-based alliances worldwide, through both scale and scope advantages. Another example of this type of alliance can be found in the early phase of the strategic alliance between Hitachi Construction Machinery, and FiatGeotech (for the European market), and John Deere (for the North American market) in hydraulic excavators. Hitachi was the dominant player through its technological advantage, particularly in hydraulic systems, which it also manufactures for its partners. Here Hitachi enjoys a scale advantage (See Appendix to this chapter.)

A third example is Arco Chemicals. This firm has strong patent protection in a particular chemical component and process technology. It has a series of local joint ventures in various Far Eastern countries with a number of partners to manufacture and distribute in each local market an ingredient for gasoline. Here Arco Chemicals enjoys a scale advantage in R&D. Of course, when the firm owns its own brand and has a proprietary technology as well, such as Coca-Cola, it is possible to obtain both scale and scope advantages – a particularly advantageous situation.

We can see from these examples that a dominant strategic alliance can have strong similarities to a franchising system, where the dominant partner is the systems designer and integrator. Each local partner will have to live with something analogous to a franchising package. This very explicit global dominant strategic alliance design does not, however, have to be the only example of a global dominant strategic alliance. This is illustrated in the following paragraphs.

The development into a global structure of the Japanese consumer electronics industry provides an interesting evolutionary picture of how to use strategic alliances to advantage. In a first step towards globalization several of these firms gained scale advantages through extensive use of OEM agreements with partner firms in Europe and in the US. In fact, the aim was not so much to achieve market share *per se* but, rather, to gain global manufacturing volume, or scale advantages (Prahalad and Doz 1987). In a second step, after the scale advantage had been established, these firms moved downstream toward the market, pushing their own brands based on the companies' ability to now offer a high quality product at low cost – using scale advantage in the pursuit of scope. In this example we see how an informal, temporal and only in part strategic alliance ultimately can lead to global strategic advantages.

A strategic alliance may, of course, also be motivated by the fact that a particular host country insists on local participation.

Examples of such practices can be found in several south-east Asian countries, in India, in Mexico, and in several other parts of the world. Here, the local partner may become part of a network that, consists, in part, of wholly-owned subsidiaries and, in part, of joint ventures.

It may also be practical to have local participation because of entirely different local business practices in a given country. Local contacts, access to governmental relations, etc., may be very important and hard to gain unless done through a local partner, as in particular countries in the Middle East or Asia.

In the commercial airline industry we see how Scandinavian Airline Systems (SAS) has turned the potential disadvantage of a small home country base into an offensive global strategy. The airline has a small, peripheral home base with weak bargaining clout on landing rights. Still, it has managed to orchestrate a network of strategic alliances through its links with British Air Holdings, Finnair, and Swissair in Europe; with All Nippon and Thai in Asia; and with Continental, Canadian Pacific, and Lan Chile in America. This has allowed SAS to offer its passengers one-stop services to most parts of the world with a minimum waiting time. To further strengthen its ability to serve its business customers, SAS has also developed a worldwide hotel chain mostly through strategic alliances with local hotels but also through a 40 percent ownership stake in Intercontinental Hotels.[2]

Having an ownership stake in a network partner is a practice that SAS seems to follow when it can. Swissair and Finnair also have the potential to gain an ownership stake in SAS. Such cross-ownership arrangements have particularly strong stabilizing effects on a cooperative network. We see that SAS has been able to create a global strategy by means of putting together a series of strategic alliances into its own overall meta-system. This is a global position which would have otherwise been impossible to achieve because of regulatory constraints, resource limitations, and time.

The archetype of a global dominant strategic alliance between firms based in different home countries is depicted in exhibit 8.1. We see how firm A has linked itself through separate bilateral arrangements with firms B and C. The total of all of this becomes a global network for A. However, it remains a bilateral, two-company relationship for each of the other firms.

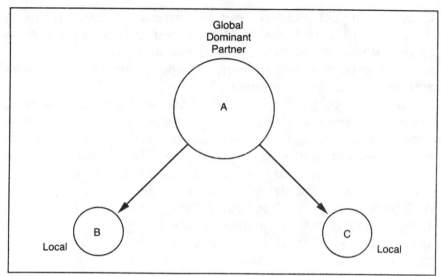

Exhibit 8.1 Global dominant strategic alliance network.

We may, of course, have situations when various substantial parties have different prospective complementary roles in a global strategic alliance, and where dominance by one partner may not be acceptable or appropriate. Strong firms may complement each other in co-developing and sharing new technologies, co-developing and sharing new products, and sharing markets. An example of this, although not entirely based on strategic alliances between separately-owned firms, but rather between different entities in a large multinational conglomerate, is General Electric's global medical equipment business. In the US organization, large and complex computer tomography (CT) scanners are developed and manufactured. In Japan, lighter and less expensive CT-scanners are developed and manufactured through the joint venture with Yokogawa Electric, Yokogawa Medical Systems. In Europe, the French-based Thompson, an acquisition, develops and manufactures the complementary ultrasound equipment. Taken together the three product lines represent one complete range of products and services. All three organizations sell this complete range in their home continents.

The archetype of a global shared strategic alliance between three firms in different home countries is depicted in exhibit

8.2. Here, the three partners (A,B,C) complement each other by offering technologies and products that, taken together, may represent a superior range of offerings. The parties also represent the other two in their own home territory, selling the entire range of products and/or services.

The Emergence of Shared Global Strategic Alliances

The dominant type of strategic alliance has a number of advantages over the shared type. For one, it represents a quick way to implement a global strategy that might be more difficult to do with equal partners. To go it alone might not be an option. It definitely can be easier to adapt locally by means of a strategic alliance with a local partner. Indeed, this mode represents a true transnational that can often provide a capability for better general political adaptability; a firm can be both local and global

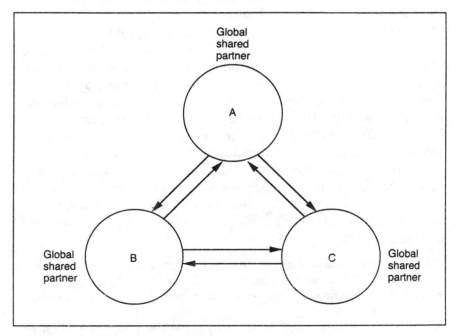

Exhibit 8.2 Global shared strategic alliance network.

whenever needed. It can be easier to obtain a first mover advantage by using dominant strategic alliances.

Typically, it will be an advantage for the dominant partner to maintain this type of an alliance over time, but the local partners may come to see it differently. Several factors, however, contribute to keep the alliance intact. It may be hard for the local partner to develop its own full-scale advantages. FiatGeotech, for example, would have had a hard time manufacturing the hydraulic components for its excavators on its own, and would not have been able to achieve sufficient scale in its own operations. In fact, Hitachi Construction Machinery, the Japanese partner, does supply the key components for the hydraulics systems, thus preventing the joint venture from developing full integrated scale advantages.

The dominant partner may also have the capability to continue developing its scale and/or scope advantages through maintaining a strong technology, new products that the partners can see are in the pipeline, extensive OEM agreements, and/or integrating itself with the partner. Also, of course, continued maintenance of its brands and image can be an important factor in preserving a partner's dominant role.

For this type of strategic alliance it is important to institute extensive planning and control, so the various parties can cooperate in developing common plans and control of the strategic alliance. In fact, we may want to adopt planning and control practices similar to those we see in wholly-owned global strategies as used by well established multinational firms such as ICI, IBM, and DuPont. The coordination tasks in such global strategic alliances can be formidable.

It is difficult to see how such alliances can continue to perform well if the dominant partner remains over an extended period of time. We see several different reasons for deterioration, all of which lead to the creation of gradually more and more shared strategic alliances:

- Lack of territorial discipline, that is, the dominant partner may have little control over exports from a local partner
- Easing of resource inputs – the dominant partner can no longer afford this role
- The local learning from the dominant partner is accomplished and it is no longer needed as extensively.

We will elaborate on each of these issues.

First, it may be difficult to control the sales activities of a local strategic alliance and get the partner to stay within a certain local territory. A partner will often want to export, particularly if there is excess capacity. This may, however, infringe on the global marketing rationale of the dominant partner. Caterpillar, for instance, created a joint venture with Mitsubishi in Japan in 1963, primarily to serve the local market. This joint venture developed a high quality line of products at reasonable prices. At some point, the joint venture decided to export some of its products to British Columbia which was an infringement of the territorial agreement and created temporary stress in the strategic alliance. As previously mentioned, Arco Chemicals has joint ventures with separate local partners in Korea, Japan, Thailand, Taiwan, and Indonesia.Each of these joint ventures has manufacturing plants with installed capacity just large enough to supply its local markets. Through careful capacity planning in each of the joint ventures, Arco Chemicals hopes to avoid a situation where one local partner might wish to look at exporting in order to utilize unused capacity. This latter scenario would, of course, create potential problems vis-à-vis Arco Chemicals' other local joint venture partners, who might suffer from disturbances in their local markets which would create competitive instability in the overall marketing of Arco Chemicals gasoline additives worldwide.

Second, when it comes to resource inputs, the domineering partner might not be able to afford the necessary investments to dominate a partnership over an extended period of time. This can lead to the easing of the dominance role by welcoming more resources, or intensive inputs, from former local partners. For example, Xerox Corporation developed a dominant global strategic alliance network through its joint ventures with Rank Xerox (for Europe) and Fuji Xerox (for the Far East). The alliance included the development of new products and technologies. Over time the partner organizations have taken on added roles in product development; not least because of a need to share the extensive costs of research. Today Fuji Xerox is, in many ways, an equal partner with Xerox. The strategic alliance network has evolved into a shared one.

Finally, we consider the effects of learning on the development of a strategic alliance. Extensive learning from a partner may lead to an adjustment in roles. For instance, General Motors' extensive job-rotation program in NUMMI, their California based strategic alliance with Toyota, may gradually lead to a lessening of General Motors' dependence on the Japanese partner. If not, one should expect more shared roles, or the termination of the alliance may result. Strong firms may complement each other in co-developing and sharing new technologies, co-developing and sharing new products, and/or sharing markets. Realistically, it is hard to see how one partner can sustain dominance over time.

Management of Global Shared Strategic Alliances

From the previous discussion we see that global strategic alliances, where one partner is dominant, often evolve into network constellations where the roles become more balanced. We refer to this constellation as globally-shared strategic alliances.

We see two fundamentally different approaches to the management of global shared alliances. The first approach is to have in place a conventional management team which runs the alliance on behalf of the partners as if it was an integrated freestanding firm. An example of this is the merger-like strategic alliance that was formed in 1987 between the Swedish-based ASEA and Brown Bovery of Switzerland (ABB). ABB became a giant overnight in the electrotechnology industry. Each parent continues to exist, but owns 50 percent each in the strategic alliance. The management team consists of senior executives from both partners, located in a neutral location, running the alliance as if it were one company. Another example is SAS. Each national airline in this alliance is 50 percent publicly held and 50 percent owned by each local government. This strategic alliance is also run as if it was an independent company.

A second approach is to manage the alliance more as a network of truly involved partners, with each playing an active and complementary role. An example of this is the evolutionary development of the FiatGeotech–Hitachi Construction Machinery–John Deere strategic alliance (see Appendix). As noted previously, Hitachi has been playing a dominant role owing to its technological lead in the hydraulics area. Each of the three parties has primary responsibility for the marketing activities in the continent in which it is are located: Asia, Europe, and North America. Each party also has increasingly taken on particular R&D responsibilities, the results of which will be shared among all parties. Manufacturing of hydraulic excavators is done in two joint venture facilities in Europe and North America. However, other manufacturing activities might be done by each party on an OEM basis for all the others. A relatively balanced network of give and take has, therefore, gradually emerged. Hitachi undoubtedly has played a major role in forming this network, and might have been seen as the dominant partner during the initial stages. Over time, a more shared network seems to have emerged.

Summary

When it comes to global strategic alliances, there seem to be several advantages which can make such arrangements prototypes for successful future global firms. First, such alliances represent a vehicle that can create scale and/or scope advantages necessary to be competitive on a global basis against wholly-owned global firms. This strategic alliance alternative also requires fewer resources and can be put together in a shorter time than a wholly-owned global strategic organization. Second, the global strategic alliance approach allows for local identity, in that local partners from various parts of the world are involved, thereby giving the strategic alliance more of an adaptive clout vis-à-vis the various national environments. This can give the strategic alliance an advantage over wholly-owned global business organizations.

The wholly-owned alternative to a global dominant strategic alliance is a multidomestic strategy. Here, certain potential scale and/or scope advantages have been traded off against a strengthened ability to adapt in the various local environments. Many multinationals may wish to evolve their wholly-owned multidomestic structure towards a more globally integrated set of businesses, so as to achieve further scale and/or scope advantages. They may, however, be slowed down in making such moves due to local resistance and local requirements for adaptation. A global shared strategic alliance may be able to avoid local resistance while still being positioned to capture the global scale/scope advantages.

A globally-shared strategic alliance has the possibility both to achieve scale and/or scope advantages and to have the local adaptation characteristics in tact. This may ultimately be a more feasible organizational form than the wholly-owned global strategy alternative.

Appendix
FiatGeotech–Hitachi Construction Machinery[1]

Introduction

Fiat S.p.A. of Turin, Italy, with 1989 sales of more than $40 billion, was one of Europe's leading industrial groups. One of its wholly-owned divisions, FiatGeotech, produced and marketed tractors, combine harvesters and harvesting equipment under the Fiatagri brand, as well as bulldozers, loaders, excavators, and other construction equipment under the FiatGeotech brand. In 1989, net consolidated revenues of FiatGeotech were $2.3 billion with the Farm Equipment Division generating $1.5 billion, and the Construction Machinery Division $795 million. In 1989, Construction Machinery Division subsidiaries sold 7,800 units (a 7 percent increase from 1988). FiatGeotech's market share, on a global basis, rose from 6 percent to 7 percent, increasing from 8.5 percent to 11 percent in Europe.

After a peak in the late 1970s, the global structure of the earth-moving machinery (EMM) industry changed dramatically in the early 1980s. The general recession in the Western countries, the large debts of Third World countries, and the crisis in the oil-producing countries, resulted in a significant decrease in public works investments and large construction. The core business shifted towards maintenance, services, and city works, away from major greenfield construction activities. The crisis also shifted the relative importance of various product lines of EMMs towards smaller, and lighter, machines.

With a mature industry, with strong global competitors such

as Caterpillar and Komatsu, with strongly competitive markets characterized by overcapacity and low margins, FiatGeotech re-examined its strategy. Could it realistically continue to pursue its own full EMM line strategy – or was this becoming prohibitive in terms of resources that would be required? The outcome of these deliberations was the pursuance of a cooperative strategy. At the same time, Hitachi Construction Machinery Company (HCM) was actively searching for a joint venture partner in Europe in order to avoid anticipated increasing European protectionism and to increase further its market share. In January, 1987, the two firms established a joint venture in Italy, Fiat–Hitachi Excavator, S.p.A., to manufacture and market hydraulic excavators.

The present case study takes its starting point in a brief historical description of the earth-moving machinery industry and its globalization. Then follows a discussion of FiatGeotech and its relatively weak competitive situation in the early 1980s. We then discuss how the company came to pursue a cooperative strategy and delineate FiatGeotech and Hitachi's approach to forming such a joint venture. Finally, the joint venture's operations during its early stages are discussed.

Evolution of The Earth Moving Machinery Industry

The EMM industry in Europe took off in the late 1940s. The main product then was, in principle, an adapted agricultural tractor, and the markets were national. Based on the band wagon concept, the first bull-dozers and crawler loaders were introduced. In general, the machines had relatively weak engines, only 40–50 hp. The machines were typically sold and distributed through the same marketing channels as agricultural tractors. Caterpillar arrived in Europe with the US Army, and another strong US manufacturer, Allis Chalmers, was also becoming known. At that time, Fiat had only a agricultural tractor division, where simple EMMs were manufactured.

During the 1950s, the EMMs were still derived from the agricultural tractor, but the number of models had increased. The postwar reconstruction of Italy resulted in a strong domestic demand, and Fiat produced approximately two thousand units per year. Fiat introduced the 60/C, FL/6, and AD/7 models and began to market its product in other European countries. At that time, the European market was still visited, but by some international competition and the major US suppliers, and no Japanese companies.

In the 1960s, product development took off in earnest and the EMMs no longer had much similarity to the agricultural tractor. The distribution channels were also becoming different, new dealers were appointed, and new assembly branches were opened in France and in Germany. The international competition was increasing. Fiat's presence in Europe increased and the annual production was some eight thousand units. In 1964, Fiat acquired 60 percent of a smaller Italian manufacturer of excavators.

In the 1970s, the world market for EMMs reached its highest level ever. In 1979, a total of 198,000 units per year was produced, in several product lines. Of this, Fiat produced some ten thousand units. The production know-how was mainly American, particularly when it came to larger machines, such as bull-dozers and wheel loaders. In the mid-1970s, however, the two Japanese firms Komatsu and Hitachi also aggressively started to manufacture bull-dozers and excavators. The degree of internationalization further increased and global marketing presence became more and more of a must. As a consequence of the pressure to be present in the US market, Fiat formed a Chicago-based joint venture with Allis Chalmers in 1974. The purpose was mainly to develop and manufacture larger EMMs, and Fiat was to own 74 percent and Allis Chalmers 26 percent of the joint venture. Through the joint venture, Fiat was able to complement its product lines with wheel loaders, large bull-dozers, scrapers, and graders. Hence, Fiat could now finally offer a more or less full line of EMMs. Severe demand turn-downs in the markets served by the joint venturer, coupled with a number of unexpected management problems, led to disappointing performance for the joint venture, however. A massive attempt to turn its performance around failed, and in 1985 Fiat had to acquire the remaining Allis Chalmers's share of the joint venture as part of a general salvaging effort. This led to a restructuring and scaling-down of the latter firm's activities.

Changes in the Competitive Situation

In the early 1980s, the situation in the EMM industry became even more fiercely competitive. Demand declined rapidly, with 1983 being the worst year. The main reasons for this recession were the general recession in the Western countries, the debt crisis in the Third World, and the slow-down crisis in the oil-producing countries due to depressed oil prices.

In general, the recession had two major effects on the EMM industry. First, there was a dramatic decrease in public works investments and large greenfield construction projects in the world, which in turn resulted in a significant drop in large contractors' demand for EMMs, particularly when it came to heavy equipment. The global production of EMMs fell from some 200,000 units in 1979 to fewer than 150,000 units in 1983, a decrease of more than 25 percent in a few years. Even though production increased somewhat after 1983, the high levels of sales from the late 1970s did not come back until 1988. It should be noted, however, (see exhibit A8.1) that the main markets did not all decline, or recover at the same rate.

In addition, not only were fewer EMMs needed, but these were also typically smaller and, consequently, represented less value per unit. One result of this new situation was that many EMM manufacturers left the industry: Massey Ferguson withdrew in 1981, IBH in 1984, and International Harvester in 1985. The recession also changed the relative importance and size of the product lines in the industry. As can be seen from exhibit A8.2, excavators and backhoe loaders, these being typically smaller vehicles, became relatively more important. The volume of wheel loaders remained approximately the same.

The excavators and backhoe loaders gradually became the two most important product lines in the industry, while bulldozers and crawler loaders lost ground. The composition of demand by products did, however, also differ between the major geographic areas, as can be seen from exhibit A8.3. These differences reflect underlying variances in infrastructure, the construction industry's structure and practices, and economic climates.

Globalization of the EMM Industry

In the early 1980s, the EMM industry accelerated in its evolution to become even more global. There were at least four reasons for this. First, the industry had become more capital intensive and less labor intensive. This was primarily due to the need for increasingly sophisticated robotization. Consequently, this increased the industry's need for capital. Second, the level of technical development was accelerating quickly. It was necessary to increase R&D spending significantly in order to keep at par with the competition. Third, it increasingly became necessary

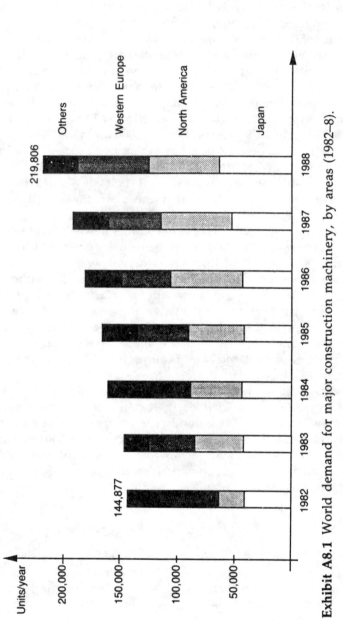

Exhibit A8.1 World demand for major construction machinery, by areas (1982–8).

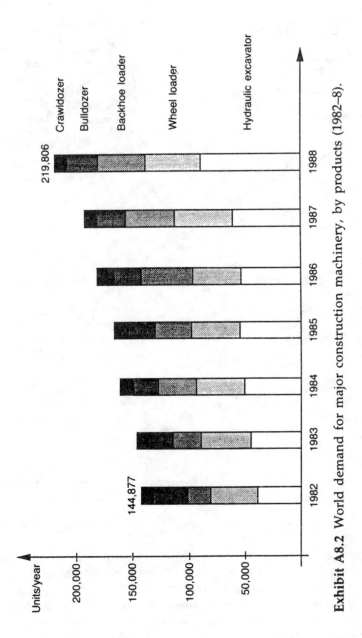

Exhibit A8.2 World demand for major construction machinery, by products (1982–8).

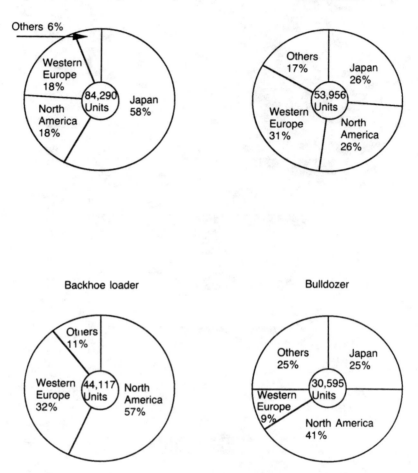

Exhibit A8.3 World demand for major construction machinery, by products and areas (1988).

to be able to offer a full line of EMMs. Customers often purchased several types of EMMs; therefore, it was preferable that all equipment could be supplied by one manufacturer, through one distributor, and with a standardized service function and aftermarket support to back it up. Finally, there was no longer much difference between EMMs offered in various parts of the world, the product had become global, and global scale and scope advantages were increasingly needed to succeed.

Over time, it became more and more obvious that it was necessary to be present in all three major trading blocks in order to survive. Marketing-wise, one of the key issues was to be recognized as a local company in each of these markets. Of all the players in the industry, only Caterpillar had fully succeeded in gaining this image.

Caterpillar was the major global company in the industry. The company was the major actor in the US and European markets and was also present in Japan through a joint venture with Mitsubishi. The second largest manufacturer, Komatsu, was also global, and had manufacturing facilities in Europe and the US in addition to its home base.

Exhibit A8.4 gives a list of the major EMM manufacturers and their involvement in the four major product line categories. As can also be seen from this, there are a number of collaborative arrangements among major companies to allow them to be able to serve a fuller line within affordable resource limits. Fiat ranked third in the world among EMM manufacturers excluding the Caterpillar–Mitsubishi joint venture. The sales volumes for each product indicate clearly also that after the big two there are a number of much smaller producers, each likely to struggle to provide a global line as an economically viable business undertaking.

The relative leadership position and degree of dominance differed among the firms regarding major product categories. Caterpillar, for instance, had always been an undisputed leader in the bulldozer segment, but had been relatively weaker in hydraulic excavators. Until 1975, the technological leadership in excavators has been European, with Poclain and Leibher as leading companies. At the same time as the European market was declining in the late 1970s, the Japanese market had increased significantly. The Japanese manufacturers of hydraulic excavators, dominated by Hitachi Construction Machinery and Mitsubishi, had started with technical license from European companies in the 1960s. Over time, the technological edge had, however, shifted towards these Japanese companies.

Alliances were formed between partners from all three major trading blocks. The cooperative agreement between Caterpillar and Mitsubishi, the entrance of Komatsu on the European market, and the increasing presence of Hitachi in Europe, made the future situation of a firm such as FiatGeotech very delicate.

Exhibit A8.4

	Construction machinery sales (billion Yen)	Bulldozer	Hydraulic excavator	Wheel loader	Dump truck	Remarks
Caterpillar	1,070	Own development	Collaboration with Mitsubishi	Own development	Own development	Worldwide full line manufacturer
Komatsu	450	Own development	Own development	Own development	Own development	Worldwide full line manufacturer Collaboration with Dresser
Shin Caterpillar Mitsubishi	290	Own development	Own development	Own development	Own development	Subsidiary of Caterpillar and Mitsubishi Heavy Industries
Fiat	285 (agricultural machinery included)	Own development	Collaboration with Hitachi	Own development	–	Worldwide full line manufacturer
Case	250	Own development	Invest to Poclain	Own development	–	Worldwide full line manufacturer
Hitachi Construction Machinery	220	–	Own development	Joint development with John Deere & Furukawa	–	Promoting sales mainly with hydraulic excavators in world
John Deere	450	Own development	Collaboration with Hitachi	Joint development with Hitachi & Furukawa	–	Sales of full line products mainly in North America
VME	450	–	Invest to Ackerman	Volvo Clark	Volvo Eucrid	Worldwide full line manufacturer

FiatGeotech Position

The competitive situation of FiatGeotech was that of a not quite global, medium-size, full line manufacturer with a strong base in the domestic Italian market. Owing to the fact that the company offered a full line of products, its position was also relatively strong on some international markets, notably in several European countries and in Brazil. Its manufacturing plants for EMMs were located in Italy, in Brazil, in the UK, and in the US – the latter a consequence of the joint venture with Allis Chalmers in 1974.

By the mid-1980s, FiatGeotech had significantly restructured its manufacturing activities in the UK and in the US, as well as in the production units in Italy. Plants were consolidated, modernized, or closed down. The product lines were also modernized and simplified. Certain models were phased out.

In the excavator segment, FiatGeotech was a medium-sized European manufacturer with an annual production of some 1000 excavators. Its competitive position in the Italian home market had traditionally become strong, but was perceived as weakening, and it was weaker in most of the other European markets. Even though the excavators had the reputation of having relatively good quality, the line was still not sufficiently technically sophisticated to compete effectively with the other leading EMM manufacturers such as Caterpillar and Komatsu. The company had problems in living up to the need for accelerated technical development, and had estimated that it would only have capacity to develop one new model per year. The technological gap between FiatGeotech excavators and those of the major competitors was thus rapidly widening. Further, one core component of the strategically critical and sophisticated hydraulic system was not manufactured within the Fiat Group, but had to be purchased from competitors. Only Caterpillar, Hitachi, and Komatsu manufactured their own hydraulic systems. This gave them distinctive advantages in quality and costs. It should be noted that FiatGeotech had never taken an interest in manufacturing such hydraulic systems, because of its own recognition of its size limitation.

It was becoming increasingly difficult to find the internal resources within FiatGeotech to be able to compete with the emerging strong competitors and strategic alliances in a viable long-term perspective. This led its management team to start considering seeking out strategic alliance themselves. It took a lot of agonizing discussions to reach this stage, given the negative experiences the group had had with its joint venture with Allis

Chalmers. Increasingly, there were three main reasons that made FiatGeotech management conclude that the company would have either to withdraw from the hydraulic evacuator segment of the EMM industry or to upgrade its lines through a cooperative strategy:

- the requirements to be global in this industry
- the costs of the necessary technical improvements of the products
- the emerging cooperative tendencies among the other main actors

A Joint Venture with Hitachi Construction Machinery (HCM)

In April, 1986, a delegation from the Sumitomo Group visited FiatGeotech. Prior to this meeting, Fiat's Vice-Chairman, Dr U. Agnelli, had contacts with the Chairman of the Sumitomo Group. During this visit, executives from both companies discussed Fiat-Geotech problems and possibilities, including the desire to find a joint venture partner. These discussions were relatively detailed.

At that time, HCM produced annually some 15,000 hydraulic excavators. These were generally sophisticated, with very advanced technology. Owing to its advanced technical know-how and experience, HCM's overall competitive position in the domestic Japanese market was very strong. As already noted from exhibit A8.3, the Japanese market in this EMM segment was much larger than both the European and the American markets together. It was dominated by HCM, Komatsu, and Mitsubishi. HCM exported some one thousand excavators per year to Europe, approximately equal to FiatGeotech's total European sales.

Several reasons had, however, also made HCM interested in considering a cooperative strategy. The company ultimately wanted to be able to offer a full line of EMMs. There was also a strong wish to increase its global market shares of its existing excavator products. This was, however, seen as increasingly difficult, not only because of the emergence of the EEC, but also because of increasing European protectionism in the form of anti-dumping tariffs of 12–32 percent on Japanese goods in the excavator segment. In conclusion, the company decided to search for a joint venture between FiatGeotech and HCM's partner in Europe. Initial discussions with VME (Volvo/Clark) did not materialize in any cooperative agreement, however.

During May and June, 1986, Sumitomo discussed the possibilities of a joint venture between FiatGeotech and HCM. In July, 1986, FiatGeotech's top management went to Japan and was introduced to HCM by Sumitomo, and a letter-of-intent was signed between the parties. Dr P. Sighicelli, who subsequently became President of the joint venture, remembered that Sumitomo took an active role as catalyst in the negotiations, and thereby helped the parties overcome initial negotiation difficulties. This was seen as particularly helpful given the fact that the parties had virtually no in-depth prior experience with each other. HCM's management team, in particular, had come to put a lot of emphasis on knowing its partner and developing a deep two-way trust. Its long-term cooperation with John Deere had contributed to this (see exhibit A8.4). Despite such prior relationships the parties decided to go ahead.

At that time, FiatGeotech had contemplated building a new manufacturing plant for excavators on its own. HCM did not have a plant in Europe. It became obvious that, through a joint venture, the parties could both share in risks, investments, and future development.

The joint venture, Fiat–Hitachi Excavator S.p.A., was established in November, 1986, with a new plant in San Mauro outside Turin. Ultimately, the plans were to manufacture between 2,500 and 3,000 units of 12 to 45 ton hydraulic excavators for the European market, Mediterranean basin, and some African countries. The excavators were to be marketed through an integrated sales organization under FiatGeotech responsibility. In principle, both parent companies were to withdraw as separate players from these markets. They were to meet the competition jointly through the joint venture.

FiatGeotech owned 51 percent, with four Board Members, Hitachi had a 44 percent ownership share with two Board Members, and Sumitomo a 5 percent share with one Board Member. The staffing of the joint venture was almost exclusively Italian. In addition to the President, Mr Sighicelli, Mr K. Ogimoto from HCM served as the Executive Vice-President, with responsibility for technology. Between seven and ten additional executives were assigned to the joint venture from HCM at different times, all functioning as technological advisers. Sumitomo's role was to be responsible for importation of key components from HCM to Italy. Exhibit A8.5 provides a summary of the joint venture's activities.

Based on its initial performance, the joint venture turned out, by most measures, to be a success. The San Mauro plant was set up in a way similar to a typical Hitachi plant, and high quality levels – at par with Japanese standards – were achieved for the

Exhibit A8.5 The joint venture's activities in Europe and America

	Deere–Hitachi Construction Machinery Corporation	Fiat–Hitachi Excavators S.p.A.
Business	Production and sale of hydraulic excavators	Production and sale of hydraulic excavators
Company foundation	May, 1988	November, 1986
Scale of business	Billion Yen	Billion Lire

Year	1989	1991	1988	1989	1991
Sales	35.5[a]	41.7[a]	163	224	321
Units	208	3,400	1,462	1,943	2,600

	Deere–Hitachi Construction Machinery Corporation	Fiat–Hitachi Excavators S.p.A.
Sales territories	North, Central, and South America	All European Mediterranean countries & Africa
Capital	$30.8 million (¥4.3 billion)	73.8 billion Lire
Share	Deere 50%, Hitachi 50%	Fiat 51%, Hitachi 49%
Employees	140	775

[a]Includes both imported machines and local production

products. The productivity levels were also at par with Japanese standards. A key reason for this was the extensive investments in state-of-the-art robotics.

Both parties felt that the duration of the joint venture contract would have to be long, in order for such a strategic alliance to work. Both parties recognized that they contributed important complementary inputs to the joint venture, thereby justifying the fairness of benefits. HCM continued to provide the most advanced technology, enabling the joint venture to produce the most competitive and reliable machines. FiatGeotech on the other hand was responsible for marketing, including after-sales service and spare parts supply, as well as the overall management of the joint venture. A potential problem – the integration of dealers in Europe – was resolved in an amicable way. The basic principle was to make use of both dealership organizations wherever these were complementing each other, and to choose the strrongest dealer where there would be duplication. The costs of dealer integration were shared in proportion to the capital contributions to the joint venture.

The marketplace responded very favorably to the new product. Demand was indeed so strong that the plant's capacity had to be increased.

Cooperation between HCM and Deere

In May, 1988, HCM and Deere signed a joint venture agreement to produce hydraulic excavators in North America. Hitachi had been the original equipment manufacturer/supplier for Deere for many years, and the two organizations thus knew each other well. It was therefore felt that as combination of a long cooperation, the two parties should enter into this joint, more binding, venture agreement. The particulars of the Hitachi Deere joint venture are

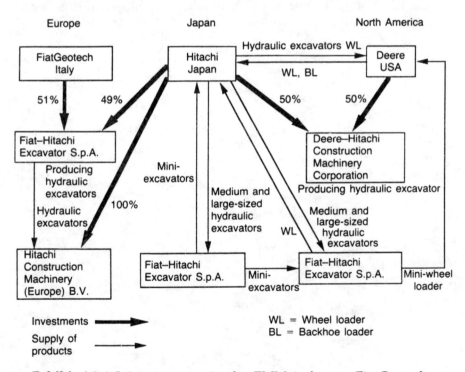

Exhibit A8.6 Joint ventures in the EMM industry: FiatGeotech, Hitachi, and John Deere.

shown in exhibit A8.5. HCM executives reflected on the fact that in retrospect it had indeed been quite easy for them to get involved in this joint venture with Deere given their long-term relationship. In contrast, they felt that the joint venture with FiatGeotech, where the parties had not known each other for any considerable length of time, had been a tougher choice to make. Despite this, however, HCM executives felt that the FiatGeotech joint venture had developed extremely well.

With the joint ventures with Deere and FiatGeotech, HCM had indeed developed a global network of cooperation. This is delineated in exhibit A8.6.

A further development along this pattern of global cooperation was an agreement signed in November, 1989 between Deere and FiatGeotech to jointly develop a backhoe loader based on joint research. Another agreement was signed with Deere which called fo the development of new medium-sized track-type loaders and bulldozers. This perhaps signaled the emergence of a more inte-grated pattern of global cooperation between these three strong players, not only within the hydraulic excavator segment but within the EMM industry as a whole.

PART V
Conclusions and Implications

9
Conclusions

Introduction

In this book we have examined the role of strategic alliances as a strategic vehicle. The strategic alliance is positioned between traditional wholly-owned organizations on the one hand and market-based interaction among several firms on the other. We have seen that there are many types of strategic alliances, and we have proposed that decision-makers should make specific choices regarding strategic alliance type, based on the particular strategic position at hand as well as on the resource base that can be drawn on. Several aspects of strategic alliances have been analyzed both through the text and through case studies. The purpose has been to discuss strategic rationales, how these are formed, implemented, and evolve. Key questions now, in conclusion, are: What are the new and important insights? Are strategic alliances something new, or merely old wine in a new bottle?

We feel that certain types of strategic alliances, such as joint ventures, have at times been focused on as something unique, and relatively out of context from mainstream strategic analysis and processes. Many strategy theorems are based on developing competitive advantage, often implying a win–lose proposition regarding the outcome for the two actors involved, implying adversary interests. In reality, however, when one examines the direction among various parties in business life and sees various actors as elements of a larger network of interaction, one finds that there is much more of a cooperative stance, and gets a quite typical picture of what many aspects of strategic management are all about. As such, the present book does not offer anything radically new; it merely provides a way to analyze how decision-makers can articulate and implement strategies within cooperative networks.

Still, with this book, we feel that we have offered several important insights into how strategic alliances get formed and operate. Even though not all of our insights are new, they confirm ideas that, so far, seem to have been tentative. The insights can be grouped into four areas:

- In contemplating how to determine what might be one of the many types of strategic alliances to go for, a contingency-based network should be applied, focusing first on the business position that the strategic alliance is part of (internal strategic importance and external strategic strength being the major considerations), and second on input/output of resources to/from a potential strategic alliance.
- The formation of a strategic alliance takes place as a multi-step, gradual process, leading up to a commitment to go for an alliance over time, rather than being a clear-cut decision-making phenomenon, where analytical and political dimensions both play important roles.
- Strategic alliances tend to be a means to an end, in that they always tend to evolve towards something else, making important issues that impact the evolution of a strategic alliance such as control processes, human resource considerations, concerns for maintaining or even building core competencies, and cross-cultural issues.
- The pursuit of strategic alliances as a strategic management mode is an advanced, complicated way of executing strategies, requiring a keen understanding of how to handle a series of typical problems as well as an ability to sort out major challenges that also tend to emerge.

In short, we have developed a view of cooperative strategies that underscores the importance of viewing strategic alliances as a dynamic phenomenon, that recognizes the strategic intent of both parties as the driving force behind it, and that recognizes that strategic alliances in many ways can be a particularly offensive tool for firms with ambitions in the global arena – offering opportunities both to gain scale and/or scope advantages and to keep a profile adapted to local conditions.

A Contingency-based View

The fact that we have taken a contingency-based view regarding the choice of appropriate form for a strategic alliance has several important implications. First, it underscores the fact that no particular type of strategic alliance is better or universally more correct than others; what matters is to make the appropriate choice of strategic alliance form, given the particular conditions at hand. One cannot say, for instance, that a full-blown joint venture is universally more desirable than a loose, ad hoc pool type of venture.

Second, rather than one set of contingency considerations to consider for determining the choice of strategic alliance form, we have proposed that there are actually two different sets of contingency-based considerations that should be assessed in sequence in order to arrive at the particular recommended form of alliance. A first consideration is to assess properly the strategic positioning context within which the contemplated deal might be classified. Here, one critical issue is whether a particular party considers the proposed deal one where it already has a dominant business position or whether the business position at the outset is quite weak. Further, it will be important to consider whether a particular strategy is part of a central strategic thrust for the firm as a whole, when considering its overall portfolio, or whether it is more peripheral.

A second set of contingency considerations deals with the strategic resources available for pursuing the strategic alliance. Here, the issue has to do with in what ways a particular party is able to dispatch, as well as retrieve, specific, identifiable strategic resources to and from the strategic alliance based on whether this resource allocation represents a reversible or irreversible move. This contingency issue deals with whether future strategic flexibility regarding a partner's resources will be at stake or not.

It should be pointed out that we have taken a parent's (there can be several parents, but generally there are two) view regarding how the particular form of a strategic alliance should be determined. Needless to say, there will have to be some symmetry regarding the contingency viewpoints of the two parents when it comes to the formal strategic alliance; this is a major negotiation point, and there might easily be situations where a strategic alliance simply will not be feasible based on the diametrically opposite viewpoints regarding choice of strategic form.

It should finally be pointed out that we have rejected the notion that the strategic alliance, as a project, should itself represent the primary basis for choosing the strategic alliance form. Our strong contention is that it is the strategic intents of the parents, and the way they see strategic alliances as part of the pursuit of their own strategies, that will primarily matter.

Formation of Strategic Alliances

A second major insight of this book is the fact that strategic alliances cannot easily be classified as phenomena that are decided upon in a clear cut way, in terms of a yes or no based on analytical proposals, analagous to many wholly-owned business propositions such as major new project investments, acquisitions, etc. Rather, strategic alliances tend to be formed over a period of time, often a considerable length of time, and this formation process generally goes through several stages. For instance, there is a preliminary stage where major considerations having to do with identifying the basic win–win rationale for the strategic alliance are at stake. Failing to focus on the basic win–win considerations for the alliance early, typically leads to a breakdown or delay at subsequent stages, where the parties can easily get bogged down in details without seeing a common vision for what they are doing.

Further, the careful detailing of a strategic alliance as a joint business proposition should represent the final steps towards negotiating the alliance. Needless to say, each party will be required to have reasonable common sense when it comes to the financial considerations around the alliance so that the quantified benefits can be seen in a broad sense earlier on. Too much detailed analysis at an early stage paradoxically tends to weaken the likelihood of reaching an agreement, in that other options can then become harder to pursue and the overall strategic rationale can get lost, risking a bogged-down view on details.

Another important feature of the formation process, as we have seen, is that strategic alliances are not decided on in a purely analytical way, but also necessitate complex stakeholder involvements, where various forms of consensus must be reached at various stages of the formation process. For instance, during the early phases of a strategic alliance negotiation, it is particularly crucial that the key stakeholders on both sides support the alliance. This might include key executives, key ownership groups, and even key financial backers. At later stages of the strategic alliance negotiation it is fundamental that the various organizations are informed earlier rather than later so that a positive motivation and selling in of the alliance can take place. The challenge here, of course, is to balance the need of confidentialty against needs for pro-active selling in of the employees-cum-stakeholders.

The formation process is a much more important part of the strategic alliance phenomenon than one might expect. Specifically, we feel that a well-balanced, properly executed formation process will strengthen the likelihood of subsequent success. We feel that success is not solely a matter of pursuing the joint organization's strategic opportunities based on the newly combined strength of the alliance to create business value as a new organizational entity, it is also a matter of having a firm basis for the joint alliance based on a proper formation process. This can represent a frustrating realization later on, when the parties realize that what could have been a strong business success does not materialize because of an inappropriate formation process.

A Means to an End: Theories of Evolution

A third major insight that we feel has been offered in this book has to do with the fact that few strategic alliances, if any at all, can be seen in a static position. Rather, they always tend to evolve towards something else. We feel that an overly focused concern for a legal contract defining the static scope of a strategic alliance tends to be counter-productive.

What tends to be important for securing a proper evolution of a strategic alliance so that the parents benefit from it, rather than get bogged-down in fruitless frictions and delaying conflicts, has to do with accepting the fact that strategic alliances tend to mature over time and take on a life of their own, quite analagously to children growing up and parents/partners becoming older. Anticipating what might be a likely outcome of a strategic alliance is a key managerial consideration that should be made before the alliance is even entered into. Needless to say, such a view can never become thoroughly precise. Still, to anticipate where everything might end up, and to assess ways to exit the business activity at this late stage, is crucially important.

Realizing the dynamic nature of a strategic alliance provides added importance for a partner in the various ways of impacting the evolutionary path of an alliance. Control issues become ones of how to impact and influence the alliance, rather than issues of show-downs regarding technical power, veto votes, etc. Control becomes a matter of establishing a base for impacting and persuading rather than becoming a punitive, reactive activity.

Similarly, concerns for the human resource and for developing a unique black box protection so as to have a degree of discretion over one's own strategic resources, become critical, when seen in an evolutionary light. The development of core competencies that can be applied in future deals are major parts of the criteria for judging the goodness of a strategic alliance. It is thus not enough that the financial end result is satisfactory. Indeed, financial end results might be unsatisfactory if future strategic options have been greatly depleted through giving up critical strategic resources such as discretionary marketing know-how, or R&D know-how.

Finally, cross-cultural considerations become particularly important when it comes to evolutionary issues. Here, the ability to cooperate over time by building trust and by having appropriate interactions on business matters that lead to cooperation and common learning, becomes essential. If the cultures of the partners are such that evolution of the strategic alliance cannot take place, because the partners end up playing watch-dog against each other, the alliance will, of course, not be a success. To be successful in implementing strategies through the strategic alliance form requires a considerable amount of organizational maturity when it comes to both parties. It is this perspective that should prevail, manifested by the fact that a party actually relishes the fact that the other party also gets a considerable share of the benefits from the alliance.

An Advanced Working Mode

The management of strategic alliances represents an advanced working mode. We have seen that there are several unique insights that must be mastered when it comes to successfully going through a strategic alliance formation process and when assessing one's ability to implement it and allow it to evolve. Needless to say, hands-on experience building and practice is important. We have seen plenty of evidence that strategic alliance management becomes easier for corporations that already have relevant experience. Learning pertinent issues relating to the formation, implementation, and evolution of strategic alliances is critical. It is a mistake to underestimate the unique body of specific know-how pertaining to strategic alliances which complements the more general body of management practices.

We have seen that strategic alliances do not have to be defensive or last resort types of decision tools. In fact, many of the more successful alliances are offensive and pro-active in nature. For instance, when it comes to developing a global strategy, it may simply take too long to do it on one's own.

We have also seen that a strategic alliance provides unique opportunities to achieve both the advantages from a global strategy, such as scale and/or scope advantages, and the local adaptive profile so important to gain acceptance in each area. A firm might achieve comparable scale and scope advantages this way, given that the ownership and responsibility of the strategic alliance is shared among many partners around the world. We see that this type of global strategic alliance could be the prototype for future transnational corporations. Management insights from global strategic alliances, especially from shared alliances, may be of increased importance for the global firm of the future. Or, to underscore this with a statement from de Benedetti (1990):

> For an entrepreneur, it is not quite enough to acknowledge the network corporation as the reference model for the future, as the most appropriate structure for moving towards the global

corporation. This type of corporation requires a different organizational structure and, more importantly, a different management style. There is a great difference between the qualities you need to guide a hierarchical system and the ones you need to make a network system work. That difference is often detrimental for large companies.

We have observed how important the strategic intents of the various participants are in shaping a strategic alliance, and we have outlined several aspects of the strategic intent issue. It is clear that strategic intent must be seen as a management team issue, not as one resting in a particular executive's mind. Reaching some sense of political group consensus regarding the strategic intent is crucial. We have also observed that the stakeholder/political aspects of strategic alliance management are critically important, paralleling the more analytical aspects of managing such alliances.

In addition, strategic intent cannot be established by rational analysis alone. Rather, it must be crystallized through the appropriate combination of inputs: the strategic opportunities and complementarities seen in the strategic alliance itself; the fit with the strategic rationale of a given parent; and the assessment of the managerial capabilities to pull off the strategic alliance. And the intent must be based on an assessment of a firm's partners as well as own organizational capabilities. Strategic intent, consequently, represents an amalgam of these factors. A strategic alliance is driven by selfish interests. If a prospective partner does not see "what's in it for us", the alliance is unlikely to work. Cooperation through strategic alliances must thus be motivated by realistic, opportunity-seeking strategic intent.

Summary

In conclusion, we consider strategic alliances from a retrospective viewpoint, from a current perspective, as well as from a future perspective. In retrospect, it seems as if strategic alliances in the past were seen as a last resort. Considerable time has been spent on arguing why one should use strategic alliances when one does not have to, when a dominant ownership share would be preferable, and when there are various negative conflicts and adversarial challenges to overcome. In short, strategic alliances from a retrospective point of view are often summarized as stressful, and, in general, not a desirable way for pursuing a firm's strategies.

Currently, the view on strategic alliances has shifted quite dramatically. Now, the issue is much more one of recognizing that complementary activities, leading to a win–win situation for both parties, can represent considerable savings in time and pooling of resources (particularly brain-driven), which otherwise might not occur. In short, strategic alliances, in our view, represent opportunities that elsewise *de facto* might be out of reach. Thus, even large, resource-drawn organizations see strategic alliances in a generally more positive mode with emphasis on the benefits side (the upside potentials) rather than the negative and problem-laden side. As such, one might say that the current perspective on strategic alliances is one of considerable more maturity, representing more of an open mind toward their positive aspects. A can do attitude rather than a be aware attitude seems to prevail under the current perspective, that is, win–win rather than win–lose.

From a future-oriented point of view one can, of course, only speculate how strategic alliances will be seen. We feel, however, that the needs of the modern corporation in an increasingly integrated global world will dictate a considerable emphasis on strategic alliances. It looks as if industries increasingly are being globalized (in a true global sense, as well as in regions of the world such as the European Community), requiring the successful firm to have scale and/or scope advantages at least at par with its competitors. At the same time, however, the need for local business control, adaptation to local conditions, adherence to national requirements and sentiments, etc., represent concerns that can be seen to be in conflict with the call for globalization. Thus, the firm of the future might see itself in a considerable dilemma having to be both global and local at the same time. We see the strategic alliance form as the principal way of resolving this dilemma, allowing the scale and scope advantages to accrue through cooperation among several partners, while at the same time allowing each partner to maintain a local perspective. We feel that from a prospective-oriented point of view, strategic alliances represent the business approach of the future.

Notes

Notes to Preface

1 Earlier results from this research are reported in Lorange, P. and Roos, J. (eds), 1987: *The Challenge of Cooperative Ventures*, Institute of International Business, Stockholm School of Economics, Stockholm, Sweden.

Notes to Chapter 1

1 This is based on the so-called transaction cost theory introduced by Williamson (1975).
2 Jack Welch, CEO of General Electric, insists that a business must be in a number one or two position worldwide, in terms of market share, to remain in GE's portfolio. If not, a divestiture or strategic alliance would be the line GE would want to pursue. GE's radio telephony business was, for instance, not among the world leaders. As such, one might argue that GE classified this business as suitable for a full-blown joint venture and was perhaps prepared to restructure or unload.
3 Based on data on 140 full-blown joint ventures.
4 For instance, Hamel, Doz and Prahalad (1989), Harrigan (1985; 1986), and Kogut (1989).
5 In his study, "strategic alliances" included joint ventures, licensing agreements, minority equity investments, co-marketing agreements, co-development agreements, cross-licensing agreements, joint bidding, and consortia. The CEOs were involved in approximately 386 domestic and international strategic alliances.

6 See the case study "Swedpartner–Norpartner" at the end of Chapter 7.
7 For instance, Janger (1980), Killing (1983), Beamish (1985), Kogut (1986), and Harrigan (1986). It should be noted that these studies mainly concern joint ventures, i.e., stand-alone entities, not strategic alliances in general.

Notes to Appendix

1 Copyright Paul Olk 1990. This case was prepared by Paul Olk as a basis for discussion rather than to illustrate either effective or ineffective handling of an administrative situation. Any use of this material without the written consent of the author is prohibited.

Notes to Chapter 2

1 Following Porter's (1980) framework.
2 For instance, Tomlinson (1970) and Lecraw (1984).
3 For instance, Franco (1971), Stopford and Wells (1972), Killing (1983).
4 For instance, Gomes-Casseres (1987).
5 For a fuller discussion of measurement of strategic performance see Chakravarthy (1986).
6 It should be noted that Anderson's (1990) article discussed full-blown joint ventures as stand-alone entities.

Notes to Appendix

1 This case was prepared by Research Fellow Thomas Cummings, under the supervision of Professors Per Jenster and Francis Bidault, as a basis for discussion rather than to illustrate either effective or ineffective handling of a business situation. Contributions from Michael Horner, Digital Europe, are gratefully acknowledged. Copyright 1990 by the International Management Development Institute (IMD), Lausanne, Switzerland. Not to be used or reproduced without permission.

Notes to Chapter 3

None

Notes to Appendix

1 This case was prepared by Dr Johan Roos as a basis for discussion rather than to illustrate either effective or ineffective handling of an administrative situation.
2 This does not include the 1988 acquisition of the French company Peaudouce.
3 It should be noted that the technology is changing rapidly in this industry. Thus, it is of great importance to have access to continued technological improvements.

Notes to Chapter 4

None

Notes to Appendix

1 Copyright 1987 by the President and Fellows of Harvard College, Harvard Business School case 9 1987 104. This case was prepared by Research Assistant Agnes Connolly, under the supervision of Lecturer James T. Rhea, as a basis for discussion rather than to illustrate either effective or ineffective handling of an administrative situation.

Notes to Chapter 5

1 Other authors have emphasized different human resource management issues. For instance, Cascio and Serapio (1990) stress the importance of the following issues: blending of cultures and management styles, job design, orientation and training of new hires and current employees, performance appraisal, compensation benefits, career issues, and labor–management relations. Frayne and Geringer (1990) discuss human resource issues as control mechanisms in strategic alliances. They found that four sets of mechanisms are most significant in this respect: recruitment and staffing, training and development, performance appraisal, and compensation and reward strategies.
2 See Hamel and Prahalad (1989) for a fuller discussion of core competencies.

Notes to Appendix

1 Copyright 1973 by the President and Fellows of Harvard College, Revised 1985, Harvard Business School case 9 373–348. This case was prepared by Dr Michael Yoshino as a basis for discussion rather than to illustrate either effective or ineffective handling of an administrative situation. Reprinted by permission of the Harvard Business School.

Notes to Chapter 6

1 The literature points out significant differences in management practices between Western and Japanese firms, attributed by many to be largely the result of fundamental cultural differences (McCraw 1986; Kagono, Nanaka, and Okumura 1985; Clark 1979; Ouchi 1981; Kono 1984, and others). This suggests that US and Japanese firms may be characterized by different managerial practices that might give rise to different strategic alliance formation processes.
2 See Cameron and Whetten (1983) or Kimberly, Norling, and Weiss (1983) for a fuller discussion of how to measure performance.
3 See Anderson (1990) and our discussion in Chapter 1.

Notes to Appendix

1 This case was prepared by Gary Jacobson and John Hillkirk for their book, *Xerox: American Samurai*, Macmillan Publishing Company. It is not intended to illustrate either effective or ineffective handling of an administrative situation.

Notes to Chapter 7

None

Notes to Appendix

1 This case was prepared by Dr Johan Roos as a basis for discussion rather than to illustrate either effective of ineffective handling of an administrative situation.
2 The names of companies and persons are disguised in this case description.

Notes to Chapter 8

1 For instance, see Prahalad and Doz (1987), Bartlett and Goshal
   (1989), Ohmae (1985; 1989), and Porter (1986).
2 SAS is currently trying to divest itself of this business.

Notes to Appendix

1 This case was prepared by Dr Peter Lorange and Dr Johan Roos as
   a basis for discussion rather than to illustrate either effective or
   ineffective handling of an administrative situation.

References

Abegglen, J.C. 1984: *The Strategy of Japanese Business*. Cambridge, MA: Ballinger Publications.

Anderson, E. 1990: Two firms, one frontier: on assessing joint venture performance. *Sloan Management Review*, Winter, 19–30.

Argyris, C. and Schon, D. 1978: *Organizational Learning*. Reading, MA: Addison-Wesley.

Athos, A.G. and Pascale, R.T. 1981: *The Art of Japanese Management*. New York: Simon & Schuster.

Bartlett, C.A. and Ghoshal, S. 1989: *Beyond Global Management: The Transnational Solution*. Boston, MA: Harvard Business School Press.

Beamish, P.W. 1985: The characteristics of joint ventures in developed and developing countries. *Columbia Journal of World Business*, Winter, 13–19.

Cameron, K.S. and Whetten, D.A. (eds) 1983: *Organizational Effectiveness: A Comparison of Multiple Models*. New York: Academic.

Cascio, W.F. and Serapio, M.G., Jr. 1990: Human resource systems and international alliances: obstacles to success? *Organizational Dynamics*, Winter, 63–74.

Chakravarthy, B. 1986: Measuring strategic performance. *Strategic Management Journal*, 7, 437–58.

Chakravarthy, B.S. and Lorange, P. 1991: *Managing the Strategy Process*. Englewood Cliffs, NJ: Prentice-Hall.

Chang, G. 1990: quoted in "Is long-range planning worth it?" *Fortune*, April 23.

Clark, R. 1979: *The Japanese Company*. New Haven, CT: Yale University Press.

Contractor, F. and Lorange, P. (eds) 1988a: *Cooperative Strategies in International Business*. Lexington, MA: Lexington Books.

Contractor, F. and Lorange, P. 1988b: Why should firms cooperate? The strategy and economics basis for cooperative ventures. In Contractor,

F. and Lorange, P. (eds), *Cooperative Strategies in International Business*. Lexington, MA: Lexington Books, 3–30.

de Benedetti, C. 1990: International alliances – a major contribution to the development of global companies. Paper given at Eksport-Forum 90, Oslo, Norway.

Fifield, G., Hanada, M. and Pucik, V. 1989: *Management, Culture and the Effectiveness of Local Executives in Japanese Owned U.S. Corporations*. Ann Arbor, MI: University of Michigan, Division of Research.

Franco, L.G., 1971: *Joint Venture Survival in Multinational Corporations*. New York: Praeger.

Frayne, C.A. and Geringer, J.M. 1990: The strategic use of human resource management practices as control mechanisms in international joint ventures. Research in *Personnel and Human Resources Management*, Suppl. 2, 53–69.

Geringer, J.M. and Hebert, L. 1991: Control and performance of international joint ventures. *Journal of International Business Studies*, 22 (2), forthcoming.

Gomes-Casseres, B. 1987: Ownership structures of foreign subsidiaries: theory and evidence. Working paper, Harvard Business School, Boston.

Gupta, A.K. and Govindarajan, V. 1984: Business unit strategy, managerial characteristics and business unit effectiveness at strategy implementation. *Academy of Management Journal*, 27, 25–41.

Håkansson, H. 1980: Marketing strategies in industrial markets. *European Journal of Marketing*, 14, 5/6, 365–77.

Håkansson, H., Hagg, I. and Johansson, J. 1980: Foretags-forbindelser och konkurrenskraft. *Ekonomisk Debatt*, 2.

Håkansson, H. and Johansson, J. 1988: Formal and informal cooperative strategies in international industrial networks. In Contractor, F. and Lorange, P. (eds), *Cooperative Strategies in International Business*. Lexington, MA: Lexington Books, 369–90.

Håkanson, L. 1989: Forskning och utveckling i utlandet: en studie av svenska multinatinalla foretag. Stockholm. *IVA-PM*, 1.

Håkanson, L. and Lorange, P. 1991: Research and product development-based cooperative ventures. In Lars-Gunnar Mattson and Bengt Stymne (eds), *Corporate and Industry Strategies for Europe*. Elsevier Science Publishers, 235–260.

Hamel, G. and Prahalad, C.K. 1989: Strategic Intent, *Harvard Business Review*, 67, 3, May–June, 63–7..

Hamel, G., Doz, Y.L. and Prahalad, C.K. 1989: Collaborate with your competitors – and win. *Harvard Business Review*, Jan.–Feb., 67, 1.

Harrigan, K.R. 1985: *Strategies for Joint Ventures*. Lexington, MA: Lexington Books.

Harrigan, K. R. 1986: *Managing for Joint Venture Success*, Lexington, MA: Lexington Books.

Haspeslagh, P. 1988: Observations from the INSEAD acquisition project. Working Paper, INSEAD, Fontainebleau.

Heenan, D. and Perlmutter, H. 1979: *Multinational Organization Development, a Social Architectural Perspective*. Reading, MA: Addison-Wesley.

Hergert, M. and Morris, D. 1988: Trends in international collaborative agreements. In Contractor, F. and Lorange, P. (eds), *Cooperative Strategies in International Business*. Lexington, MA: Lexington Books, 99–110.

Houghton, J.R. 1990: Corning cultivates joint ventures that endure. *Planning Review*, 18, 5, September/October, 15–17.

Jacobson, G. and Hillkirk, J. 1986: *Xerox, American Samurai*. New York: Macmillan Publishing Co.

Janger, A. 1980: *Organization of International Joint Ventures*. New York: Conference Board.

Kagono, I., Nanaka, I. and Okumura, A. 1985: *Strategy vs. Evolutionary Management: A U.S.–Japan Comparison of Strategy and Organization*. New York: North Holland.

Killing, P. 1983: *Strategies for Joint Venture Success*. New York: Praeger.

Kimberly, J.R. 1982: Managerial innovations and health policy: theory, perspective and research implications. *Journal of Health Politics, Policy and Care*, 6, 637–653.

Kimberly, J.R., Norling, F., and Weiss, J.A. 1983: Pondering the performance puzzle: effectiveness in interorganizational settings. In Hall, R.H. and Quinn, R.E. (eds), *Organizational Theory and Public Policy*. Beverly Hills, CA: Sage Publishing Company, 249–264.

Kogut, B. 1986: *Cooperative and Competitive Influences on Joint Venture Stability under Competing Risks of Acquisition and Dissolution*. Working Paper, Reginal H. Jones Center, Wharton School, University of Pennsylvania.

Kogut, B. 1989: Joint ventures: theoretical and empirical perspectives. *Strategic Management Journal*, 9, 4, 319–32.

Kono, T. 1984: *Strategy and Structure and Japanese Enterprise*. New York: Sharp.

Lecraw, D.J. 1984: Bargaining power, ownership, and profitability of transnational corporations in developing countries. *Journal of International Business Studies*, Spring–Summer, 27–43.

Lewis, J.D. 1990: *Partnerships for Profit: Structuring and Managing Strategic Alliances*. New York: The Free Press.

Lorange, P. 1980: *Corporate Planning: An Executive Viewpoint*. Englewood Cliffs, NJ: Prentice-Hall.

Lorange, P. 1984a: Implementing strategic planning at two Philippine companies. *The Wharton Annual*, 8. Oxford: Pergamon Press, 165–76.

Lorange, P. 1984b: Strategic control: some issues in making it operationally more useful. In Lamb, R. (ed.), *Competitive Strategic Management*. Englewood Cliffs, NJ: Prentice-Hall.

Lorange, P. and Roos, J. (eds) 1987: *The Challenge of Cooperative Ventures*. Institute of International Business, Stockholm.

Lorange, P. and Roos, J. 1990: Formation of U.S.–Japanese strategic alliances: differences in management approaches. Presented at the International Symposium on Pacific Asian Business, Honolulu, Hawaii, January.

Lorange, P. and Vancil, R. 1976: How to design a strategic planning system. *Harvard Business Review*, Sept–Oct, 75–81.

McCraw, T.K. (ed.) 1986: *American versus Japan*. Boston, MA: Harvard Business School Press.

MacMillan, L.-G. and Jones, P.E. 1987: *Strategy formulation: political, power and politics* (2nd ed.). St Paul, MN: West Publishing.

Mason, R. and Mitroff, I. 1981: *Challenging Strategic Planning Assumptions*. New York: Wiley.

Ohmae, K. 1985: *The Coming Shape of Global Competition*. New York: The Free Press.

Ohmae, K. 1989: *The Global Logic of Strategic Alliances*. Harvard Business Review, 67, 2, March–April, 143–54.

Ouchi, W.C. 1981: *Theory Z: How American Business can Meet the Japanese Challenge*. Reading, MA: Addison-Wesley.

Porter, M. 1980: *Competitive Strategy*. New York: The Free Press.

Porter, M. 1985: *Competitive Advantage*. Boston, MA: The Free Press.

Porter, M. 1986: *Competition in Global Industries*. Boston, MA: Harvard Business School Press.

Prahalad, C.K. and Doz, Y.L. 1987: *The Multinational Mission: Balancing Local Demands and Global Vision*. New York: The Free Press.

Reich, R.B. and Mankin, E.D. 1986: Joint ventures with Japan give away our future. *Harvard Business Review*, March–April, 2, 78–86.

Root, F.R. 1984: *International Trade and Investment*. Cincinnati, OH: Southwest Publishing.

Root, F.R. 1987: *Entry Strategies for International Markets*. Lexington, MA: Lexington Books.

Schaan, J.-L. 1983: Parent control and joint venture success: the case of Mexico. Unpublished doctoral dissertation, University of Western Ontario.

Stopford, J. M. and Wells, L. 1972: *Managing the Multinational Enterprise*. New York: Basic Books.

Tomlinson, J.W.C. 1970: *The Joint Venture Process in International Business: India and Pakistan*. Cambridge, MA: MIT Press.

Williamson, O.E. 1975: *Markets and Hierarchies: Analysis and Antitrust Implications*. New York: The Free Press.

Zajac, E. 1990: CEOs' views on strategic alliances. Paper presented at the Marketing Science Institute's Conference on Managing Long-Run Relationships, Boston.

Zeira, Y. and Shankar, O. 1990: Implications for management and human resources in international joint ventures. *MIR*, 30, Special Issue, 7–22.

Index